MW01284562

The 1990s

The 1990s

Marc Oxoby

American Popular Culture Through History
Ray B. Browne, Series Editor

GREENWOOD PRESS
Westport, Connecticut • London

Library of Congress Cataloging-in-Publication Data

Oxoby, Marc.
    The 1990s / by Marc Oxoby.
       p. cm.—(American popular culture through history)
    Includes bibliographical references and index.
    ISBN 0-313-31615-5 (alk. paper)
       1. United States—Civilization—1970– 2. Popular culture—United States—
History—20th century. 3. Nineteen nineties. I. Title. II. Series.
E169.12.O96   2003
973.929—dc21   2003048519

British Library Cataloguing in Publication Data is available.

Library of Congress Catalog Card Number: 2003048519
ISBN: 0-313-31615-5

First published in 2003

Greenwood Press, 88 Post Road West, Westport, CT 06881
An imprint of Greenwood Publishing Group, Inc.
www.greenwood.com

Printed in the United States of America

The paper used in this book complies with the
Permanent Paper Standard issued by the National
Information Standards Organization (Z39.48–1984).

10 9 8 7 6 5 4 3 2 1

Contents

Contents

Acknowledgments

Thanks are due to the families Oxoby and Clark and Allemand for their aid during composition of this volume. Acknowledgments need also be made to Rob Kirkpatrick and Debby Adams of Greenwood Press, and to the team at Impressions Book and Journal Services, Inc., for their guidance and feedback.

Very special thanks to Marthe Clark and Robert Sickels for their assistance and moral support.

This book is for Charlene and Gerard Oxoby. Let us open the bottle.

Series Foreword

Popular Culture is the system of attitudes, behavior, beliefs, customs, and tastes that define the people of any society. It is the entertainments, diversions, icons, rituals, and actions that shape the everyday world. It is what we do while we are awake and what we dream about while we are asleep. It is the way of life we inherit, practice, change, and then pass on to our descendants.

Popular culture is an extension of folk culture, the culture of the people. With the rise of electronic media and the increase in communication in American culture, folk culture expanded into popular culture—the daily way of life as shaped by the *popular majority* of society. Especially in a democracy like the United States, popular culture has become both the voice of the people and the force that shapes the nation. In 1782, the French commentator Hector St. Jean de Crevecouer asked in his *Letters from an American Farmer*, "What is an American?" He answered that such a person is the creation of America and is in turn the creator of the country's culture. Indeed, notions of the American Dream have been long grounded in the dream of democracy—that is, government by the people, or popular rule. Thus, popular culture is tied fundamentally to America and the dreams of its people.

Historically, culture analysts have tried to separate culture into two categories: "elite"—the elements of culture (fine art, literature, classical music, gourmet food, etc.) that supposedly define the best of society—and "popular"—the elements of culture (comic strips, bestsellers, pop music, fast food, etc.) that appeal to society's lowest common denominator. The so-called "educated" person approved of elite culture and scoffed at popular culture. This schism first began to develop in Western Europe in the fifteenth century when the privileged classes tried to discover and develop differences in societies based on class, money, privilege, and life styles. Like many aspects of European society, the debate between elite and popular cultures came to the United States. The upper class in America, for example, supported museums and galleries that would exhibit "the finer things in life" that would "elevate" people. As the twenty-first century emerges, however, the distinctions between elitist culture and popular culture have blurred. The blues songs (once denigrated as "race music") of Robert Johnson are now revered by musicologists; architectural students study buildings in Las Vegas as examples of what Robert Venturi called the "kitsch of high capitalism"; and sportswriter Gay Talese and heavyweight boxing champ Floyd Patterson were co-panelists at a 1992 State University of New York at New Paltz symposium on literature and sports. The examples go on and on, but the one commonality that emerges is the role of popular culture as a model for the American Dream, the dream to pursue happiness and a better, more interesting life.

To trace the numerous ways in which popular culture has evolved throughout American history, we have divided the volumes in this series into chronological periods—historical eras until the twentieth century, and decades between 1900 and 2000. In each volume, the author explores the specific details of popular culture that reflect the general undercurrents of the time. Our purpose, then, is to present historical and analytical panoramas that reach both backward into America's past and forward to the collective future. In viewing these panoramas, we can trace a very fundamental part of American society. The American Popular Culture Through History series presents the multifaceted parts of a popular culture in a nation that has grown and is still growing.

Ray B. Browne
Secretary-Treasurer
Popular Culture Association
American Culture Association

Introduction

The American Popular Culture Through History series is a testament to a notion that has gained significantly in pervasiveness; that to truly understand a society one must look not only at its high culture, but also at its popular culture, at how people dressed, what they ate, what they did to pass the time, and the like. The last decade of the twentieth century, in fact, saw a rapid growth in the amount of critical attention cast upon popular culture and its components. There was an increase in the number of American universities with departments devoted to popular culture, or contemporary media, or various categories therein. The number of university film departments, for instance, rose notably. But the change in popular culture's reception occurred not only in scholarly circles, but also amidst the general public. Indeed, there appeared among the populace a growing need to not only consume popular culture, but also to understand it. Perhaps nowhere is this seen more vividly than with the introduction of Digital Video Discs (DVDs) during the 1990s. Although picture and sound quality of DVDs certainly spurred sales well beyond those of the older VHS video cassettes, an additional appeal of the DVD was the bonus features, those that gave insights, through short documentaries or commentaries by filmmakers, into the background and making of the movie in question.

The popularity of this one technology can be held as symbolic of a larger trend towards the almost rabid pursuit of information about popular culture. Indeed, the 1990s have been referred to as the "Age of Information." With the rapid spread of various media, carrying an ever increasing amount of information, there was a growing sense among many Americans that information was of value. And what could be of more value than information about the popular culture to which so many people devoted so much of their time, whether it be by watching television, listening to music, or deciding on an outfit to wear to school or work? The ultimate value of these things, especially as compared to, say, global or national politics, or technological advancements, remains a subject of debate. Some might question the ultimate, lasting value of DC Comics' killing and resurrection of Superman, for instance, as compared to the impeachment of a president.

One of the very premises behind this volume, however, and indeed behind this series of books, is that there is considerable value in studying popular culture. Clearly, popular culture is *not* divorced from politics and technology, and to understand one is to understand the other with greater depth. Obviously politics and technology influence popular culture, but one would be remiss in ignoring how popular culture has affected politics and technology. The computer technology developed to operate home video games, for example, has continued to push the digital envelope, and these same video games have on more than one occasion dictated political and social discourse, on everything from media violence to computerized education.

Thus, this volume operates from two basic assumptions. The first is that popular culture reflects what is going on in the world, as well as the mass psyche of its denizens. As we can look to the movies of the 1950s and sense the Cold War anxiety of Americans of the period, so too can we glean something of the pervading attitudes of the 1990s in that decade's popular culture. To look to the popular culture that Americans consumed is to look into the very concerns that drove many aspects of their lives. The second assumption is that popular culture, more than being a mere reflection, can play an important part in shaping the country and its populace. For many Americans, this is a more dubious claim than the first. Indeed, few wish to imagine that their opinions, even their worldview, are being shaped by what they watch on television in their leisure time or what clothes they throw on in the morning. Some might admit to having their views changed by events in the news, but the notion that the very conveyance of that news, via a half-hour television broadcast, for instance, effects a very real alteration in their perspective, is a notion that makes many feel uncomfortable.[1] A personal sense of self-sovereignty and self-determination makes this a tough concept for some to swallow. Yet our culture has been quick to suggest that music or movies of a kind can have a harmful effect on youths. Likewise, there is little resistance to claims of historical change due to cultural developments, be they movable type, the locomotive, or cinema.

The very term *popular culture* deserves some consideration. A quick perusal of this volume's table of contents should indicate what a large pool of information we are dealing with. While few would bat an eye at the thought of pop music, television, and video games as popular culture, the structures in which we dwell and the cuisine we consume are more often taken for granted. But the considerations of architecture and food in this volume are easily as telling about 1990s America as are those things we more quickly label as popular culture. Popular culture is a term that is often applied with limited expectations, and it is also a term that has frequently been used derogatorily. High culture has been somehow exempt of the popular culture label, as have more pragmatic institutions. Most don't think of civil engineering as popular culture, for instance. Popular culture, to some, even to those who consume it quite happily, is often thought of as synonymous with cultural trash.

But this series forges ahead with a somewhat more liberal, and, I would suggest, a somewhat more accurate definition of popular culture. In their introduction to *The Guide to United States Popular Culture,* editors Ray B. Browne and Pat Browne argue that popular culture "is far more than entertainment and leisure time activities. It is the bone and flesh of a society from which the spirit emanates and soars—or falls...Popular culture is the way of life in which and by which most people in any society live." Obviously, then, while entertainments certainly constitute a significant portion of this study, this study seeks to explore a much greater range. It seeks to flesh out the American character at the end of the twentieth century by exploring a notion of popular culture which encompasses, as Browne and Browne would have it, "the mass media, entertainments, diversions...our heroes, icons, rituals, everyday actions, psychology, and religion—our total life picture."[2]

We do well in considering that the term *popular* can have more than one meaning. The most common usage of the word indicates that what is most popular is enjoyed or consumed by the most people. But the word can also be read as meaning "of the people." With this connotation in mind, one could well argue that all culture is popular. This volume attempts to walk the line between the two uses of the term. While all aspects of culture might be popular, the scope of this book necessarily required some degree of limitation. Efforts were consequently made to highlight those aspects of popular culture that commanded the greatest amount of attention from the greatest number of people. However, efforts were also made to root out certain countercultural movements that also revealed a great deal about the American mind-set. Therefore, although the movie *Titanic* may necessitate mention due to its monstrous box office success, quirkier films and the rise of independent cinema also demand attention for what they might reveal about a specific segment of the populace or for what impact they may have in the future. After all, few at the time were aware of the early television experiments of the 1920s. Only hindsight proves what a profound effect these experiments were to have on the country and the world.

Hindsight, however, is something that, as of this writing, we have but little of when considering the 1990s. The relative lack of temporal distance between the 1990s and today presents us with both advantages and disadvantages when considering the decade's popular culture.

Time greatly affects the way we perceive a given era, especially when considering something as apparently ephemeral as popular culture. The passage of time allows one to distance oneself from a period, and this distance potentially allows for a broader perspective of that period. One looking back on an earlier decade might have a greater sense of which developments of that decade had the most lasting effect. Indeed, what may have seemed the most vital development during the period may, ultimately, have little lasting effect on the future development of American culture, and seemingly minor developments can have enormous effects. Experiments with computers in the 1960s and 1970s, for instance, generated relatively little interest amongst the majority of the American population, but given the ubiquity of computers today, those early stirrings necessarily demand careful attention. This is but one example of how the preceding decades of the twentieth century helped shape the 1990s. It should therefore always be kept in mind that while decades provide a convenient categorical system, the lines are not so sharply drawn. In analyzing the 1990s, one can't ignore developments in the late eighties and earlier, which shaped the final decade of the twentieth century as much as any developments strictly restricted to this ten-year period. The artifice of segmenting off a given decade constitutes a significant limitation to the present volume.

Another limitation that comes with writing of such recent developments in American culture is that gauging the importance of said developments requires some degree of guesswork. Obviously, some guesses are more accurate than others. This is particularly the case when considering technology. It is no stretch of the imagination, for instance, to postulate that the Internet will continue to be of enormous importance and influence on the future of American culture. Entertainment, however, provides less solid ground for prediction. Many of the best-selling books of yore, after all, are now largely forgotten. What the future holds for the most profitable books, movies, television shows, and pop bands remains to be seen. We can only offer educated guesses in measuring their lasting import.

The flipside of this limitation is that it is much easier to develop an accurate picture of 1990s popular culture, if not of its future implications. While the scholars working on the American Popular Culture Through History series seek to present an accurate picture of each decade's popular culture, it must be acknowledged that people in general tend to exhibit selective memory when considering earlier eras. The average American, if asked to describe the 1950s would likely mention rockabilly music, pompadours, Elvis Presley, and the like, essentially sketching a picture of the decade that has more to do with the TV show *Happy Days* than with the reality. Certainly these were features of the 1950s, but there was so much more. A similar query of the 1990s would likely produce a far greater variety of responses. That decade has yet to settle into a common pattern in the American consciousness as a whole. When it does, it will likely become fodder for nostalgia, just as the 1970s and even the 1980s were during the nineties. For now, the 1990s remain resistant to nostalgic memory. Instead, the decade lives in popular memory with much of its complexity and its richness intact.

If any general theme can be drawn from the decade at this point, it might be that of diversity and blending. The 1990s seem to have been a great age of mélange, of the coming together of disparate forces. This is true socially, politically, and aesthetically. This volume can be divided into two parts, each of which reflects this theme. The first two chapters, which constitute the first part, explore general demographic, political, and social trends in the context of everyday America and that specifically of youth culture. In the first, a sharp political split seems to belie the notion of a blending of oppositions. But as many have pointed out, and as a growing segment of the American population complained of bitterly, the two major political parties both moved towards the ideological center, indeed becoming more alike. The first chapter also examines the growing diversity of the American populace, due to immigration and other changes in the country's demographic makeup, which nonetheless was coupled with a growing homogeneity of cities across the nation, largely driven by media and commercial influence. The second chapter explores similar issues in the world of youth, finding a similar degree of diversity and cohesion.

The remaining chapters divide American popular culture into more specific categories, dealing with such topics as travel, literature, and architecture. Although more specific in their focus, running through them are the same themes. In the latter half of the twentieth century one can see an increasing dissolution of the barrier between high and popular culture, and this dissolution seems to reach a peak in the century's final decade. The increased use of popular film, music, and literature in classrooms across the country in the 1990s indicates that such artifacts were seen as being as valuable as works from the traditional literary and cultural canon. Likewise, Hollywood's vigorous use of classic literary works as the source for numerous film projects demonstrates a reverse impulse. The chapters in the second part, therefore, feature quite a wide, and at times disparate focus. Some chapters may seem particularly omnivorous in their coverage. A chapter covering fads, games, toys, hobbies, and sports obviously covers quite a bit. While a chapter covering the performing arts for, say, the 1910s might be quite manageable, for the 1990s one must consider not only stage performances, but also take on the gargantuan task of examining developments in the ubiquitous media of film and television. These chapters are, by necessity, rather superficial in their coverage, intended primarily as a springboard to further study.

The notes and suggested reading should provide a start for those wishing to more closely examine aspects touched upon in this volume. It might be noted that the proliferation of literature about the 1990s continues unabated, and, in fact, seems to be accelerating as more and more people seek to determine the impact of this complex decade from which we have but recently emerged. It is probable that the 1990s produced more literature on the decade itself than had any previous one. The quick pace of the decade did not stop individuals from engaging in some degree of analysis of what was happening around them and what significance these events would have. Therefore, even at this early date, much has been said about the 1990s. But much more remains to be said.

Timeline of the 1990s

1990

Iraq invades Kuwait (August 2).

Hubble telescope is launched.

AIDS activist Ryan White dies.

Beverly Hills 90210 debuts on TV.

Seinfeld debuts on TV.

Twin Peaks debuts on TV.

Henry and June becomes the first film released with the new NC-17 rating.

Luciano Pavarotti, Plácido Domingo, and José Carreras, as The Three Tenors, release the most successful classical recording in decades (43 on the pop music charts).

A Cincinnati museum director is brought up on obscenity charges for displaying work by photographer Robert Mapplethorpe.

Clean Air Act passed.

Panamanian dictator Manuel Noriega turns himself in to U.S. military forces.

Washington, D.C. mayor Marion Barry is arrested in an FBI drug sting.

2 Live Crew's *As Nasty as They Wanna Be* is ruled obscene by a federal judge in Florida.

1991

Persian Gulf War (Operation Desert Storm): air bombardment begins (January 16); Iraq accepts cease fire terms (February 28).

The Soviet Union regime collapses.

Nirvana's *Nevermind* is released.

First women's World Cup Tournament is held.

Earvin "Magic" Johnson announces that he is HIV-positive.

Street Fighter II arcade video game is introduced.

Allure begins publication.

FDA approves ddl for AIDS treatment.

Supreme Court nominee Clarence Thomas is approved despite controversy over
sexual harassment charges.

John Grisham's *The Firm* reaches the number one spot on the *New York Times* best-
seller list.

Coca-Cola advertises using dead stars resurrected through digital technology.

1992

Los Angeles race riots follow the acquittal of four police officers charged with the
beating of Rodney King.

Bill Clinton is elected president.

Art Spiegelman's *Maus* becomes the first comic book to win a Pulitzer Prize.

America's largest shopping center, Mall of America, opens in Minnesota.

Andrew becomes the most costly hurricane in U.S. history when it slams into
Florida.

Boxer Mike Tyson is convicted of rape.

Johnny Carson retires from *The Tonight Show.*

Fubu line of hip-hop clothing begins.

Image Comics begins publishing creator-owned books.

Superman dies and is reborn.

Id Software, creators of video games *Wolfenstein 3-D* and *Doom,* begins business.

Rapper Ice-T's heavy metal band sparks controversy with the song "Cop Killer."

Entertainment Weekly begins publication.

The Real World debuts on TV.

1993

Ratification of the North American Free Trade Agreement (NAFTA).

A raid is conducted on the Branch Davidian compound in Waco, Texas.

The United States Holocaust Memorial Museum opens in Washington, D.C.

Steven Spielberg's Academy Award-winning film *Schindler's List* is released.

Bombs detonate at World Trade Center.

The *X-Files* debuts on TV.

The series finale of *Cheers* airs.

Chicago Bulls basketball player Michael Jordan announces his retirement, but returns to the sport the next year.

Stereograms come to the U.S. with the publication *Magic Eye.*

A series of floods cripple the rural Midwest.

Barnes and Noble booksellers forge an agreement to serve Starbucks coffee in their stores.

The Luxor, the world's third largest hotel, opens in Las Vegas.

The first 32-bit video game console, 3DO, is introduced by Panasonic.

New Kids on the Block break up.

1994

"The Republican Revolution": Republicans gain control of Congress.

Investigation of the Whitewater scandal begins.

Kurt Cobain of Nirvana commits suicide (April).

O. J. Simpson is arrested on two counts of first degree murder (June 17).

Congress abandons efforts to reform health care (September).

Friends debuts on TV.

Jackie Kennedy Onassis dies.

A massive earthquake hits Los Angeles.

Dr. Bernard A. Harris becomes the first African American astronaut to walk in space.

Quentin Tarantino's *Pulp Fiction* is released in theaters.

Ratification of the General Agreement on Tariffs and Trade (GATT).

Major league baseball players go on strike.

Olympic ice skater Nancy Kerrigan is attacked as part of a conspiracy involving rival Tonya Harding.

NHL hockey players are locked out following a labor dispute.

1995

Oklahoma City Bombing (April 19).

Amazon.com online book retailer begins operations (July).

Cal Ripkin breaks Lou Gehrig's record for most consecutive games played in Major League Baseball (September 6).

U.S. government shuts down due to disputes between Congress and the President over the federal budget (November).

O.J. Simpson trial.

ESPN creates the *Extreme Games* (later called the *X Games*).

Toy Story, the first fully computer animated feature film, is released.

eBay online auction house is founded.

The San Francisco 49ers become the first football team to win five Super Bowls.

1996

The U.S. Government shuts down a second time as a result of budgetary disputes (January).

A welfare reform bill is passed.

Bill Clinton is reelected to the presidency.

Ted Kaczynski, the Unabomber, is arrested.

Oprah Winfrey begins an on-air book club (September).

The NAMES Project AIDS quilt is exhibited in its entirety for the final time, in Washington D.C.'s National Mall.

Marvel Comics files for bankruptcy.

Tickle-Me Elmo is introduced.

McDonald's restaurants and Walt Disney forge a ten-year licensing agreement.

Heavy-weight boxer Mike Tyson bites off part of Evander Holyfield's ear in the ring.

1997

An antitrust suit is brought against Microsoft.

Maxim men's magazine debuts in the U.S.

Dolly the sheep is cloned.

Tiger Woods wins the Masters golf tournament.

Fashion designer Gianni Versace is murdered (July).

Camel cigarettes retires its mascot, Joe Camel, in response to increasing public and political pressure.

Construction on Frank Gehry's Guggenheim Museum in Bilbao, Spain is completed.

The Volkswagen Beetle is reintroduced.

The Getty Center in Los Angeles opens.

Heaven's Gate cult commits mass suicide on the event of the passage of Hale Bopp comet.

Child beauty queen JonBenet Ramsey is found murdered.

California bans affirmative action.

Mars Pathfinder lands on Mars' surface.

World chess champion Gary Kasparov is defeated by IBM's computer opponent, Deep Blue.

1998

Newt Gingrich resigns as House speaker.

The scandal involving Bill Clinton's affair with intern Monica Lewinsky erupts.

School shootings take place in Jonesboro, Arkansas (March), and Springfield, Ohio (May).

U.S. Embassies in Kenya and Tanzania are bombed (August).

J.K. Rowling's *Harry Potter and the Sorcerer's Stone* is published in the U.S. (September).

Iraq is bombed by U.S. forces (December 17).

Bill Clinton impeached (December 19).

Senator and former astronaut John Glenn, at 77 years of age, becomes the oldest man in space.

The 5,000th episode of the TV game show *The Price is Right* airs.

Eminem's *The Slim Shady* LP is released.

Seinfeld series finale is most watched single episode of a television series.

Titanic becomes the most successful motion picture ever made.

Viagra sexual stimulant is marketed.

Mark McGwire breaks Roger Maris's homerun record.

Furby is introduced.

America Online buys out Netscape.

1999

Clinton is acquitted in the Senate.

Harris and Klebold massacre/suicide at Columbine High School, Littleton, Colorado (April 20).

The women's U.S. soccer team wins the World Cup.

John F. Kennedy, Jr. dies in a plane crash.

Hundreds are arrested protesting a meeting of the World Trade Organization in Seattle.

"Sensation" show at the Brooklyn Museum of Art opens to controversy.

Ricky Martin's "Livin' La Vida Loca" becomes the most successful single by a Latino artist.

Star Wars: Episode I: The Phantom Menace is released in theaters.

The Blair Witch Project, filmed on a budget of $35,000, becomes a box office smash hit.

Woodstock '99 music festival is marred by violence.

George W. Bush announces his presidential candidacy.

PART ONE

LIFE AND YOUTH DURING THE 1990s

The 1990s

1

Everyday America

DEMOGRAPHICS

The 1990 Census counted the American population at 248,709,873. But during the decade the country added more than 30 million to its population, reaching 281,421,906. This increase was due, in part, to a growth in the birthrate during the decade, but while the number of children born during the decade grew, the percentage of the population that they made up actually shrunk. According to the 1990 Census, nearly 36.5 million children were born in the 1980s, making up 14.7 percent of the population. The 2000 Census registered over 39.7 million children born in the nineties, which accounted for only 14.1 percent of the U.S. population.[1] Thus, there were other sources for the growing population. Particularly, growth can be attributed to an aging population and increased immigration to the United States.

The last quarter of the twentieth century saw the aging of the American populace, and in the 1990s this trend began receiving an increased amount of attention. The birth rate in the United States declined in the 1970s, and remained low through most of the eighties and nineties, and the result was a significant increase in the average American's age. By the end of the 1990s about 20 percent of the populace was over the age of 65, an increase from 8 percent in 1970.[2] Besides ensuring the elderly considerable political power, this aging of the populace also threatened to tax many of the systems meant to provide for the elderly. The federal Medicare system and private medical care saw increases in costs, as did insurance companies. There were also worries about the state of Social Security. Pensions granted by Social Security were to a large degree paid for by younger segments of the population that paid into the system. But the changing age demo-

graphics of the country led many to worry that Social Security would not
be able to provide what it promised, and that the system even ran the risk
of going bankrupt.

The loosening of immigration restrictions in the seventies and eighties
contributed to a growing number of immigrant Americans in the 1990s. By
2000, immigrants came to exceed 11 percent of the total population, num-
bering about 31 million. During the 1990s alone, more than 13 million people came to the U.S., either to become citizens or residents. Immigrants from
Latin America made up more than a third of all immigrants coming into
the United States during the nineties, and totaled about one quarter of all
immigrants living in the United States. By 2000, the number of Hispanic
Americans exceeded 35 million, or 12.5 percent of the total population. This
was a sharp increase from 9 percent in 1990. Importantly, there were several states in which the Latino population was concentrated. California,
Arizona, New Mexico, and Texas particularly saw rises in the number of
Latin American immigrants, and these populations became increasingly
potent in politically shaping those states. But an even larger segment of the
incoming immigrant population was from Asia. Constituting more than 40
percent of new immigration, people from China, Japan, Vietnam, Thailand,
Cambodia, Laos, the Philippines, Korea, and India swelled the number of
Asian Americans to more than 10 million, about 3.6 percent of the U.S. population in 2000, over 2.8 percent in 1990. Like the Latino population, these
groups frequently established centers of activity, particularly in the Western United States.[3]

The African American middle class grew a great deal during the 1990s.
A string of civil rights legislation that had started in the fifties and sixties
had contributed to growing opportunities for African Americans, and while
race disparities in the professional world had not vanished, they were less
pronounced in the nineties than in any prior period of American history.
A larger portion of the African American populace was attending college,
and many were making great strides in medicine, law, and education, as
well as in other fields that had once been racially prohibitive. In addition,
many black families were moving into suburbs and more prosperous urban
centers. Many moved into traditionally white neighborhoods, but there
was also a growing trend of affluent African American neighbors. The rise
of the black middle class spawned the term *Buppie*, for Black Urban Professional, an African American equivalent to the *Yuppie*, and helped contribute to a new kind of depiction of blacks in the media. Buppie movies
and television programs largely changed the profile of African Americans
in public life (see chapter 12.)

The black middle class constituted more than half of the African American population, but there was also a large black underclass. Almost one
third of the nation's black populace lived under the poverty line, mostly in
decaying urban neighborhoods. As middle class African Americans left

these neighborhoods, the neighborhoods became increasingly impoverished and the remaining denizens became increasingly desperate. Education and family life among inner city blacks were among the worst in the nation, and gangs, drugs, and violence became a way of life for much of the black lower class. Affirmative action programs largely focused on race as opposed to class, so many poor blacks were overlooked in favor of those of the African American middle class, and other social programs seemed just as futile to the poor black community.

This growing frustration and feeling of being trapped in poverty manifested itself in numerous ways. At its best, such anger was expressed through creative outlets such as rap music, but at its worst, it manifested itself as senseless violence. In April 1992, the anger of those living in poverty in Los Angeles exploded onto the streets. The year before, a black motorist named Rodney King had been stopped by police after leading them on a chase. A bystander with a video camera filmed what ensued, the nightstick beating of King by the officers. While some argued that King was posing a direct threat to the officers, for most Americans the beating appeared excessive, as King was prone, unarmed, and outnumbered. Charges were brought against the officers, but the initial trial, held in an affluent suburb outside of Los Angeles, seemed a mockery to most inner city blacks who claimed that police brutality in the city had become commonplace. When the officers were acquitted by the all-white jury, the anger of poor blacks found its outlet in what would become the largest racial disturbance of the twentieth century. The riots, which fanned out from South Central Los Angeles' ghettos, left more than fifty dead, and tremendous property damage from looting and arson. For many whites in the country, many of whom had assumed that racial inequality had largely vanished since it was not as prevalent in the media as it had once been, the riots in Los Angeles were a wake-up call.

ECONOMICS

Despite the rough early years, when a recession forced an increase in bankruptcy filings and mass layoffs in many industries, the 1990s will likely be remembered historically as an age of economic prosperity, and indeed, money circulated through the American economy in unprecedented amounts. It is also likely, however, that some will equate the wealth of the nineties to that of the Gilded Age of a century before, at which time most of the wealth was held by only a small number of people. Furthermore, the economic gap between labor and management increased considerably in the nineties. A study released in August 2000 showed that the pay rate for corporate executives bloated uncontrollably during the decade, increasing an average of 535 percent. Meanwhile, the stock market grew at a lesser rate, with the Standard & Poor's 500 growing only 297 percent, a fact that would come under increasing scrutiny with the corporate scandal revelations of the early years of the twenty-first century. Even more shocking is that during this period, the average pay for workers increased a mere 27.5 percent, just over the inflation rate, which put corporate CEOs'pay at approximately 475 times workers' pay.[4]

These figures represent an extreme, but the economy demonstrated sharp distinctions between financial tiers. In 1995, those without a high school education had an average income of $14,000 a year, while those who had completed high school made an average of $21,400. College graduates made about $37,000 a year and those with advanced degrees earned an average of $56,700. These pronounced differences made clear the importance of education in the working world. But they also made clear that 1990s America was not a classless society. Moreover, personal economic growth was not equal among the different tiers of the populace. From the early eighties to the mid-nineties, the average income of families in the wealthiest 20 percent of the population grew about 20 percent, while for those in the second wealthiest 20 percent it grew a bit over 8 percent.[5] But those in the lower classes did not see a similar growth in their income, leaving many, particularly those who had not completed high school, under the poverty level. Although the poverty rate was decidedly under that of the late 1980s, by the end of the 1990s about 12.5 percent of the American population still lived under the poverty line. More than 6.6 million families and nearly 33.9 million individuals lived in poverty according to the 2000 Census.

Several developments fundamentally changed the economy of the nation, and, indeed, that of the world. One of the most important of these was the force of globalization, the linking of the American economy with the economies of other nations. From 1970 to 1994, the dollar amount of exported goods went from about $43 billion to $513 billion, and imports rose from $40 billion to $663 billion.[6] The outpacing of exports by imports naturally stirred considerable concern among some Americans, many of whom worried that foreign goods would cause damage to the United States economy. Industrial America was particularly hard hit by globalization. As industries lost a share of the market to foreign companies, and as numerous American corporations constructed factories on foreign soil with low wage labor, particularly in Mexico and Asia, many American workers found their jobs threatened. But many also saw globalization as a boon for the country. Certainly, increased importation created a wider selection of goods available to American consumers, and it also tended to keep prices low. Many political leaders worked to stimulate global economic exchange by weakening trade barriers. In particular, two major trade agreements championed by the Clinton administration were passed by Congress in the 1990s. The North American Free Trade Agreement (NAFTA) was passed in 1993, and the General Agreement on Tariffs and Trade (GATT) was passed in 1994. Both were topics of fierce debate, and the ultimate effects—positive and negative—of these agreements continued to be debated into the new millennium.

Certainly, the rapid advancement of computer technology contributed to major changes in the way business was conducted, and also in how personal finances were managed. Banking came to be almost entirely computer assisted, with most Americans engaging in some kind of computerized banking by the end of the decade. Home computers could be used not only to manage finances, but also using the Internet, customers could also check on the latest details of their bank accounts. Computerized record keeping took over in all areas, from businesses, to schools, to government agencies. Libraries across the country retired their card catalogues in favor of more efficient and user-friendly computer catalogues. Cash registers in retail establishments were widely replaced by new models that integrated computer processors and monitors with cash drawers. But increasingly, purchases were made with credit cards. Cashier computers electronically processed credit cards, sending information to the credit card companies, which electronically reciprocated with credit approval. Many stores even instituted systems which allowed customers to swipe their own credit or debit cards into the computer, making the cashier nearly expendable. Even industrial manufacturing heavily utilized advanced computer technology, with computerized product design and robotic factory labor.

RURAL AMERICA

Rural America saw a thinning in population, part of a long-lived trend, begun in the 1930s, of flight away from the country into the cities. Moreover, per capita birth rates decreased in rural America, as well. The 1990 census determined that in the Midwestern Great Plains region the average population density was an average of six people per square mile. The declining population continued to have an effect similar to that of earlier decades. Political clout was affected, as were schools and hospitals. Obviously, a school or hospital in an area where the population was declining would be forced to downscale or even close if revenues failed to cover operating costs. And the closing of these institutions ran serious risk of increasing the number of people fleeing a rural region in order to be closer to the amenities offered by the city.[7]

The economic situation for farmers improved somewhat from the 1980s, but with continued growth in industrialism and urbanism, farming nonetheless suffered its share of hardships, especially for small independent farmers. The growing of crops and raising of livestock increasingly became the domain of corporations, many of them international conglomerates, with which it was difficult for the small farmer and rancher to compete. As it was, the number of independent farmers decreased. Small farmers were also affected by international concerns. The nineties saw an increase in international market competition, and farmers were also plagued by the fact that, while many foreign countries had a call for American produce, a number of them, including Russia and former Russian republics, simply lacked the funds to purchase American goods. Natural disasters also affected small farms. A series of floods in 1993, the worst recorded for the area, was disastrous for farmers in the Midwest. And while the large corporations were able to withstand the economic blow of the floods, many smaller farmers were not so well equipped. As a result of these troubles, the last half of the twentieth century saw a sharp decline in the number of rural residents making a living in the farming industry. An increased number of residents turned to other areas of employment, such that by the 1990s, the majority of those living in rural America were employed outside of the farming industry. Only about 3 percent of the nation's population was employed in the farming industry in the nineties. This was a startling reversal of figures from fifty years before, in which the number of farmers in rural areas was three to four times that of non-farmer residents.[8]

POLITICS

Politically, the U.S. populace was probably as evenly divided in the nineties as it had ever been. But more important than partisan positioning, a growing number of Americans looked to politics with increased suspicion, even disdain. The political events of the decade certainly encouraged this move, as partisan infighting and power politics seemed to eclipse the concern of public officials for the American people. And those people frequently made their dissatisfaction known.

Many viewed the federal government as lumbering and ineffective. In fact, in both the eighties and nineties, many major pieces of legislation came into being, but the battles between Republicans and Democrats made this a laborious process. Americans seemed increasingly tired of what they saw as governmental gridlock. George Bush, elected president in 1988, had particular difficulty with the Democratic Congress, especially when it came to domestic issues. Bush seemed to some commentators to have little real interest in the domestic agenda, but he had inherited a dangerous economic condition, an enormous debt and deficit which was playing a part in effecting an economic recession in the late eighties. Largely driven by these conditions, Bush promised in his campaign that there would be "no new taxes," and he consequently found himself in frequent conflict with Congress over the implementation of any domestic programs that required increases in federal spending. But in 1990, Bush was persuaded into approving a program to reduce the deficit, a program that required a considerable tax increase.

Despite this change of tone, as well as the fights with Congress over other issues, including a 1991 civil rights bill, Bush was a popular president for most of his term in office. Part of his popularity came from his involvement in several global conflicts that emphasized the United States' status as the only remaining superpower, a result of the Soviet Union undergoing a weakening and then collapsing from 1987 to 1991. The United States had had great success with the ousting of Panama's leader Manuel Noriega, accused and eventually convicted of drug trafficking. And then, in 1991, the U.S., along with an international military coalition, took action against Iraq, which had invaded Kuwait in an attempt to annex the oil-rich country. The United Nations demanded Iraq's withdrawal, even as the coalition gathered some 690,000 troops along the Saudi Arabia-Kuwait border. Iraq's leader, Saddam Hussein, failed to withdraw by the given deadline of January 15, 1991, and the next day the U.S. led coalition began a bombing campaign that would last for six weeks. A ground campaign followed. Ultimately, Iraqi forces were driven from Kuwait with relative ease. Coalition soldiers met little resistance on the ground, suffering a light casualty count of 141 fatalities. The apparent victory that came when Saddam Hussein agreed to allied cease-fire terms on February 28 was very popular with Americans back home, even though the Iraqi regime remained intact.

But although Bush's popularity was at its highest point after the war, the issue of the economy soon drove it downward. The recession was worsening and the administration was perceived as doing little to combat it. This set George Bush up for his ultimate defeat in the 1992 presidential election in which many Americans derided the Bush campaign's heedlessness of the issue with a call of "It's the economy, stupid!"

In the 1992 campaign, Arkansas governor William Jefferson Clinton, a Democrat, won a decisive victory. Economic troubles plagued the Bush campaign, and Bush had troubles trying to cater to the political right without alienating the left. But even more important to the election results was Bill Clinton's public persona. Clinton was affable, optimistic, and one of the finest public speakers that the U.S. presidency had ever seen. Clinton's clear, specific addressing of the economy also helped secure votes. In the end, Clinton won 370 electoral votes and Bush won 168.

But another election year development also revealed a great deal about the American public's view of politics. A Texas billionaire named Ross Perot entered the race as an independent candidate and at times in the spring appeared to be leading both Bush and Clinton in the polls. Perot's greatest asset was his ability to tap into Americans' exasperation with both major parties. Although Perot was far richer than the vast majority of the populace, he came across as being outside of the establishment, as not tied down by the petty power politics of the major parties. Moreover, Perot had a folksy style about him that gave many Americans the sense that he was one of the common people, like themselves, and that he would represent the people, rather than any party line or corporate interests, which, ironically, the wealthy CEO was seen as being far more removed from than his Democratic and Republican foes. Perot's full potential effect on the presidential campaign will never be known, since he effectively derailed his own efforts when he withdrew from the race in July in the face of media scrutiny and then reentered in October to much diminished support. Nonetheless, he garnered 19 percent of the popular vote, which ultimately failed to secure him any electoral votes. In truth, Perot ultimately offered very little in the way of concrete ideas in his campaign, but the fact that he gained more support than any third-party candidate in 80 years demonstrated that much of the country was tired of partisan bickering and governmental bureaucracy, and was looking for a change.

The partisan struggles of the Bush administration paled in comparison to those experienced by Bill Clinton. Coming into office with a fairly liberal agenda, Clinton found himself quickly on the defensive. His efforts to eliminate the ban on gays in the military was countered so strongly by conservatives and military leaders that the result was a largely impotent "Don't Ask, Don't Tell" policy toward gay men and women serving in the armed forces. The congressional approval process on political appointments made by Clinton early in his administration was frequently so contentious that he had to withdraw the appointment. His major efforts to dramatically reform national health care, so that every American was guaranteed affordable medical care, were met with ferocious resistance from those that believed the system would put far too much power in the hands of the government. Ultimately, the efforts of medical care reform died in late 1994.

Clinton had his share of political victories, in part aided by his ideological move from the left to the center, including a new budget, which included significant new taxation of wealthy Americans. His victory in getting NAFTA approved, however, was over the opposition of many Democrats, as well as that of the AFL-CIO. It also made a great number of working class Americans, fearful of job losses, wary of the administration.

The conflicts of government were seen by many Americans as nothing but party politics, Republicans fighting Democrats, and vice versa, not on any true ideological grounds but on partisan ones. This partisan combat suddenly became much more volatile with the elections of 1994, in which Republicans took the majority in both houses of Congress. Party leaders acclaimed this as the Republican Revolution, overstating what they claimed was a sea change in American ideology, towards a more conservative ideal. The new House speaker Newt Gingrich had, shortly before the election, released his Contract with America, a set of promises that echoed longtime Republican goals, and many in the party saw the election results as a sign that U.S. voters supported those ideals. In truth, it is unlikely that many voters were even familiar with the contract's content at the time of the election, and post-election response to it seemed as split as opinion had ever been over Republican ideals, with some in support, and plenty of detractors cynically referring to Gingrich's promises as the Contract on America.

The contract was principally concerned with fiscal issues, but opponents pointed out how the document, in some cases through pointed omission of important details, opened windows for anti-abortion legislation and the repeal of certain federal social programs. The fights that ensued between Congress and the Presidency in the years that followed were of historic magnitude, reaching their worst when the government twice shut down, in November 1995 and again in January 1996, because of their inability to agree on a federal budget. To many political commentators and the public alike, this case smacked more of election year posturing than true legislative debate, and antipathy towards the federal government rose. But it rose more for the Republicans, whose leaders had refused to pass a "continuing resolution" that would have prevented the government from shutting down during debates. Perhaps those leaders thought that this might make a positive impression of the public as a sign of Republican resolve, but most Americans were simply angered by the shutdown of federal services, and unpaid federal workers were even more exasperated.

This set the stage for Clinton's 1996 win of a second term over Republican Bob Dole, 375 electoral votes to 159. But the months before the election saw a major flurry of cooperation as the Congress and President grew concerned about how little legislation had been passed in the past two years. The legislation was largely economic, appealing to workingclass Americans. For the first time in over a decade, the minimum wage was raised. The Congress also passed legislation that further protected workers from insurance companies, and passed a major welfare reform bill, which reduced the amount of money available through welfare, and also turned much of the power to distribute those funds over to the states.

SCANDAL AND THE PRESIDENCY

In 1997, Bill Clinton proved that he could negotiate with the Republican Congress on a new budgetary plan. The smooth negotiations tempered the disgust that had been evoked by the government shutdowns, and Clinton's popularity received a considerable boost. But the greatest challenge to the presidency was yet to come. From the start of his presidency, Clinton had been plagued by rumors of scandal, from alleged banking and real estate malfeasance (the Whitewater Scandal), to charges of corruption in his cabinet, to a sexual harassment suit filed against him by Paula Jones, who had worked for him when he was governor. Kenneth Starr, a former official in the Justice Department during Ronald Reagan's presidency, was appointed as an independent counsel for the Whitewater case, which had netted several convictions, but found no conclusive evidence of wrongdoing on the part of Clinton or his wife, Hillary. Starr was again appointed to investigate allegations that had arisen during inquiries into Paula Jones's accusations, that Clinton had been sexually involved with a White House intern,

Monica Lewinsky. Moreover, it was claimed that during his Paula Jones case deposition Clinton had lied about the relationship and had encouraged Lewinsky and others to lie.

Whatever else Clinton did in 1998, the Lewinsky affair constantly cast a shadow over him. He continued to vehemently deny the relationship, and during this period the majority of the public came to regard Clinton as an embattled innocent and Starr as a vindictive villain seeking to derail a political opponent by any means possible. During this time Clinton's approval rating never dropped below 60 percent, at its peak reaching a record 79 percent. Then, as the case seemed to be losing steam, Lewinsky struck a deal with Starr, testifying to the relationship. Clinton was backed into a corner and forced to admit to the relationship. The report finally submitted by Starr created a media sensation, largely due to its graphic sexual details. The report was published in full in many newspapers across the country, and even television newscasters recounted details. Never had such salacious details been made so public. The American populace seemed simultaneously fascinated and repulsed by the particulars of the case, and even as many were distressed by the president's actions, as many or more were disturbed by what they saw as a clear-cut invasion of privacy. This latter impulse helped Clinton maintain a strong approval rating, even after the revelations. His ratings also stayed strong as Congressional Republicans called for his impeachment. Poll after poll showed that the majority public opinion was decidedly against impeachment, but House leaders continued to push for it. On December 19, 1998, in a vote that largely fell along party lines, Clinton became the second U.S. president to be impeached. The President would eventually be acquitted by the Senate, but the whole affair had left an indelible mark on the country, and disgusted many Americans.

The case was perhaps most notable in how it seemed to do away with the line between private and public life, a line that many Americans held sacred. It was also important in how it brought scandal to the forefront of American politics. And in a time when more conservative Americans were bemoaning the loosening of mores, and especially of sexual mores, the publicity given the details of the President's sexual behaviors was too much. Many blamed the media for their almost morbid attention to those details, but in truth the whole case provided few who could not be cast in the role of villain, from the media, to Congressional Republicans, to Clinton, to Starr, to Lewinsky. Americans far and wide expressed a keen unhappiness with the events that had transpired, but the source of their unhappiness was nowhere close to uniform.

CRIME

Despite the number of high profile crimes that occurred in the 1990s, the decade actually saw a decline in the rate of crime, which reached a 20-year low. The decline began about mid-decade, reversing a long-lasted trend of rising crime. In 1996 and 1997, violent crime fell 11 percent, with about a 20 percent decline in murder alone. During the same period, burglary dropped 9 percent and robbery 17 percent.[9] The reasons for the decline were hotly debated. Some claimed that the decrease was the result of better crime fighting techniques which allowed law enforcement to deter more crime, while others claimed that it was the result of an improving economy, wherein a greater number of people were financially stable. Some claimed that tougher legal penalties had a great deal to do with the reduction. Certainly the rapidly growing number of people in the United States' prisons suggested that more people were being incarcerated and that many were serving longer sentences than they might have a generation before. The growing prison population, however, was problematic. By the end of the 1990s, nearly two million Americans were in prison. Many new prisons were constructed, but they could not outpace the growing number of incarcerations, and prison crowding became a growing problem. An increasing number of individuals were incarcerated on non-violent drug charges, which led many to question the theory that tougher penalties were really the cause of the reduction in violent crime.[10]

Central to the federal government's actions against crime of all sorts was the War on Drugs, a 16-billion-dollar-a-year project designed to eradicate illegal drug use in the United States. The largest dollar amount of this war went to the Bureau of Prisons, the Justice Department agency that oversaw the operation of 90 prisons across the country. Another five billion a year was spent by state and local government on drug user and dealer incarceration. Over forty other government agencies also received moneys to fight the nation's drug epidemic. Included in these was the Department of Defense, which took active action against suppliers of illegal drugs in the Caribbean and in Central and South America. The U.S. Department of Health's Substance Abuse and Mental Health Services Administration also received considerable funding from the War on Drugs, equaling about $1.3 billion in 1997. This agency was the primary organization to be involved in prevention and treatment programs, and was instrumental in distributing funds to local treatment and prevention facilities. Such, many believed that it was deserving of even greater funding, and that the reduction of drug use through these kinds of efforts served the populace better than increases in incarcerations.

By the end of the decade, however, many were questioning the efficacy of the War of Drugs. Use of illegal drugs did not diminish during the 1990s, and the federal government's efforts to stifle the drug trade led not to fewer drugs on the street, but rather to higher prices for those drugs, thereby making the drug dealing business even more lucrative. The War on Drugs was also attributed with triggering an increase in violence, more so than had the drugs themselves. The crackdowns on drug solicitation prompted many dealers to arm themselves to a greater degree. While the early criticisms of the War on Drugs came from a fringe political minority, as the decade progressed, and as the drug problem seemed as widespread as ever, a greater number of mainstream figures, including some in law enforcement, came forth with their opposition to the war's agenda. Though it remained a minority, an increasing number of people even suggested that the legalization (coupled with firm government regulation) of drugs might be a better solution. In some states, the first steps towards legalization were taken with public voting on the issue of legalized medical marijuana. Such legislation would make it possible to use marijuana as a prescribed medication. States that passed such legislation, however, were faced with a hurdle: regardless of what state law might allow, marijuana remained illegal under federal law.

Even though the decade's decline in crime comforted many Americans, certain crimes gained widespread media attention. This attention created for some Americans a sense that the country was more dangerous than it ever had been. A 1994 Associated Press poll reported that 52 percent of men and 68 percent of women held high fears of falling victim to crime. The murder trial of O.J. Simpson garnered more attention than did any other trial of the decade, but it was not the only high profile case. A series of high school shootings and other violent acts by suburban teens also caught the media's attention. So too did a growing number of acts of domestic terrorism. These were naturally extreme cases, but although conventional crime dropped, it also remained a significant problem in the United States. The statistics in crime were a sobering reminder that a reduction fell far from solving the problem of crime, and meant little indeed to the victims. In 1996, for instance, there were 9.1 million Americans who fell victim to violent crime. A murder was reported to police somewhere in the country an average of once every 27 minutes, a rape every six minutes, a robbery every 59 seconds, and an aggravated assault every 31 seconds.[11]

DOMESTIC TERRORISM AND THE MILITIA MOVEMENT

Ted Kaczynski, dubbed the Unabomber by the FBI, mailed a series of bombs from May 1978 to April 1995, killing several men and injuring numerous others. The Unabomber's identity had remained a mystery for most of this time period, but in 1993 the otherwise silent Kaczynski began to write letters to the press and sometimes to his targets. In 1995, the *New York Times* published a 35,000-word essay by Kaczynski, which ultimately led to his arrest when a family member recognized his writing style. In 1998, Kaczynski was sentenced to life in prison without parole.[12] The essay published by the *New York Times* was a long political manifesto detailing Kaczynski's beliefs that American society was corrupt and rationalizing his desire to rebel against it. But most Americans who followed his story were convinced that he was mentally unstable, especially after a court-appointed psychologist deemed him a probable paranoid schizophrenic.

But other acts of terrorism were less easily explained away. The most striking of these was the bombing of a federal building in Oklahoma City on April 19, 1995. The bombing, which killed 168 people, including many children, was the worse act of terrorism of the nineties. While initial speculation had it that it was executed by Middle Eastern terrorists, many Americans were shocked to find that it had been perpetrated by one of their own. The principal figure in the bombing was Timothy McVeigh, who had ties to a militia group. This brought attention to the growing number of such groups across the country. The Oklahoma bombing was in part a response to a clash with a similar group, a well-armed religious cult calling itself the Branch Davidians, exactly two years before. The standoff with the Branch Davidians ended when the group's Waco, Texas compound caught fire, killing most within. Most Americans who followed the story agreed with federal officials that the deadly fire was ignited from within the compound, possibly intentionally set by cult members. But others, including McVeigh, believed that federal law enforcement officials were responsible for the blaze. For those in the country's growing militia movement, the tragedy at Waco was a sign that the federal government had overstepped its bounds. Centered mostly in rural areas, and composed largely of disaffected citizens, militias saw the federal government as a fascistic institution, one that sought to trade in the rights of the common man in exchange for international power (though the concept of the "common man" was sometimes a narrow one given that some militia groups also exhibited strong white-supremacist tendencies). These notions bore some similarities to those presented in the Unabomber's Manifesto, but here they were being extolled not by a single man, easily dismissed as insane, but by a growing number of working-class Americans. Ultimately, the percentage of Americans involved in militia movements was quite small, but those militias nevertheless succeeded in making a name for themselves, and acts like the Oklahoma City bombing showed that these were people not to be ignored.

MEDIA EVENTS & O.J.

The 1990s may well be remembered as the great age of the "media event." For instance, the political events that rocked the nation grabbed most of the populace's attention not merely for their inherent importance, but also for their significance as stories, as television dramas as compelling as anything that network producers could come up with on their own. Certainly the scandal that led to Bill Clinton's impeachment, with its salacious details, became a favorite story for television reporters. Likewise, the dynamic pictures from the front lines of the American invasion of Iraq kept viewers glued to their TV sets. As important as these events were, in and of themselves, also of major significance was the way that they were treated by the media. In short, as the media covered the stories, the manner of coverage itself became a major story.

Perhaps nowhere was this so clear as in the case of former football great and actor, O.J. "The Juice" Simpson. Simpson's wife, Nicole Brown Simpson, and her friend Ronald Goldman had been found brutally murdered on June 12, 1994 outside of her Brentwood townhouse in Los Angeles. The murders immediately garnered considerable media attention, for their location, their brutality, and for their celebrity connection. But the early attention soon seemed minute in comparison to the bizarre, almost surreal events that would follow. Five days after the killings, O.J. Simpson was charged with two counts of first degree murder. Simpson's lawyer negotiated a time for his surrender to authorities at police headquarters, but when the hour arrived Simpson did not, becoming, in effect, a wanted fugitive. That evening Simpson was spotted. Then began the strange scene of Simpson riding his white Ford Bronco, driven by his friend A.C. Cowlings, up Los Angeles freeways, followed by a parade of police cruisers. News helicopters covered the chase from the air. In fact, the whole affair was traveling at well under the speed limit, resembling a ceremonial procession more than a high-speed chase.

More striking than the actual chase was the nature of the television coverage. Regularly scheduled programs were interrupted by newscasters who filled the viewership in on what was happening, and presented live video footage from the scene. Informed of the news, a mass of residents crowded to the side of the freeway to watch, and even to cheer Simpson on, in some cases holding signs reading "Go, Juice, Go!" and the like. The cameras followed the chase along the freeways until the Bronco finally pulled into the driveway of Simpson's multimillion-dollar estate. The cameras stayed on the parked Bronco as Simpson spoke to police through a cell phone, and as the sun went down, with cameras still rolling on the darkness. Eventually, Simpson surrendered himself, but the affair of the chase and siege took hours, equaling hours of interrupted television programming. As across the country Americans watched rapt.

What ensued was the Simpson trial which lasted for many weeks, and ended in Simpson's acquittal, though he was later found guilty in a civil suit filed by Goldman's family. The trial itself became far more important than Simpson himself. As popular as Simpson was as an athlete and an actor, it was the trial that became a sounding board for pundits and average Americans, about race, about the justice system, about media, about celebrity, about spousal abuse. The whole of the Simpson case brought commentators out in droves. The case became a major theme of discussion in all media.

The Simpson case was only the most notable of the media events of the 1990s. Other crimes fell under public scrutiny, from the Menendez brothers' killing of their parents, to the high school shootings of the decade (see chapter 2). The Gulf War became a television spectacle, and notably one that boosted CNN to paramount importance among news-gathering organizations. The cable network's video footage of the initial U.S. air invasion of Iraq entranced TV audiences with its otherworldly, video-game-like appearance. Nearing the end of the decade, more people than perhaps ever before followed the actions of Congress, as the House of Representatives leveled an impeachment at President Bill Clinton, complete with sexual details that were reported on TV news broadcasts and in newspapers across the country.

Key to these events was the way they were packaged by the media, especially television. More than simply relating the details of a given news item, the media increasingly compartmentalized information. Roy F. Fox, in his book *MediaSpeak,* explored how "the Gulf War was a serious, deadly experience, but it was nonetheless wrapped in media messages akin to a TV mini-series, complete with titles, logos, musical sound tracks, computer graphics, controlled press conferences, and star reporters wearing field jackets."[13] This was true of many news stories, which consequently went well beyond being mere reportage, instead becoming "events," with television networks putting as much thought into their presentation as went into the content of such presentations. That the packaging of these events borrowed so much from entertainment programs did not go unnoticed.

NEWS, REALITY TV, AND THE AMERICAN WORLDVIEW

As hard news appeared increasingly as entertainment to many, there was a consequent rise in the amount of television entertainment programming that walked the line between reality and fiction. So-called reality television came to full fruition in the 1990s, and reached a peak in the early 2000s. Shows like *A Current Affair* (1986–1996) and *Hard Copy* (1989–1999) presented themselves as news shows, yet even a casual viewer of these programs could tell that they were very different from the traditional network news broadcasts. Although the programs certainly dealt with select important news items, their coverage was geared towards maximum sensationalism. For instance, the details of Bill Clinton's sexual misconduct were a popular subject for these shows, while the rather dry details of impeachment proceedings gained less attention. In short, then, the entertaining aspects of a story were emphasized more than the aspects that might prove educational.

Reality TV was also shaped by several crime and justice shows. *America's Most Wanted,* first aired in 1988, presented dramatizations of true crimes and actually marketed itself as a crime fighting tool. Photographs of fugitives were shows on screen, accompanied by a phone number which viewers were urged to call if they had any information on that fugitive. On the other hand, *Cops,* first aired in 1989, did not rely on dramatizations whatsoever, and urged viewers to take a passive role in crime fighting. In *Cops,* a cameraman with a shoulder-held video camera, would ride with police officers while they responded to calls. The show captured car and foot chases, fights, public drunkenness and nudity, and anything else that might be exciting to the viewers. Although the show included a disclaimer that all suspects were innocent until proven guilty, they were nonetheless a subject for mockery in a program that showed them at their worst, and some argued that *Cops* ultimately had already judged the subjects in its methods of depicting them.

The irony of reality television was that it really didn't depict reality. *Hard Copy* and *A Current Affair* were not only very selective about the stories they chose to cover, but also about what footage they included in their coverage. On occasion, these programs utilized video footage not of the actual story being covered, but of earlier similar, and generally more sensational footage. *Cops,* though filmed in the streets as an allegedly true document of "the men and women of law enforcement," was heavily edited. Only the most exciting or sordid outings by the police were included in the broadcasts, most of them notably taking place at night. Additionally, suspects' reactions to the police officers were shaped by the cinematography and editing. A growing concern about *Cops* and similar programming was the way the cameras shaped the behaviors of the police officers. Some claimed that the number of potentially dangerous car chases depicted on these shows was an encouragement for officers on camera to act in a like manner. Indeed, the number of high-speed car chases occurring in the country did increase during the 1990s, though there was no evidence definitively tying this rise to reality TV. Many media experts were concerned about how this kind of programming manipulated the public's worldview, so that what the public took for reality was, in fact, a performative alteration of reality. But on the other hand, many, perhaps even most, Americans took these shows for what they were: pseudo-reality. This, however, posed another problem for many media-savvy Americans, in that it cast considerable doubt on what they saw in the media. Although media manipulation had existed as long as had media, its rapid proliferation at the end of the century created a growing suspicion on the part of the public, not only of the media, but of those using the media, including public officials. (Note: Reality TV took two basic forms. Those mentioned in this chapter, though largely created and consumed as entertainment, deliberately tried to sell themselves as pseudo-news, that is to say, that which was actually happening in the world outside. Another form of reality TV unapologetically presented itself as entertainment, and also presented a "reality" that was much more transparently shaped by the shows' producers. MTV's *The Real World* set a precedent for this kind of programming by candidly filming the interaction amongst a group of young, good-looking strangers living together under one roof.)

THE AIDS EPIDEMIC

The very term *epidemic* was one that only came into wide use in respect to AIDS (acquired immune deficiency syndrome) in the 1990s. The 1980s saw a rapid spread of the disease, both in the United States and overseas, but many Americans still considered it a virus that only affected the fringes of society. But as the number of AIDS-related deaths increased in the 1990s, and as a growing number of high profile figures, from sports stars to actors, contracted HIV (human immunodeficiency virus), the virus that led to AIDS, a different attitude developed. Indeed, it became increasingly hard to dismiss AIDS as something that only affected promiscuous homosexuals and intravenous drug users as it became one of the leading causes of death among Americans between the ages of 35 and 44. In 1997, the Centers for Disease Control estimated the number of Americans infected with HIV as being as high as 900,000. Moreover, they estimated that only about half of those infected were aware that they were.[14] Worldwide, the number of HIV-infected individuals reached a staggering 22 million in 1997 and global concern about the epidemic increased accordingly. One problem with such estimates was that AIDS, despite growing education, was still considered by many to be a syndrome that should be hidden. It is true, however, that conditions were better in the 1990s than they had been even a few years before. AIDS patients were less likely to be left untreated due to fears of contracting the disease, and generally they were not so ostracized as they had been before. But the popular image of AIDS was not one that was easily shaken by the general public or by the patients themselves.

However, the public face of AIDS certainly did alter somewhat in the nineties. In 1990, over 121 thousand people died of AIDS, including Ryan White, who posed a real problem to those who preferred to regard AIDS as a fringe disease. White, a teenager with all-American looks, had contracted the virus via a blood transfusion, and in his short life became one of the most recognized AIDS activists, showing that the disease's reach was far longer than some thought. The year 1990 was also when former president Ronald Reagan issued an apology for his administration's neglect of the AIDS crisis, signaling a change in official concern over the issue. As the decade progressed, other well-known figures fell to AIDS, including actor Robert Reed, tennis pro Arthur Ashe, dancer Rudolf Nureyev, and rapper Easy-E. Perhaps the figure who most contributed to a change in the popular perception of AIDS was basketball great Earvin "Magic" Johnson, who announced in 1991 that he had contracted HIV. He retired from basketball and became a major rallying figure for those who wished to show that AIDS could be contracted by anyone. Possibly the greatest change in perspective on the disease occurred when Johnson returned to professional basketball. The thought of an infected player on the court would likely have been scoffed at a decade earlier when most Americans had a lesser understanding of HIV, but now Johnson's return was celebrated, and Johnson's popularity remained undiminished.

COMPUTERS AND THE INTERNET

Undoubtedly, the most important technological innovations of the decade had to do with computers. Computers had been gradually increasing their impact on society over several decades. Intel's introduction of the microprocessor in 1971 opened the door to increasingly compact and powerful computer systems. Then, in the late seventies, Apple Computers introduced the first mass-market personal computer (PC), which was followed by a gradual growth in the PC market throughout the 1980s. But in the 1990s the proliferation of the personal computer accelerated to a new and astounding level. Computers very fundamentally changed the way the country operated, and there was no area of American life that was untouched.

Throughout the decade, the most powerful company in the computer business was Microsoft, the company that had devised the operating system MS-DOS for IBM's first personal computer. MS-DOS and later Microsoft's Windows operating systems dominated the computer industry, and the company also produced highly popular software, turning the company into a giant corporation and making CEO Bill Gates one of the country's richest executives. Not all were happy with Microsoft, however, and several smaller companies accused the corporation of unfair business practices. In 1997, the U.S. Justice Department filed a number of antitrust suits against Microsoft, which was deemed to have monopolized the market. In particular, Microsoft's Windows '98 operating system, it was argued, worked so well with Microsoft programs, including its Internet Explorer, that it effectively stifled the market for other software creators' wares.

As much as the computer market expanded in the 1990s, so too did Internet use. The Internet had existed in some form or other since the creation of the Arpanet for the government's Advanced Research Projects Agency in 1963. Expansion from that point had been gradual, but starting in the late 1980s, the Internet grew tremendously. In 1984, there were fewer than a thousand computers hosting Web sites networked into the Internet, but by the mid-nineties, there were over six million host computers. Each host computer in turn serviced many individual personal computers, and consequently an enormous number of individual users. There were several reasons for this rapid acceleration in Internet use. Certainly, the general proliferation of personal computers contributed to it considerably. So too did the development of the World Wide Web, created in 1989 in Geneva, Switzerland. The WWW, frequently referred to simply as "the Web," allowed individual personal computer users an unprecedented opportunity to post their own sites online, and generally brought a greater sense of order, for both dissemination and retrieval of information. Most users accessed the Internet via phone lines, though with the growing amount of data contained on any given Web site, many, especially later in the decade, turned to fiber optics or other systems of information transference. E-mail (or electronic mail) also contributed to the growth of the Internet in the way it allowed individuals to communicate with ease and at very little expense with other users across the globe. By the mid-nineties, observers were estimating that the rate of e-mail use had overtaken that of the telephone or traditional postage. As a result, by decade's end many phone companies also began offering Internet service. Other companies, feeling threatened by the Internet, also jumped aboard. Media outlets particularly exploited the Internet, and in 1998, there were more than 3,250 newspapers and 1,280 television stations with Web sites.

The appearance of commercial Internet service providers probably contributed the greatest popular boost to the Internet. America Online (AOL), CompuServe, and other companies offered access to the Internet with a good deal of friendly assistance. The Internet was potentially overwhelming for many Americans, but these services provided customers with a user-friendly interface to the Internet, and helped the user search for and organize information more easily. AOL began as a self-contained online system. Users were able to send and receive e-mail from virtually any Internet user and were able to access a great number of features contained in America Online's host systems, but were unable to browse the Web. AOL, however, quickly amended their systems, adding Internet browsing software to later versions of their service. This helped to make AOL the largest Internet provider in the world, as did its reputation as a "safe" way to access the Internet. AOL marketed itself as the most family oriented of the service providers, offering strong juvenile protections from potentially objectionable online content. By 1998, AOL was reporting that it had 14 million users.

COMMUNICATIONS

Communications technology advanced to such an extent in the 1990s that, perhaps more than any other technological advancements of the decade, it altered the way of life for most Americans, and perhaps even effected a significant shift in worldview. More than a few scientists, writers, and politicians would refer to this as the age of information. More importantly, it was the age of information dissemination.

Besides e-mail, cellular phones, introduced publicly in the 1980s, became pervasive as their capacity grew and their size shrank. In 1994, there were about 16 million people in the U.S. using cell phones, but by 2001, there were a staggering 110 million users, according to the U.S. General Accounting Office. The increase was due to many factors, including the fact that what had earlier been bulky could fit easily in the palm of one's hand and in any pocket. Likewise, as the phones became more popular, retailers like Motorola, Nokia, Verizon, and Erikson were able to reduce prices not only on the phones, but on service, leading to still more consumers leaping on the cell phone bandwagon. Early in the decade, having a cell phone was a distinct status symbol, suggesting wealth and fashionability on the part of the user. But as the number of users increased, cell phones became less of a status symbol and more of a necessity. Many eschewed traditional phone service, keeping their cell phones as their only phone. So pervasive was the cell phone that even youths had them, with cell phone companies advertising cell phones not only to adults, but also to teenagers. One series of ads even depicted the advantages of a cell phone for every family member. Moreover, with the popularization of cell phones, they became something of a fashion accessory. As the phone itself was no longer a means of self expression, the design of phones, now available in a multitude of colors, was. The ring of a cell phone also became a means of self-expression. Early traditional digital tones were replaced by musical passages, at first a singular one and then by a electronically stored menu of selectable tunes. At decade's end, some cell phones could even be tapped into the Internet where they could download a seemingly infinite number of musical rings. The most advanced models offered e-mail capacity, direct Internet access, and even video games. In short, they became portable computers as well as telephones.

CONCLUSION

Given these developments, the United States was a distinctly different place by the end of the 1990s from what it had been at the dawn of the decade. Politically, it had been a volatile decade and changed how many regarded the American political system. Cynicism towards the process was certainly nothing new, but in the 1990s that cynicism reached a new peak. Likewise, the technological innovations of the decade changed the world and how many regarded it. The coming of a new millennium led many to believe that the country was on a kind of threshold, and that the 1990s were a gateway to a new world. Some religious fanatics anticipated great cosmic developments with the coming of the new millennium. More secular alarmists expected a great technological breakdown driven by the feared Y2K bug, a computer system problem resulting from a two-digit system of denoting years. These individuals feared that important computer systems would read the year 2000 as the year 1900 and shut down, resulting in widespread technological system failures and casting global society into utter chaos. In fact, January 1, 2000, seemed very much like December 31, 1999. Life in the United States continued as it had. Yet the import of the turn of the millennium was marked not only by fanatics and alarmists, and one can well understand the excitement and anticipation that infected even the most average of citizens. American society and culture had developed rapidly in the prior 10 years. While dramatic overnight change was not to be had on New Years' 2000, the volatility of the nineties electrified the imagination of a populace as to what the next 10 years would hold.

2
World of Youth

GENERAL FIGURES AND TRENDS

Unfortunately, the popular image of youth in the nineties is not a particularly positive one. Rather, it is one of violence, sex, and drugs. Certainly, there has long been a generation gap between American adults and their children, but in many respects, that gap seemed widened at the end of the twentieth century. It is true that certain events seemed to confirm this popular portrayal of youth, but it would be a mistake to generalize. Whatever images may have planted themselves indelibly in the popular consciousness, American youth were a diverse group and, on the whole, instrumental in shaping American culture.

Unlike the youths of the 1950s or the 1960s, those of the nineties were a group that was actively courted by older generations. While earlier generations tried to figure out youths, in the 1990s there was an active effort to let them speak for themselves. Never before had the youth of the nation been submitted to so many polls and surveys to find out what they thought about the world around them. It's true that many of these surveys were conducted by corporations interested in determining how best to market to a generation that generally was more affluent than any before them. But there was also a great concern over youths', and especially teens', views of themselves and their place in society because of the seemingly growing gap between them and parents.

A study by the Federal Interagency Forum on Child and Family Statistics found that in 1999 there were some 70.2 million children 18 years old or younger in the United States. This number accounted for more than a quarter of the national population. The study also found that American youths were becoming increasingly diverse. The stereotype of 1990s American youth tended to focus on those of the white middleclass. But this stereotype neglected the very real diversity of nineties youth. In fact, according to the 1990 census, about 35 percent of American youths from 10 to 29 years of age were non-white or Hispanic. The number of Hispanic youths increased the most quickly, reflecting the rapid growth of American Hispanics in all age groups. By 1999, 16 percent of America's youth were Hispanic/Latino, as compared to only 9 percent in 1980.[1]

In the 1990s, family structure and dynamic were often different from the traditional. Marriage came to be regarded in a very different light than in the 1950s, for instance. Whereas in the 1950s the divorce rate, as well as the percentage of individuals who never married, was fairly low, in the 1990s divorce became quite common. In the 1960s, about 90 percent of children lived with both parents, but by 1993 that number had decreased to about 70 percent.[2] Most children living with a single parent lived with their mothers, but the number living with fathers increased somewhat over the last two decades of the century. Although only about 2 percent lived with fathers in 1980, this number increased to 4 percent by 1999. Perhaps as a result of these figures, many youths expected to marry and have children at a later age, if at all.[3]

Despite the changing family dynamic, surveys suggest that the youth of the 1990s were actually returning, in many ways, to traditional valuation of the family. While family structures varied to a greater degree in the 1990s, many young people placed greater import on family ties than earlier generations of youth. Additionally, more youths seemed to return to traditional religion. While it is true that many youths continued to remain non-religious or religiously inactive, enrollment in religion-based youth groups mounted steadily during the decade. It may be that these inclinations were a reaction to growing up in a time of moral relativism, wherein values seemed largely undefined. Many youths sought some kind of moral structure in their lives, and traditional values provided this.

A 1998 *Rolling Stone* survey asked youth, "How do your moral standards compare with your parents?" In response to this, only 15 percent of youth said their moral standards were higher, and about 24 percent said they were about the same. But 58 percent saw their moral standards as below those of their parents.[4] Several things are suggested by these results. It is possible that the responding youths generally had higher regard for their parents, unlike the youth of the sixties, for instance, many of whom saw adults, including their parents, as culpable in the social and political problems of the era. Even more importantly, the survey suggested that nineties youth had a rather poor image of themselves. Why this self-image developed is open to debate, but it may well be that young people were somehow directed to think of themselves in this way. Certainly, youths were often depicted in the media as unmotivated and apathetic, and the repetition of the

notion that this was a less moral generation than the lionized ones of the
past (whatever the reality might have been), may well have implanted itself in the psyches of American youths. As Barbara Schneider and David
Stevenson pointed out, "Popular media images often portray adolescents
as 'slackers,' drug users, and perpetrators of violent crimes." But they continued, noting that "The overwhelming majority of teenagers, however,
graduate from high school, do not use hard drugs, are not criminals, and
do not father babies while still in their teens. Many of them are willing to
work hard to get good grades and assume this will make them eligible for
scholarships at the college they plan to attend."[5] Most also saw their relationship with parents as generally strong. A 1997 Gallup survey found that
96 percent of teenagers claimed that they got along with their parents, and
three out of four agreed that they shared their parents' values and morals.
About 82 percent ranked their home life as good or better.[6]

Interestingly, the notion of popularity, ever a vital force in shaping students' self-perception, changed somewhat in the latter half of the twentieth century. According to one study conducted in the early 1990s, 10 percent
of students considered themselves to be very popular and 65 percent considered themselves somewhat popular. It has been suggested that this trend
is the result of a gradual decentralization of the high school elite. Whereas
once a single small group of students may have been seen as the most popular, by the 1990s, this notion had become weakened by the development
of numerous smaller social cliques. The growth of these groups can certainly in part be attributed to the growing multi-ethnicity and multiculturalism of many schools. These smaller units of social organization allowed a greater number of youths to feel as if they were part of a group,
rather than to aspire to be a part of one single exclusive group. This greater
sense of acceptance, if only in one small social grouping, may well have
contributed to a rising sense of a youth's own popularity, and perhaps to
a diminished sense of wide-scale popularity's importance. Of course, in
many cases, some groups were seen as better than others, particularly by
those within the so-called better group. As in the popular mythology of
high school, for instance, the jocks were frequently the more celebrated
niche of a student body than, say, the nerds. Additionally, even as alternative culture began to gain acceptance and be welcomed into mainstream
culture, certain individual alternative cliques continued to feel ostracized.
Consequently, the same kind of unhappiness that developed as a result of
being outside of the elite was still wont to occur. This seemed to be the case
with those students involved in school violence during the nineties.[7]

By the 1990s, youths of middle and high school age spent nearly half
their waking hours in school or working. On average 43 percent of their
time was spent in school, and 4 percent at work. They also spent about 9
percent of their time with friends, and 19 percent with family. But youths
also spent an increasing amount of time alone, as much as 20 percent of

their waking hours. The average amount of time spent alone increased considerably as they aged. Students in the twelfth grade typically spent nearly 50 percent more time alone than did sixth graders. Most of this time was spent on typical youth activities: eating, dressing, schoolwork, and the like. But an average 19 percent of alone time was spent watching TV and movies as well as playing video games. Another 9 percent was spent on the phone. Computers in general consumed a growing amount of the average youth's alone time, with not only games, but also the Internet rapidly gaining popularity with young people. In addition, electronic activities, particularly games and television, occupied an increasing amount of time spent with friends.[8]

In 1993 the poverty rate for children reached a high of 22 percent, though social programs, as well as the improving economy, lowered this rate somewhat in the latter half of the decade. The 1990s ended with a child poverty rate of about 18 percent. Although this was certainly an improvement, child welfare specialists nonetheless found this percentage alarmingly high. Moreover, the poverty rate was compounded by inadequate housing and diet for an even larger percentage of the country's youth population. In 1997, the percentage of children living in problem housing—physically inadequate housing, overcrowded housing, or *high cost burden* housing—reached 36 percent, an increase of 6 percent over a 1978 study. Lack of food was a lesser problem, and the rate of child hunger actually decreased during the 1990s. However, about a third of the children living below the poverty line still suffered food insecurity.[9] Additionally, while fewer American children were actually starving, there was increased concern about the healthiness of diet. A large number of children did not meet nutrition standards, and there was an alarming increase in the number of obese children in the U.S.

The number of *latchkey* children, those who returned home after school to an empty house, also increased in the nineties. The growing number of single parents certainly contributed to this increase, but so too did many families' need for two incomes. In many cases, both parents were required to work in order to support the family. On the positive side, growing attention showered on this issue led to many school districts establishing latchkey programs, which provided parents with a supervised after-school program for their children. Such programs began to surface in the late eighties, but quickly proliferated, until they were to be found in most school districts. Also on the increase was the number of parks and recreations programs designed to give youths safe and positive activities in which to participate. Of course, the problem with leisure time programs for youths was that they were not free. Said programs frequently imposed an additional financial burden on parents. In poorer areas, community and governmental support, not always easily attained, was central to the effective implementation of such programs. Still, few could deny the positive impact of such programs on individual youths, and the efforts to provide positive alternatives to drugs or gangs was a major issue at the end of the decade, as youth crime gained visibility and American jails, adult and juvenile, filled at an accelerating rate. In the 1990s, more than half of all children third grade or younger received non-parental child care, increasingly needed by the growing number of households in which both parents worked.[10]

NAMING A GENERATION

The elder group of teens in the 1990s was given the label Generation X. This name, applied roughly to those born between 1965 and 1976 (or as late as 1980, depending on which sources one consults), was initially applied to suggest a certain degree of mystery about the generation, "X" equating an unknown factor, as in mathematics. The notion was held that this generation was an aimless one, lacking direction in their lives, and one whose ultimate contribution to society was unknown. This was the first generation to be born into the postmodern era, wherein values and truths seemed much more ambiguous than they had before. This was, more or less, the crux of the novel *Generation X,* by Douglas Coupland, which had given this generation its name. Although the X may have initially been regarded as an unknown factor, there was no shortage of people attempting to define this generation, particularly in terms that could be used in marketing. Corporations engaged in major efforts to commercially court Generation X, using music, fashion, and other cultural motifs that were seen to be definitive. Ultimately, however, by the mid-1990s, most individuals in this age demographic were rejecting the Generation X label. Even Coupland, in a 1995 *Esquire* article, claimed "that 'X' is over. Kurt Cobain's in heaven, *Slackers* is at Blockbuster, and the media refers to anyone aged 13 to 30 as Xers. Which only proves that marketers and advertisers never understood that X is not a chronological age, but a way of looking at the world."[11]

The following teen generation, those born after 1976 and just coming into their teens in 1990, posed a greater problem for the name-makers. Certain segments of this generation had an even bleaker, more directionless view of life, while others seemed to come full circle from the Generation X malaise, with stronger ties to parents and greater valuation for religion and formal education. In short, this generation seemed as difficult to define, if not more so, than the preceding X generation. More negative pundits labeled the generation Y, following X, naturally, but also echoing the question "why?," and suggesting a kind of nihilistic pointlessness. But since this generation was also the product of a new baby boom, many sought parallel labels to that of the Baby Boomers, many of whom were now entering middle age. Echo Boomers, some called them, others, the Baby

Busters or the Baby Boomlet generation. Others still thought of them as the
Thirteenth Generation, or Thirteeners. Ultimately, however, most of those
in this generation rejected the terms, suggesting, as did Generation X before, that to apply a single label to them all was a fruitless and even unfair
endeavor. A 1999 book by Barbara Schneider and David Stevenson tried
out a different label, which seemed to encompass both the good and bad
aspects of this generation. The book was called *The Ambitious Generation:
American Teenagers, Motivated but Directionless.*

EDUCATION

The American educational system came under fire in the 1990s, but while
many argued that the quality of education had dipped considerably in the
decade, these arguments largely echoed those that had permeated educational debate since the 1950s. Then, with the launching of the satellite Sput-
nik, commentators argued that America's failing schools had allowed the
U.S.S.R. to take the lead in the conquest of space. The eighties and nineties
saw a similar fear of international inferiority, but this time the fear was economic, in light of the substantial technological advancements of Japan and
other East Asian nations.

In 1989, George Bush and state governors across the country forged a
plan called Goals 2000, intended to make the United States the world leader
in education. Then, in 1993, Bill Clinton and the Congress passed legislation calling for voluntary national standards in numerous subjects, including English, mathematics, science, and history. This legislation was
stalled in the mid-nineties as legislators and educators quarreled about
what standards should be used, but in 1997, Clinton again called for higher
standards. This time more specifics were offered, including the implementation of standardized national testing of students, as well as the establishment of national standards to be applied to educators. At the end of
the decade there was also a push on the part of legislators, particularly Republicans, to establish a system of school vouchers. Supporters of the plan
claimed that it would give parents greater choice in what schools their children attended. The selected school would receive federal funds, in the form
of vouchers, which ultimately meant that the better schools, that is, the ones
that parents preferred, would be rewarded. Opponents claimed that this
system ran the risk of draining money from already under-funded schools,
especially those in poor neighborhoods. Indeed, some worried about federal funds being taken away from public schools, and granted to private
schools. Disputes arose around the possibility of religious schools receiving vouchers, which some claimed was a clear violation of the separation
of church and state. The 1990s would not see the end of the debate. Indeed,
by 2000, the rhetoric about failing schools was virtually identical to that
which began the decade, the ideals of Goals 2000 a distant memory.

The failing of schools was largely blamed on school administrators, but also on educators themselves. While it remained politically unpopular to criticize teachers in general, political figures nonetheless called for the removal of bad teachers. Conservative thinkers attacked the educational system for what they saw as a growing trend towards liberalism and progressivism in schools, as well as unchecked grade inflation. But these problems were openly blamed not on the individual teachers, but on organizational bodies, specifically education administrators and teachers unions, which these same critics claimed had ceased to represent the concerns of the actual educators in the classrooms.

But the truth of the American education system in the 1990s was probably quite different from the message conveyed through political rhetoric. Few would deny that the country's school systems could stand improvement, but the claim that schools were in their worst state ever was problematic. Indeed, American education was often negatively compared to a fictional golden age of education, typically the same 1950s in which alarmists likewise claimed that the country's schools were failing. In fact, the 1990s, due largely to reforms instituted in the eighties, saw notable improvements on many fronts of public education.

Approximately 82 percent of the population in 1997 had completed four years of high school, which marked a distinct rise over the course of the last few decades of the twentieth century. In 1992, the high school drop-out rate was less than 6 percent, a considerable improvement over the 11 percent of 1980, and the 20 percent of 1972.[12] Studies of current high school students suggested that up to 90 percent of them planned to attend college, and a large number of them were also already planning to continue into graduate school.[13] Moreover, an increased number of students seemed to be interested in taking more challenging classes, and the number taking Advanced Placement classes grew significantly. In 1996, about 535,000 American high school students took and passed AP tests in a variety of subjects, as compared to only 98,000 in 1978. A greater number of high school students were also taking the Standard Aptitude Tests (SATs). While scores for these tests slumped somewhat in the nineties, it should be noted that a wider breadth of students actually took the exam, not only those with the highest ranking in their class.[14] Despite claims to the contrary, there also appeared to be evidence that students were generally working harder in school in the nineties than they had earlier. One study reported that in 1981, the average student aged six to eight spent 52 minutes on homework a week, but that in 1997, the average was over two hours a week.[15]

More students were also attending college than ever before, in part due to the Echo Boom, but also because of a greater emphasis in high schools on preparing students for college. College education in the last several decades of the twentieth century became something that was within the reach of nearly every student. This, of course, posed the problem of what to do with

all of the college graduates, especially when there was a dearth of jobs re-
quiring that level of education. A 1995 survey conducted by the University
of Illinois found that of its 1994 graduates, almost 40 percent believed themselves to be overqualified for the jobs they now found themselves working.[16]

The Internet provided a convenient realm in which to post useful study
guides, but it was also targeted as a potential aid to cheating. Students
could, for instance, post test answers or completed papers online, which
others could download and pass off as their own work. Instructors were
therefore required to exercise a new level of vigilance against academic dis-
honesty. Even honest students were at risk when using Internet material,
and some teachers reported an increase in the number of disjointed com-
positions utilizing unprocessed and superficial Internet information. In
general, however, computers were received with great enthusiasm in
schools. In part this was due to an increasing reliance on computers in the
professional world. A 1996 survey found that many teachers found computer skills more important than biology, chemistry, physics, European history, and classic literature. One problem with classroom computer use,
however, was the rapidly accelerating technology, which forced schools to
spend more money on keeping up with the latest software and hardware.
The expense of computers often meant a tightening of the budget for music
or arts classes. Schools in rural or lower-class urban areas had even less of
an opportunity to keep up with the technology, and in some cases, were
unable to acquire computers at all. This, it was feared, would only increase
class discrepancies in the country.[17]

Other important trends also had significant impact on American education. One of these was that a growing number of schools began imple-
menting dress codes. It was believed that a dress code would eliminate
certain problems in the schools, including gang violence, as gang members
were often identifiable by certain articles of clothing, and the general clas-
sism that frequently accompanied fashion choice. Another important development was the proliferation of year-round schools. Many of these were
multi-track, meaning that different groupings of students started school at
different times of the year. Rather than a single long vacation, students instead took several shorter ones throughout the year. Although multi-track-
ing did successfully reduce class sizes, a growing problem in the largely
under-funded public school system, the staggered vacation times often
proved difficult for working parents.

WORK

Part-time work was a very common experience for high school students
of the 1990s. Approximately 80 percent of students worked at some time
during their high school years, with many of these actually working 15 to
20 hours during the academic year. The summer and winter school breaks,

of course, provided considerably larger numbers of teens looking for work. The winter holiday time especially provided many openings for temporary employment, especially in the retail industry as it geared up for the Christmas shopping season. Still, employment during the school year accelerated during the eighties and nineties, almost catching up to summertime and holiday statistics. A greater number of part-time jobs—most of which were low-wage service jobs as cashiers, retail salespeople, fast-food workers, waiters, and the like—became available to youths during this period. Many of these businesses created more positions as they expanded operating hours, and this general trend towards longer business hours also made joining the workforce easier for youths, who could take on late afternoon or evening work, which did not interfere with school hours.[18]

To much of America's youth, college became increasingly important, in part due to the changing job market. Coming on the heels of the Baby Boomers, those of the so-called Generation X had to contend with the fact that the large preceding generation was still working, and would, in fact, likely be occupying those jobs for some time yet to come. Although the 1990s saw no severe scarcity of jobs, the Boomer occupation of professional life was nonetheless often seen as a threat to the incoming labor force. This may well have in part driven the greater interest in attending college. Young people were able to spend time in college rather than entering a potentially hostile job market, all the while improving their education, and consequently their credentials upon entering the job market. Of course, this created a greater pool of the college educated to compete in the job market. As a result, college education came to be seen as increasingly necessary. Students entering college were far more likely to admit that their paramount, if not only, motivation for pursuing a higher education was the desire to secure a better job than would otherwise be available to them. Indeed, for most youths with only high school education, the available jobs were by and large fairly menial. There were exceptions to this, but the safe bet was seen to be the attainment of a college degree. Those who eschewed a college degree, perfectly willing to take on blue-collar employment, frequently found that this avenue, too, presented new challenges. The latter decades of the century had seen a gradual decrease in the number of available blue-collar jobs, particularly in the field of manufacturing. Many who went directly from high school to work found themselves involved in the same kinds of low-paying service jobs that they had worked while in high school, particularly those in retail sales and the food industry. The manufacturing job decline was, in part, due to an increasing reliance on the part of industry on computers and automation technology. More than the natural flux of the job market, then, youths were forced to contend with fundamental changes in the nature of business and industry. Technology, of course, forced a considerable change in the market. Indeed, with the boom in high tech industry, many youths saw that a higher education was absolutely necessary to compete. Computer science, for instance, became a major field of study. But even for those entering professions not directly tied to high-tech industries, the need for basic computer skills became vitally important.

One study suggested that youths, particularly in the latter half of the decade, faced a fairly volatile professional life, but that this was something that they expected to face, and something for which they were, in some respects, prepared. Teenagers, the study claimed, "believe that they will change jobs frequently and change careers occasionally. Teenagers accept the volatility of the labor market and believe that the way to create a personal safety net is to obtain additional education."[19] There was considerable truth to the argument that education and work was, in general, much more complex for the youth of the nineties than for any prior generation. In certain respects, it was much more exciting due to the great number of choices facing most youths. The range of subjects available for study expanded considerably, as did the means of putting oneself through school. As there were more students attending college, so there were more scholarships and financial aid programs available. Of course, for many of those youths in rural and lower-class urban areas, the possibilities were frequently more limited.

SEXUALITY

A 1995 study reported that more than 80 percent of Americans had lost their virginity during teenage years, and this trend was also visible among the teens of the nineties. The average age for males' first sexual experience was 16, and for females 17. Most teens claimed that their sexual experiences were not driven by peer pressure and that they had come out of serious emotional relationships. Yet about a quarter of women between the ages of 15 and 24 nonetheless gave their first sexual experiences low ratings when asked about how much they had wanted the encounter to happen. Likewise, another study found that 55 percent of females and 40 percent of males reported having felt pressured to engage in sexual activities.

Active sexuality among teens came with several serious social problems as well. Date rape was a growing problem among teens, and surveys of youths suggested that not enough was being done by educators and parents to enlighten teens about this issue. About 8 percent of girls and 5 percent of boys in high school reported having been forced to have sex against their will, and these numbers were not surprising given the attitudes held by many teens toward the subject of date rape. One study reported that almost a third of high school students believed that a boy was not at fault if he forcibly had sex with a girl provocatively dressed. A quarter surveyed responded that if a boy were to get a girl drunk and have sex with her after her refusal, the act would not constitute rape. These notions might well have been responsible for the general figures on rape, which by the early 1990s most often victimized teen girls. About one quarter of rape victims were girls aged 11 to 17.

Another issue facing sexually active teens was sexually transmitted diseases. One in four sexually active teens, about three million individuals, contracted a sexually transmitted disease each year, most commonly gonorrhea, and chlamydia. HIV and AIDS were also major problems. As education about the diseases spread, the general rate of HIV contraction in the United States declined somewhat. But among the teen population of the U.S., there was no comparable decline. Throughout the decade, AIDS was one of the leading causes of death among 15- to 24-year-olds, and in 1998, the Centers for Disease Control estimated that about half of all HIV infections occurred in men and women under the age of 25, many of them in their teens.

Teen pregnancy was also on the rise in the nineties. The teen pregnancy rate among 15- to 19-year-olds reached nearly 10 percent by the end of the decade. About one third of these girls had abortions, while about half had successful full-term pregnancies and childbirths. Teen pregnancy frequently had long-term repercussions. Girls who gave birth before the age of 18 had an elevated high school dropout rate, and also appeared to have a harder time establishing financial stability and maintaining successful marriages. About three quarters of teens who gave birth were unmarried, and the lack of a proper paternal figure provoked considerable worry. A single parent household, especially one headed by a teenaged girl, was much more likely to encounter economic difficulty than a two-parent household.[20]

TEEN VIOLENCE

In 1991, the United States had the highest rate of teen homicide in the world, with murder the third leading cause of death among white teens and the first among young black males. Teens who lived in urban ghettos had become increasingly acclimated to a lifestyle of violence in the 1980s, and this pattern continued throughout the nineties, as well. Many took to arming themselves with guns easily attained through the gang underworld. A 1991 survey found that 57 percent of black teens knew someone who had taken a gun to school, and 87 percent knew someone who had been shot. A 1996 study found that of the teens who owned guns, 84 percent of them had attained them before they were 15 years old, and that in many cases they had been given unsolicited firearms by older teens or adults.[21]

In ghettos, violence had become a way of life. But for many Americans, ghetto violence seemed far away. Consequently, when a wave of teen violence struck America's largely white suburbs, a different kind of hysteria erupted. In March 1998, two boys, allegedly in retaliation for one's rejection by a female classmate, became the first in a series of high-profile teen murderers. Thirteen-year-old Mitchell Johnson and 11-year-old Andrew Golden of Jonesboro, Arkansas, went to school armed with automatic weapons and shot and killed four students, all female, and one teacher. For most Americans, it was easy enough to discount the two boys, who were sentenced to serve time until they were 21 years old, as monsters, as aberrations. But as similar cases grabbed headlines, the country began to suspect that there was something more to this violence, that something was seriously wrong with American boyhood. Just months after the Jonesboro shooting, in May 1998, in the town of Springfield, Ohio, a 15-year-old boy named Kip Kinkel followed in Johnson and Golden's footsteps. Kinkel shot and killed his parents, then, using knowledge gained mostly from the Internet, rigged their house with explosives. He then went to his school heavily armed with two handguns and a rifle and started shooting. Two students were killed and 22 others injured.

The worse case of school violence, however, came on April 20, 1999, when Eric Harris and Dylan Klebold conducted an assault on their Littleton, Colorado, high school. The boys were far more heavily armed than those involved in the earlier school shootings, carrying a semiautomatic handgun, a semiautomatic rifle, two shotguns, and more than 50 bombs. By the time the rampage was ended, they had killed 12 Columbine High School students and one teacher, and injured many others. They then took their own lives. Across the country, viewers saw television footage of students fleeing the school and law enforcement moving in. They saw footage of a bloodied student desperately escaping the school from a second story window. In short, the media brought the shooting graphically into the homes of the whole of America, leaving the country in shock at the savagery of the assault. No specific rationale was ever discovered for Harris and Klebold's actions, though they had been victims of hazing from certain classmates who were on the football team. As a consequence, many painted the shooting spree as a kind of war between cliques, though friends of the shooters pointed out that the cliques were not as strong as the media made them out to be and that Harris and Klebold had acted not as members of a group but as individuals.

Interestingly, these cases occurred during a period in which the rate of violent crime in the United States was dropping significantly. As the suburban high school shootings stirred the passions of many Americans, the number of adolescent deaths by firearms dropped enough to effect significant declines in the mortality rate of youths between 15 and 19 years old. In fact, in 1998, about 27 per 1,000 youths between 12 and 17 years old were involved in perpetrating violent crime. This marked a decrease by more than half from 1993. The 1998 measure also marked the lowest level of youth crime since such studies were first conducted in 1973.[22] Much of the decline, however, was in lower class and ethnic minority neighborhoods. It was perhaps a sign of continued social inequity that the violence committed by suburban, white youths garnered much greater public and media attention than did the day-to-day violence suffered by inner city children.

YOUTH AND MEDIA

There was a unprecedented rise in the amount of media actively directed towards teens. Of course, MTV had established itself as extremely popular among that demographic, proving that teens accounted for a substantial amount of media consumption. Consequently, the 1990s saw an increase in the number of radio stations that were geared at a teen demographic. Additionally, a great deal of television programming targeted that audience, as well. The early nineties saw shows like *Beverly Hills 90210,* and these set a precedent for *Dawson's Creek, Felicity, Buffy the Vampire Slayer,* and the like, in the latter half of the decade. These shows, in depicting young people frequently dealing with the same kinds of problems their teen audience faced, if in a somewhat less melodramatic way, tapped into an important psychological dimension of the audience. These shows were about the teens, and less often about the teens' interaction with their parents. Indeed, teenagers commonly fended for themselves, maturing not so much with the benefit of advice from elders, but through experience faced individually. This was also true in a number of motion pictures geared at teens, including horror movies, like the *Scream* series of films, and teen sex comedies, like the *American Pie* films. These productions have been read as tapping into several aspects of teen psychology. They certainly found resonance with the teen exasperation at being caught between childhood and adulthood, a stage in life when many teens longed for a state of independence so well depicted in the media. But it may well be that these shows also appealed to a sense of abandonment on the part of teens, who had increasingly grown up with a single parent or two working parents. Some experts worried that the popularity of shows about independent youths was in part due to the fact that teens were increasingly living lives that forced them to be independent at an earlier age.

Attention to the media's effects on youths also experienced a considerable rise with the growing publicity of teen violence, especially the series of school shootings. While some were exploring social and psychological factors that might have led to such violence, others were looking elsewhere. The search for a scapegoat in mass media was nothing new to the nineties, with other precedents throughout American history. The greatest targets in the 1990s, music, television, and movies, had all previously been accused of corrupting morality.

Gangsta rap was targeted from its onset. The violence and frequent misogyny of the lyrics caused many to denounce it as immoral. But gangsta rap had received relatively little national publicity until it found a listen-ership among suburban white youths. In 1995, Republican senator and presidential candidate Robert Dole even took on gangsta rap as a political issue, and efforts by Dole and others were in part responsible for the Time-Warner media conglomerate's severance of ties with rap label Death Row. Likewise, heavy metal and Goth bands, especially Marilyn Manson, came under fire. But ultimately, for most youths, these kinds of aggressive and even antisocial recording artists provided only a limited outlet. Listening to the anger of a hard-core rapper might have provided a youth the op-portunity to blow off steam, but a very few would even think to take the lyrics as instruction.

Television and movies were also denounced, in part due to increasing sexual explicitness, but mostly because of their portrayal of violence. A brief fantasy sequence in the 1995 feature film adaptation of Jim Carroll's book, *The Basketball Diaries*, depicted a student walking into a classroom wearing a trench coat and carrying a gun, which he proceeded to discharge at his fellow students. Opponents of film violence cited this scene as an influence on the rash of high school shootings. Other movies, especially the ultravi-olent spate of films, such as *Pulp Fiction* and *Natural Born Killers*, were also accused of contributing to youth violence. Television's effect on youth also became a major issue, which led to the development of a TV ratings sys-tem similar to that used by movies, and to the creation of the V-chip, an electronic device installed in some televisions that could be used to block out violent programming. Ultimately, these protections probably contrib-uted to the loosening of television standards. Since networks could now claim that the rating system and V-chip gave parents an unprecedented amount of power in controlling what their children watched, they could concern themselves less with self-policing. Similarly, video game manu-facturers created a rating system in order to fend off the claims that their games contributed to real world violence.

Many experts marked these moral panics regarding the media as little more than scapegoating. The facts were that youth violence was still rela-tively rare. There had been no increase in the number of violent acts on the part of teens, but the scale of those acts was sometimes far worse, as in the case of the Columbine High School massacre. Some argued that the kind of disaffection felt by teen killers was no different than it had been in ear-lier eras, but that the access that teens had to weapons was much greater. And many felt that to target media as the source of violent impulses was irresponsible and that scapegoating left the real causes of the problem un-treated. Certainly, youth violence remained at its worst in poor, urban areas, in which teens tended to play fewer video games and go to fewer movies than those in middle-class suburbs. Clearly, however, there were uncontested cases where youths imitated what they saw in the media, and the debate centered on how widespread and how dangerous this influence actually was. Ultimately, the debate about media's effect on youth remained a contentious one throughout the decade.

DRUG USE

A 1997 study found that drug use among youth had increased substantially during the decade. A steady increase in underage smoking and drinking was also registered in the nineties. Survey results showed that one in four twelfth graders had smoked cigarettes on a daily basis during the previous 30 days, and one in three admitted to heavy drinking. In 1999, 31 percent of twelfth graders, 26 percent of tenth graders, and 15 percent of eighth graders reported having had five or more drinks in a row at some time during the previous two weeks. In addition, the number who had used illicit drugs increased as well, rising from 14 percent in 1992 to 26 percent in 1997. Of even more concern was that youths seemed to be discovering tobacco, alcohol, and illicit drugs at a younger age. The rate of illicit drug use among eighth graders more than doubled, from 7 percent to 15 percent from 1992 to 1997, dropping slightly, to 12 percent, by the end of the decade. And drug abuse among youths was not limited to urban areas. Indeed, drug use, as well as gang involvement, began increasingly affecting suburban and even rural areas.[23]

One of the most fashionable drugs among the young was MDMA (methylenedioxymethamphetamine), better known as Ecstasy, which became extremely popular at the rave scene. At many raves, large all-night dance parties, Ecstasy became as central as the driving techno music. Along with the alleged feelings of peacefulness, the drug was also popular for its stimulating effects. Ecstasy provided youths with the energy to continue dancing all night without growing tired. But that also came with serious risks. The drug allowed youths to push their bodies beyond normal limits, and often led to serious dehydration and other health problems. Ecstasy was connected to a loss of body temperature control, as well as to elevations in heart rate and blood pressure.

Even as parents, politicians, and health officials were crying out their alarm at the growing use of illicit drugs by American youths, prescription drugs were being given to those same young people in record amounts. The nineties saw a sharp increase in the number of children being diagnosed with Attention Deficit Disorder (ADD) and Attention Deficit Hyperactive Disorder (ADHD). As a result, there was a concurrent rise in prescriptions for the behavior-altering drug Ritalin. The drug came into popular use in the 1980s, but really hit stride in the 1990s, as diagnoses and Ritalin production both leapt. From 1990 to 1997, Ritalin production increased seven-fold, to about 30,000 pounds a year.[24] Although for some parents and teachers Ritalin was a godsend, some questioned the rise in diagnoses and prescriptions. Why, it was wondered, were there more ADD children now than there had been in the past? Were children being over-diagnosed with a condition that many before them had had and outgrown without the influence of Ritalin?

YOUTH AND POLITICS

The youth of the nineties were generally seen as apathetic towards politics and world affairs. The 1992 Bill Clinton presidential campaign made an active effort to court young voters, including several gracious appearances by Clinton on MTV. The efforts perhaps boosted youth participation in politics somewhat, but surveys throughout the decade showed that youths were increasingly disengaged. Many of these surveys also showed that youths generally had less confidence in governments, both local and federal, political parties, and the overall electoral process. These attitudes manifested themselves in small voter turnout among the young. Not even one in five eligible young voters took part in the 1994 midterm election, and the 1996 presidential election drew only about 32 percent of young voters. For those so inclined, this provided more ground to criticize the nation's youth. Young people didn't engage in politics because they were lazy, apathetic, cynical, and self-centered. The truth, however, was considerably more complex. Numerous reasons were cited for the growing political apathy of the nation's youth. Some blamed the breakdown of traditional family structures and values or excessive television viewing for detracting from youths' civic education. Others claimed that young Americans' distaste for politics was a result of their growing up during a period of partisan bickering and widespread criticism of government. A kinder reading suggested that these youths had a clear vision of problems facing the country—educational, environmental, and economic—but didn't see anything in the government and political process that was addressing these issues.

A 1999 article appearing in *The Atlantic Monthly* suggested that America's youth was, in fact, developing a new sense of politics, one which was not party driven, but a hybrid of political ideas, especially in regards to economics. The article suggested that "Like conservatives, they favor fiscal restraint—but unlike the conservative leadership in Congress, only 15 percent believe that America should use any budget surplus to cut taxes. Like Democrats, they want to help the little guy—but unlike traditional Democrats, they are unwilling to do it by running deficits."[25]

From its 1998 nationwide survey of American youth, *Rolling Stone* magazine concluded that this generation was not, in fact, as apathetic as the popular wisdom held. The poll in part focused on the Monica Lewinsky scandal that was plaguing the president, but also sought to determine general political leanings. They found that opinions largely echoed those of American adults. Youths did appear slightly more Democratic in their inclinations, with 33 percent identifying themselves as "Mostly Democratic" or "Leaning Democratic." Yet about 29 percent identified themselves as

U.S. President Bill Clinton and Mrs. Clinton hold hands as they leave Air Force One at Moscow's Vnukovo-2 airport Sept. 1, 1998. With Russia reeling from a political and economic crisis, President Bill Clinton arrived for a summit with Russia's leader Boris Yeltsin.
© AP/Wide World Photos.

"Mostly" or "Leaning Republican." A full 30 percent regarded themselves as completely independent, reflecting the same distaste and distrust towards government to be found in the adult population. The poll also measured general political interest. About 24 percent claimed to have very little or no interest in politics. 34 percent claimed to have "just some" interest, and 42 percent cited themselves as having "quite a bit" or "a great deal" of interest. The results, however, could not be taken as a sign of political activism on the part of youth, given that the preceding presidential election brought out less than 40 percent of American voters, and an even smaller percentage of young adults eligible to vote.[26]

The growing disinclination towards joining one of the major political parties manifested itself repeatedly, as in the youth support for political candidates like Jesse Ventura and Ralph Nader. Even Ross Perot, whose background and political stance had little real relation with those of young

Americans, enjoyed significant youth support, primarily on account of his third party status. A large number of politically active youths opposed the two-party system, and were eager to embrace any third party candidate. Additionally, many were highly supportive of campaign finance reforms and changes in the electoral system to more accurately represent the will of the American populace.[27]

Interestingly, many surveys concluded that young people's attitudes towards race were torn. While most respondents claimed that the civil rights movement still had a long way to go, few registered any support for affirmative action programs. In fact, 68 percent opposed affirmative action in college admissions. It may be that youths responded negatively to affirmative action because they were among the first generations to actually be affected by it. The perception of some white youths was that affirmative action reduced their chances of getting admitted to the college of their choice, although this notion overlooked the fact that a larger percentage of youths, white and otherwise, were attending college than in previous generations.[28]

Ultimately, if political engagement was to be measured only by voting turnout, then the criticisms leveled at American youths may very well have been valid. But perhaps the youth of the 1990s simply rejected traditional politics, which many saw as having failed them. Even as many young people rejected traditional politics, there was evidence suggesting an increase in civic engagement on other fronts. Volunteerism, boycotts, and demonstrations appeared to rise among young adults during the 1990s. In 1996, approximately half of all high school students reported engaging in some sort of volunteer activity. This increased in the latter years of the decade, reaching 55 percent in 1999.[29] These kinds of activities had a more noticeable effect than engaging in conventional political practices, and offered visible results. In the end, it may be that the youth of the nineties were indeed civically engaged, then, but in a way different from previous generations, and in a way that the conventional ways of measuring political activity simply failed to register.

YOUTH SPORTS

Growing enrollments and reduced public education spending forced many American schools to tighten their budgets in the 1990s. As schools sought to reduce expenses, high-school sports and other extracurricular activities were frequently targeted as expendable. And with the decrease in funding of sports programs, schools were forced to turn to other means of financial support. Parents were asked to help foot the bill, and fundraisers were held by the participating students themselves with increasing frequency. Some schools even turned to corporate sponsorship, with sporting gear companies frequently contributing equipment. Still, despite the financial crunch, high school sports did experience an increase in participants, partly due to the baby boom of the late seventies and early eighties.[30]

According to a University of Michigan's Institute for Social Research study, children aged 3 to 12 spent less time playing indoors. Between 1981 and 1997, the amount of indoor play time declined by 16 percent. Moreover, the amount of time spent watching television also declined by about 23 percent. A 20 percent increase in time spent studying and a 27 percent increase in time spent partaking in organized sports were also registered. Youth soccer, for instance, experienced a boom during the eighties and nineties. In 1981, U.S. Youth Soccer registered about 811,000 players, but by 1998 that number had grown to almost three million.[31]

With the institution of Title IX, the 1972 legislation guaranteeing females equal access to sports, there was a sharp increase in the number of girls involved in high school sports. The number leveled out for most of the 1980s and the early 1990s, until it experienced another surge. By 1997, girls constituted about 40 percent of high school sports participation. It should be noted, however, that certain high profile sports, like baseball and football, remained dominated by male participants. Girls typically dominated sports like softball, volleyball, and field hockey. But basketball, which had once been a male-dominated sport, now experienced something resembling gender equality, perhaps driven in part by the successes of professional women's basketball during the nineties. The increase in female participation in sports was even more pronounced at the college level. From 1982 to 1996, the number of women competing in college sports increased over 45 percent, while the number of men only increased 4.5 percent. In some fronts, this development was praised, but it was also not without controversy. As women's sports were added to accommodate demand, colleges were frequently required to cut the less popular male sports, including wrestling, skiing, gymnastics, and lacrosse.[32]

In general, there was an increase in youth interest in individual sports. This trend may in part have been the result of a growing interest in involving youths in athletics that could be continued for a lifetime, which was less often the case with team sports. But it may well have also been the result of youths generally spending more time alone, than with family or friends. Certainly, it must be partly attributed to the general trend in sporting activity towards adventure sports. Activities that tapped into the notion of the rugged individual, like rock climbing and camping, increased in popularity, as did extreme sports, and most of these activities emphasized the goal of the individual doing for themselves, rather than depending on others as part of a team effort.

CONCLUSION

The 1990s, ultimately, involved the intersection of two generations of youths, as those labeled "X" came into adulthood, and the "Ys" stepped up to take their place. This generational crossover certainly makes it difficult to draw many across-the-board conclusions about the decade's youth, but the definitional difficulties are also far more permeating than this. Indeed, each of these generations—and in truth there was no distinct break between them, but rather they blurred together—contained multitudes in and of themselves. The country as a whole had seen an increase in diversity over the last several decades of the twentieth century, with an increase in immigration and the growing influence of American subcultures. Additionally, as the denizens of earlier subcultures, from the sixties and seventies, aged and entered the mainstream of economic and social America, diversity began to manifest itself increasingly in the media. These images most certainly suggested to the youth of the late twentieth century that there was room for many different types of people.

Commonalities that were easily visible in earlier generations of youths became less apparent in these latest generations. As a consequence, no writing on 1990s youth can truly capture the makeup of these generations. To suggest, for instance, that 1990s youths listened to grunge and hip-hop overlooks the growing number of youths disdaining these genres in favor of country music. And the differences were not merely superficial, as youths from different regions of the country adopted very different worldviews. No single statement of how youths responded to authority, or tradition, or ideology, could possibly do justice to the youth of this decade. Indeed, as American youth became increasingly difficult about which to generalize, it came to reflect, perhaps more than ever before, mainstream American diversity.

PART TWO

POPULAR CULTURE OF THE 1990S

3
Advertising

THE ADVERTISING BUSINESS

In the 1990s, the business of advertising became increasingly complex. The number of possible outlets for advertising increased dramatically, but so too did fragmentation of potential audiences. Thus, advertisers had to explore many different avenues—television, radio, magazines, the burgeoning Internet, and others—in order to find the broadest possible audience for their advertisements. Nearly every venue for advertising seemed to flourish in the nineties, with the possible exception of the billboard industry, which had to compete against a growing interest in highway beautification.

The sheer volume of advertising, as well as that of the money involved in advertising, became truly staggering in the 1990s. On the one hand, there was a great deal of profit to be made by advertising, a major stimulant to the American economy. On the other, advertising became so ubiquitous that some worried about the psychological effect it might have on the population at large. Companies spent more than $150 billion on advertising per year at the end of the decade. Some experts even claimed that the number was over $200 billion, and indeed, it is a difficult number to settle on given the diversity and subtlety of advertising. Advertising accounted for more than 60 percent of magazine revenue, some $30 billion a year, and the $40 billion generated by the electronic media accounted for almost all of its revenues.[1] It is estimated that American consumers were exposed to about twelve billion ads each day, about three million of which were broadcast ads. A 1991 estimate placed the number of ads targeted at the average American at a daily rate of 3,000.[2]

The top advertising agency of the nineties was the WPP Group, but other advertisers also thrived, including Saatchi & Saatchi, Omnicom, Interpublic, and Dentsu. But these companies had been strong since at least the mid-eighties. More interestingly, many mid-sized American and international agencies broke into the top twenty-five, though some found themselves being absorbed by their peers. Such was the case for Chiat/Day, which merged with another company to become Chiat/Day/Mojo.

In general, the volume of spending on advertising by major corporations grew significantly from year to year. In part, advertising outlets were charging more for space and airtime, but the larger companies were also simply spreading the word about their products with greater intensity. In addition, television commercials became, in essence, short movies peddling a product. It was not uncommon for the actual production costs of a TV advertising spot to rival that of the television program during which it aired. Large corporations routinely spent as much as $250,000 producing a single commercial, and then another $250,000 to air it.[3]

Certain big ticket broadcast events, like the Super Bowl or the Academy Awards, naturally made for prime advertising time. These events drew larger than normal audiences and consequently drew top dollar advertising. An ad for the Academy Awards, for instance, would typically cost over a million dollars for 30 seconds of airtime. And advertisers were more than willing to pay such prices, with the understanding that such exposure would easily prompt compensating consumption on the part of viewers. Of course, these events also developed a reputation for the quality of their commercials since viewers knew that companies would be investing terrific dollar amounts to make these commercials the best of the best. It was not unusual to hear nearly as much about the commercials the next day in the media and in conversation than about the Super Bowl game itself. An ad campaign for a financial services company produced by the Arnold Communications ad agency for the 1999 Super Bowl demonstrated just how much time and effort was put into utilizing such advertising slots. Eleven months of planning went into the campaign, as did 12,000 man hours and 30 hours of film footage, which all boiled down to a brief 30-second spot.[4]

American companies also began marketing to other countries much more intensely in the nineties. Particularly, Eastern Europe, after the widespread fall of Communism, provided fruitful advertising ground for companies like Procter & Gamble, Phillip Morris, and Coca-Cola, three of the more vigorous exploiters of the new market.

GENERAL TRENDS

Several general trends, though not new to the decade, accelerated in the 1990s. One of these was the celebration of American individualism in advertising. Many ads went back to the very source of individualism and in-dependence in exploiting the natural world. The rugged outdoors was an ideal arena to peddle certain products. Automobiles, especially trucks and sports utility vehicles, were frequently depicted tearing through the most hostile of environments. The 1996 Nissan Pathfinder, for instance, em-ployed a campaign that took the vehicle on an African safari, all the while emphasizing the interior luxury and comfort that the would-be adventurer enjoyed. But other products also enjoyed the outdoors in their ads. Food, clothing, telephone service, and virtually any other product could be sold by depicting individuals in the wilderness. Panasonic, for instance, demon-strated the use of its camcorder in a rain forest. Besides appealing to the impulse toward individuality, these ads also endorsed the growing envi-ronmental concerns of many consumers, and they provided an appealing setting for individuals who felt frequently trapped by urban life.

Nostalgia was also exploited by advertisers. In general, American cul-ture seemed to have a renewed interest in the recent past, as evidenced by a rise in "retro" fashions. Consequently, many ads sought to capture the look of the fifties, sixties, seventies, or even, near the end of the decade, the eighties. These eras were almost universally idealized in the ads, though the 1950s were certainly emphasized as kitschy rather than cool.

As young people of so-called Generation X and also of the following gen-eration of youths aged and increasingly developed their own sources of disposable income, advertisers began increasingly to target them and their interests. These young people had often been seen as defining themselves in opposition to mainstream society, and the advertising directed at them exploited this concept. It expounded on the idea that older individuals were somehow out of touch, and also implied that the products under scrutiny were somehow rebellious. Extreme sports, like skateboarding and snow-boarding, were frequent visuals of these ads, even if bungee jumping, or what have you, had very little to do with breakfast cereal, or whatever product was being sold. A Nike campaign targeting skateboarders asked "what it would look like if other athletes were harassed ... the way skate-boarders so routinely are?" As a result, the company appeared to have em-pathy with the skateboarders who felt themselves marginalized by society at large.[5]

INNOVATION IN ADVERTISING

The common themes aside, the 1990s nevertheless allowed for a great degree of experimentation in advertising. Indeed, many advertisers ap-proached the market with the idea that startling, unusual ads would catch consumers' attention far better than the same tired approach. A print ad for the Porsche 911 Turbo, for instance, downplayed the technical features of the car, and even downplayed the status that was associated with such a vehicle. Instead, it featured a photograph of the car underscored by the slogan "Kills bugs fast."

One of the more unusual ad campaigns of the decade was Benetton's $80 million spring and summer clothing line promotion which first ran in the March 1992 issue of *Vanity Fair.* The ad was composed of three news photographs. The first depicted a car on fire, the second, refugees climbing the side of a ship, and the third a dying AIDS patient surrounded by loved ones. Each photograph was accompanied by the slogan "United Colors of Benetton," but nothing else was said about the clothing or company. The campaign produced much speculation. What exactly did it all mean, and what had it to do with fashion? Roy F. Fox, author of the book *MediaSpeak: Three American Voices,* offered his own analysis of how the ad drew the viewer in with its gradual move from distanciation from the depicted events to intimacy, thereby effecting an emotional transformation, thereby hitting "closest to home, closest to the heart of our emotional lives."[6]

Surprisingly, one of the strongest advertising campaigns of the 1990s was for one of the most traditional of products: milk. The California Fluid Milk Processor's Advisory Board (CFMPA), in seeking to improve the rather lackluster image of milk stumbled upon not one, but two wildly popular campaigns. The television campaign was kicked off by a commercial in which a young man sat eating a sandwich in a library filled with memorabilia related to Aaron Burr's shooting of Alexander Hamilton. He received a phone call from a radio station which offered him a chance to win $50,000 if he could answer a trivia question. The question, of course, was "who shot Alexander Hamilton?," but the man, mouth full of sandwich and his milk carton empty, was unable to answer. The spot ended with the words, "Got milk?" More commercials followed with similar situations, in which protagonists were confounded by the absence of milk. The print campaign was as simple as it was popular. The ads depicted various celebrities wearing milk moustaches, accompanied by brief descriptive copy. The CFMPA was surprised by the clamor on the part of celebrities who wanted to be a part of the campaign, and it soon came to depict actors, sports stars, musicians, and other celebrities, all sporting the moustache.

TELEMARKETING AND INFOMERCIALS

There was considerable growth of telemarketing in the 1990s, a trend which also contributed to the growth in phone call screening devices and services. Calls from marketers selling phone service plans, magazines, credit cards, and other products and services proliferated. And in the process, telemarketing gained a reputation as one of the most infuriating forms of advertising. The general anger of consumers, who were particularly vociferous about being called during meals and showers, ultimately did nothing to reduce the sheer number of telemarketing calls. In fact, the industry grew during the 1990s, largely because it continued to be profitable. Tele-marketing itself was an extremely inexpensive form of marketing, and therefore returns did not have to be so high as for television and print ads. Annual sales for telemarketers reached $650 billion by 1999, and the 1,000 telemarketing companies employed nearly four million Americans.[7]

Due to limited deregulation of commercial time restraints in the mid-eighties, the late 1980s and 1990s saw the rise of the infomercial, television commercials expanded to 30 minutes or an hour's length. One of the first products to exploit this kind of advertising was the Soloflex, and exercise device, the infomercials for which became dominant late night broadcasts in the 1980s. Its success led to a flood of exercise equipment infomercials which aired through the 1990s. Exercise programs, or rather the books and video cassettes that came with them, also proved popular subjects for these long advertisements. Exercise guru Billy Blanks largely made a name for himself and his Tae Bo exercise program through infomercials. But exercise equipment was only one of many products to make good use of the form. Juicers were only moderately popular in America before the infomercial, but due to this new form of marketing, over the course of 1991, juicers went from a 10-million-dollar industry to one that raked in $380 million a year. The key to the infomercial was that it tried, to some extent, to hide its ultimate purpose of selling a product. Certainly, infomercials frequently showed the 800 number by which you could order the product at alleged fantastic savings. But they also frequently exhibited a parade of celebrities chatting about the wonders of the product. Many conducted themselves like the television talk shows that were so popular in the nineties. In short, the infomercial sought to entertain as well as sell, because keeping the audience entertained for 30 to 60 minutes, might well translate into a sale, or at very least the imprinting of a brand name in the viewer's mind.[8]

CELEBRITIES

With the unrestrained spread of advertising in the closing decades of the twentieth century, there came a new fervor to advertisers' desires to stand out from the crowd. The average American was exposed to advertisements so frequently, that it was easy for a less-than-gripping ad to go all but unnoticed. Even advertising on TV, interrupting a consumer's favorite shows, was no longer safe from a commercial-saturated public. In fact, a 1994 poll suggested that up to 74 percent of Americans switched channels during commercials , and that 50 percent occasionally muted the sound during them. One solution was to give viewers something they would actually want to watch, regardless of the fact that it was selling to them. Naturally, then, nothing seemed better for the advertising industry than a celebrity. One of the most commercially fruitful celebrity/advertiser relationships

Michael Jordan and Bugs Bunny appear in a Nike ad during the 1993
Super Bowl telecast on Jan. 31, 1993. In this frame from the 90-second
commercial, Jordan and Bugs go to Mars in search of Jordan's shoes.
© AP/Wide World Photos.

was that between Nike and basketball star Michael Jordan. Jordan was estimated to have been worth $5.2 million to Nike, maker of sports shoes, in-
cluding the Air Jordan brand. Moreover, during the time he was appearing
in Nike ads, the company went from earning 18 percent of the retail sales
for sneakers, to 43 percent.[9]

Naturally, celebrity advertising was of limited effect if viewers were not
familiar with the personality in question. An ad featuring John Elway, for
instance, would carry little weight with a viewer who never watched and
had little care for professional football. As a result, where and when these
ads appeared mattered a great deal. Ads with sports figures appeared in
greater volume in sports and men's magazines than in women's magazines,
which would typically feature more attractive television and movie stars,
including the occasional soap opera star, who would have little sway in the
men's magazines. Likewise, television ads during sports programming
were dominated by sports-related advertising and celebrities. An episode
of *Seinfeld*, might very well feature a credit card or fast food commercial
featuring one of the show's stars. Candice Bergman's commercials for
Sprint phone service regularly appeared during broadcasts of her sitcom

Murphy Brown. There were, however, celebrities that reached such high profile that ads featuring them could successfully appear virtually anywhere. Michael Jordan was one of these, and so too was Tiger Woods, who came to be recognized nationwide, even by those who had never followed amateur or professional golf.

Celebrity endorsements didn't always work as well as planned, however. Pepsi had several bad experiences with celebrity ads. Madonna and Mike Tyson were both tapped as Pepsi spokesmen, but the controversies that followed them forced Pepsi to discontinue their ad campaigns. Likewise, Michael Jackson was a controversial figure, even before Pepsi sponsored his 1993 tour, but Pepsi felt compelled to distance itself from the singer after Jackson cancelled the tour due to dehydration.

PRODUCT PLACEMENT

A subtle form of advertising, known as product placement, infiltrated television shows and movies. Product placement involved the exclusive use of certain products in a show so that if one were to watch carefully, one might note that all of the characters, regardless of their role in the drama, happened to drink the same brand of soda. Naturally, the products were not openly advertised, as they might be in a standard commercial, but the expectation was that these brand names would imprint themselves on viewers' minds, thereby increasing the likelihood that consumers would select that product brand over another. In her essay "We Can't Duck the Issue: Imbedded Advertising in the Motion Pictures," Linda K. Fuller pointed out how the 1994 movie *Reality Bites* contained product placement promotion for The Gap, Seven Eleven's Big Gulp, Rolling Rock beer, Minute Maid orange soda, Continental Airline, BMW, Snickers, Pringles, Pizza Hut, Eastman Corporation, Camel cigarettes, and more. She cited no less than forty-eight product placements in the 1990 film *Days of Thunder.*[10] The practice even gave rise to placement companies, who received scripts in advance of filming and could determine the best way to slip products into the scenes. The TV drama *Seven Days* featured a clearly placed can of Coca-Cola and a Wells Fargo Bank billboard. What made this particular case a standout over the ubiquitous product placement in the entertainment industry was that these images were actually digitally placed into the scene, and were not there when it was first filmed.[11]

It was this same digital technology which in 1991 allowed for television advertisers to exhume dead stars to sell their goods. An ad for Coca-Cola seamlessly used old movie footage to compile a party scene featuring Louis Armstrong, Humphrey Bogart, James Cagney, Cary Grant, and Groucho Marx. The reanimated celebrities were depicted having a wild and wonderful time, and drinking diet Coke all the way. The commercial itself was a masterpiece of technology, but many found the use of deceased personalities distasteful, and the technique was not widely embraced by advertisers. In 1996, however, Coors Light similarly borrowed footage from the 1966 movie *Cast a Giant Shadow* in order to have John Wayne expound upon the superiority of the beer.

CHILDREN AND ADVERTISING

There was considerable controversy about how ads for certain adult goods were geared towards children and young adults. Advertisements for alcohol, particularly beer, advertised a good life of parties, women, and loud rock 'n' roll. These ads typically featured people in their twenties, but certainly also celebrated a lifestyle that appealed to those in their teens, and this, according to critics, was a thinly veiled invitation to underage drinking. Cigarettes were also attacked on these grounds. Many attributed the disturbing upward trend of teenaged smoking to the way cigarettes were marketed. While some cigarette ads utilized the same key features to be found in alcohol ads, one advertising figure was attacked with particular vehemence. Camel cigarettes employed in its print and poster ads a cartoon character named Joe Camel. Joe, an anthropomorphized camel, was the ultimate smooth character, dressed in a sharp suit, eyes hidden behind sunglasses. He was perpetually surrounded by beautiful women and fast cars and was inevitably the center of attention. The fantasy of Joe Camel's life certainly appealed to a broad (if mostly male) demographic, but the fact that he was a funny animal cartoon character stoked fears that he would have at least as much appeal to children as he would to adults. In fact, a 1991 study found that Joe Camel was as familiar to American six-year-olds as Mickey Mouse.[12] Camel staunchly denied that they were selling to minors, but in 1997, after much criticism from political leaders, advocacy groups, and the public, the company finally retired its mascot.

Obviously the notion of selling tobacco and alcohol to children was met with rancor, but there were some who attacked the advertising industry for its methods of advertising to children in general. Children, particularly susceptible to the persuasion of marketing, were singled out as advertisements sought to create a need for their products. Advertisers emphasized the coolness of their products, understanding that children could be extremely persistent in their demands to the parents who actually had the disposable income. It should also be noted that children themselves had more disposable income in the 1990s than ever before. Estimates place the amount of money spent by children and teens between the ages of 4 and 19 at $66 billion in 1992 alone, with $36 billion of that being parents' money.[13] Furthermore, advertisers understood the value in creating a desire on the part of children for certain events and activities, including dining, especially at fast-food restaurants which thrived on their family image. The sale to a child was accompanied by the additional spending of parental accompaniment.

It was a common practice for advertisers to hire psychologists in order to exploit the psychology of children in their ads. In 1999, a group of 60 psychologists drafted an open letter calling for the American Psychological Association "to expose and challenge this abuse of psychological knowledge."

A disturbing trend in the marketing to minors was the infiltration of advertising into forums that had previously been barred against such efforts. Advertisers now snuck into schools, and were frequently met with open arms by administrators. Many school districts were struggling in the 1990s, facing financial shortfalls and growing student bodies. Classes were getting larger, and teachers were frequently underpaid. In addition, with wealthier schools acquiring computers and other high-tech facilities, the financially strapped districts felt woefully inept. For some, advertising seemed the ideal means to improving their lot. In 1993, a Colorado Springs school district became the first to allow ads in hallways and on the sides of school buses. The initial ads for Burger King ended up making the district a disappointing $37,500 a year. But in 1996, the district hired a marketing expert who eventually negotiated a 10-year contract between the school and Coca-Cola for around $11 million. The success of the Colorado Springs district enticed many other districts across the country to follow suit. One school even negotiated a deal with Dr Pepper to place an ad on the school's roof in order to market to overhead planes from the nearby airport.[14] And these were by no means the only examples of advertising in schools. The school district of Derby, Kansas, accepted one million dollars from Pepsi-Co., and in exchange they agreed to serve only Pepsi products and name its elementary school resource center the GenerationNext Center, echoing the Pepsi slogan. Another school district in Texas was sponsored by the Dr Pepper Bottling Company of Texas, and included this information on its administrative answering machine and elsewhere.[15] Perhaps the most egregious example of corporate advertising in schools was the case of a Georgia school that implemented an official "Coke in Education Day" after signing a deal with the Coca-Cola Company. At one point, the 1,200 students of the school, dressed in red and white, formed human letters spelling out the word Coke. Their picture was taken by a photographer held overhead by crane, but one student revealed a Pepsi T-shirt just as it was shot. The student was suspended for his actions. The suspension was for only one day, amidst nationwide publicity and controversy, but the incident was a dramatic demonstration of the influence that advertising could have on school administration.[16]

Advertising even wheedled its way into textbooks, with math books, for instance, including word problems designed around the saving of money in order to buy a certain name-brand product, or the number of trademarked food items able to fit into a package.[17] The nineties also saw the widespread introduction of Channel One, a satellite TV service ostensibly designed to bring students news and other features, but which was also riddled with advertising. Channel One typically charged advertisers as much as $200,000 for a 30-second spot, which companies were only too happy to pay given the large, captive audience of Channel One. And as more and more computers came into classrooms, so too did advertisers. At the end of the decade, a company called ZapMe! Corporation offered full computer labs, complete with Internet servers and teacher training, with the condition that the computers would contain "brand imaging spots" and marketing research software. In effect, the computers would conduct marketing focus groups in the schools. Around 6,000 schools signed up for the service by 2002.[18]

THE ANTI-DRUG CAMPAIGN

In 1998, Bill Clinton and a bipartisan Congress decided to allocate a billion dollars, $195 million a year for a five-year period, to go towards an anti-drug campaign, a large degree of which concerned itself with advertising. One of the major forces behind the move was the Partnership for a Drug-Free America, which had earlier created a number of television advertisements in which a spokesperson held up an egg with the words, "This is your brain." The then pan-fried egg was to represent "Your brain on drugs." As a part of the new campaign, a new variation on these ads appeared in which a young girl bypassed the egg frying, instead smashing the egg with the pan as a representation of "Your brain after snorting heroin." This was followed by a vigorous smashing of everything else in the kitchen setting, the girl swinging her pan with fury, all the while yelling, "This is what your family goes through! And your friends! And your job! And your self-respect! And your future!" In conclusion, the girl stared directly into the camera, making the same inquiry seen in those earlier ads: "Any questions?" This was probably the highest profile ad to ever be produced by the Partnership for a Drug-Free America, but it was, in fact, the latest in a long line of such ads. The partnership had produced more than five hundred anti-drug ads from 1989 to 1998, and managed to wrangle nearly $3 billion dollars worth of free media time. Some of the ads, however, were attacked for conveying misleading information about drugs and distorting the truth, particularly in their consideration of all drugs as equally harmful. Moreover, the potency of these ad campaigns was questioned. A New York advertising agency, Mad Dogs and Englishmen, conducted focus groups in the late eighties and came to the conclusion that these ads had little effect on their target audiences, suggesting that "many of today's ads aren't provocative enough to catch the attention of their audience." Moreover, many questioned the ultimate effectiveness of scare tactics in advertising and pointed out that such advertising probably had more of an effect on parents than on the intended teen audience, and therefore did little to reduce the demand for drugs.[19]

POLITICAL ADS

During the decade, there was increased concern about politics and money, about how corporations financed political candidates and how much contributors gave to a particular party or candidate running for office. Correspondingly, concern also increased about just how that money was being spent. Political advertising became a hot topic, and rightfully so as politicians were spending more on ads than ever before. A 1998 study conducted by the Annenberg School for Communication at the University of Southern California revealed that, in the three months leading to the gubernatorial election, major TV stations devoted an average of half of one percent of their news broadcasting to the race. With so little time being granted them in the news, candidates naturally turned to paid advertising to get their names out. Another 1998 survey found that the result was that viewers were four times as likely to see a political commercial than they were to see a political story aired on their local news.[20]

The results were apparent earlier in the decade. In 1992, the average amount spent on advertising for each contested House of Representative seat was about $735,000. During the 1994 presidential election campaign, nearly a billion dollars was spent on advertising, most of it on television commercials and mailing circulars. That election also came to be seen as one of the sleaziest. Fewer ads argued the merits of their candidate so much as they lambasted their opponent. Sensing the distaste felt by the American public towards such ads, the 1998 campaign's negativity was somewhat more tempered, at least at the start. But as the election came closer, and the candidates and their parties grew more anxious, advertising became increasingly negative.

NICHE MARKETING

There was greater emphasis on niche markets in the nineties. While it's true that advertisers spent the greatest amount of money and effort marketing to a general audience, they also realized that there were significant revenues to be made by advertising to marginalized groups. One ad in the trade magazine *Advertising Age,* for instance, made the point that "At $446 billion, African American buying power is more than the GNP of Switzerland." The message of the ad was quite clear, and indeed, estimates at the end of the decade were that ethnic minorities would soon be making 30 percent of all consumer purchases.[21] Advertisers then found profitable markets targeting ethnic minorities. African American controlled media grew considerably in the nineties, as did media directed towards black audiences. Television networks found tremendous success with sitcoms featuring African Americans, and so too did the advertisers who bought commercial time during these shows. Likewise, an increasing number of magazines produced by African Americans and with large black audiences also provided excellent advertising territory. Advertisers took to diversifying the kinds of people who appeared in their ads on the premise that the depiction of a multicultural world not only drew in an ethnic audience, but also made all consumers feel a little better about the world and consequently better about the product being pitched. Asian Americans, Pacific Islanders, Latinos, Arab Americans, and other ethnic groups, however, had fewer unique outlets for advertisers to exploit. They also constituted smaller segments of the consumer market, but many advertisers nonetheless sought to reach those demographics, as well. Spanish language television provided an opportunity for advertisers to reach the Hispanic community, and though some English language ads were dubbed, more were created in Spanish specifically for this outlet.

Even the gay community was targeted as a valuable consumer demographic by some advertisers. Gay media in general grew during the 1990s, as did the number of gays depicted sympathetically in print and television entertainment. A 1998 campaign for Hartford Financial Services Group was created with the gay media in mind, but the growing visibility of the gay media allowed it to cross over to the mainstream media with relative ease. In 1997, American Express invested some $250,000 in researching the gay and lesbian market, and then came to the conclusion that this was indeed a strong market and committed more money towards its development.[22] Of course, the depiction of gays in advertising, as well as the depiction of ethnic minorities, was intended to accomplish one goal over all others: sell the product. If these weren't substantial consumer groups, it's unlikely that advertisers would pursue them so vigorously. But even the crassest critic of advertising would note that these ads increased the visibility of gays and ethnic minorities, and they may very well have contributed to a more diversified perception of the American people.

ONLINE ADVERTISING

What may be the most important development in the world of advertising in the nineties was the rise of the Internet. For the first time since the birth of popular television, here was an altogether new medium through which to advertise. And with the innovation of the Internet came innovations in advertising. Agencies had to think about new ways to market their wares in this dramatic new terrain which had its own advantages and disadvantages. The great challenge of the Internet was that it was so thoroughly under the control of the surfer. Companies wondered: how could consumers be drawn to their particular Web site on which they marketed their goods? Of course, many consumers went online specifically in order to seek out certain goods. For these consumers, companies had only to post their Web sites and wait for the visitors. However, companies and their ad agencies were also interested in how to grab the attention of consumers who were not looking for the specific product or service they were selling. Several ways of marketing to this kind of surfing consumer developed. Association proved to be the most popular of these. The best association a company could make was with one of the major Internet providers. If, for instance, a company could strike a deal with America Online, then when Web users signed on to AOL, they might well be exposed immediately to an advertisement for that company's goods. Additionally, search engines might favor a site with which they had an agreement, so that a search, say, for shoes would rank their corporate associates top in their list of Web site hits.

Advertisers might also buy time on sites that bore some relationship to the product they were selling. If one were to browse a Web site dedicated, for example, to a specific model of automobile, it was more than likely that they would see advertisements for the company that manufactured that car, for part suppliers, for books about the vehicle, for company memorabilia, and other related products and services. Small sites provided particularly fruitful ground for advertisers, since they provided relatively inexpensive advertising rates and small but extremely focused interest groups to target. Since there was virtually no question that those online had some interest in computers, it is no surprise that computer-related advertisements dominated the Web. The top four online advertisers were in fact computer related. Microsoft topped the list, followed by IBM, Digital Equipment, and Excite. Ultimately nine of the top 10 were computer related. Interestingly, many of the top advertisers were also among the top publishers of ads. Excite, for instance, advertised on other Web sites in order to bring surfers to their site, where Excite would in turn expose them to numerous other advertisements. In the first half of 1998, Excite spent nearly five million dollars on advertising but brought in over $47 million in revenues from publishing the ads of others. Yahoo, the top ad publisher, spent over three million dollars on ads but brought in $54 million.[23]

The most common form of advertising was banners or buttons, spots allotted on a Web site through which the advertisers' Web site could be reached. Banners frequently topped Web pages, and were therefore the first thing that consumers saw. Additionally, advertisers might utilize a "pop-up" ad. Pop-up advertisements came unbidden to a computer user's screen when they clicked on a particular link. The very act of closing the pop-up window forced users to engage with the ad, registering it even if only in annoyance. These advertisements, typically placed with the approval of the linked Web site, seemed to be inescapable for some time. But by the end of the decade, their use had diminished somewhat. The reason for this was that, more often than not, Internet users found these ads annoying rather than appealing. The creation of an antagonistic relationship between consumer and ad was a cardinal sin of advertising.

The Internet was a new arena of advertising, and it is only natural that, as companies set about determining its potential, mistakes would be made. One was the marketing to newsgroups. Newsgroups, online discussion forums generally focused on a single topic, seemed an excellent way to reach a great number of potential customers at very little expense, since posting messages on most newsgroups was free. In 1994, law firm Canter and Siegel posted an advertisement to over 7,000 newsgroups. Many newsgroup users were enraged to be receiving a message that had nothing to do with the stated topic of the newsgroup, and Canter and Siegel suffered damage to its reputation among the online community. Even worse, the firm's Internet service provider crashed 15 times under the weight of some 300,000 letters of complaint, or "flames." Most large companies consequently avoided the posting of unsolicited ads on newsgroups. These ads became known as "spam," a term equally applicable to unsolicited ads e-mailed to Internet users.[24] Ultimately, although the practice was not the goldmine that Canter and Siegel and other companies had hoped, spamming was far from extinct at the end of the nineties, and many e-mail users complained that they spent as much time deleting irrelevant advertisements, constituting as much as 80 percent of the mailings, than actually reading their e-mail.

There was no shortage of critics of online advertising, of course. The idealists who had once regarded the Internet as a great equalizer, a democratic forum where everyone could make their voice heard, now found it hard to find those voices amidst all of the advertising. Likewise, many simply found the overwhelming assault by images and text trying to sell something to be offensive. Others complained that the flood of advertisements made Web surfing increasingly inefficient, and slowed down loading time for the Web sites that they actually wanted to peruse. Not surprisingly, then, several companies marketed software designed to block out most online advertising. However, these products, Junkbuster, @tGuard, WebWiper, and the like, had limited success since many consumers found online advertising only mildly annoying, and not aggravating enough to merit the effort required to download and install these services. A 1998 survey found that 43 percent of respondents found online ads less obtrusive than either direct mail ads or television commercials, which they had already put up with for years.[25]

The Internet also provided an unprecedented opportunity for companies to learn about their target audience. Typically, an advertiser could quite easily target a potential customer according to the region from which they signed online. In addition, Web sites could be used to keep track of how customers progressed though a site, thereby gauging what features grabbed the surfer's attention the most readily, and what kind of topics and what kind of displays had the most positive effect on an individual or specific groups of individuals. A number of Web sites and online surveys gave surfers questionnaires. The short surveys frequently had nothing directly to do with products, instead focusing on public opinion. A survey might ask about politics or other issues in the news, or about entertainment and sports events. The surveys provided a degree of amusement for surfers who could compare their opinions and predictions to the online community at large. But they also provided information to Internet service providers and other companies about the attitudes and demographics of their audience, and those companies could subsequently design ads to appeal to these demographics. A 1998 government study discovered that of Web sites aimed at children, 89 percent asked for personal information in order to market to kids, and this directly led to the April 2000 passage of the Children's Online Privacy Protection Act.

Ultimately, despite the trials that came with exploiting this new media, online advertising staked its claim, and became as much a part of life to many Americans as the commercials on network television. Online advertising began in earnest about 1994, and by 1999 had grown into a $1.8 billion industry, with no end to its growth in sight.[26]

4
Architecture

URBAN SPRAWL AND SUBURBANIZATION

Perhaps more than any other art form, architecture has always experienced the conflict between art and commerce, between aesthetics and utility. Architects have endeavored to flex their creativity, but the nature of the building industry has insisted that the practicality of structures comes first. At first glance, it might well appear that in the 1990s, commerce clearly won out over art. Indeed, more apparent than any single architectural marvel, is the rapid development of urban landscapes, not only on the fringes of the large cities, but also in rural communities. Small communities found themselves expanding tremendously as national corporations came to realize the significant untapped markets in such areas, and, while shopping malls remained a force, *superstores,* most notably Wal-Mart, were brought to new markets, changing landscapes enormously. Such constructs were brought to various kinds of areas—urban, suburban, and rural—contributing to an architectural homogeneity across the country. Meanwhile, this urban sprawl was further encouraged by the continued growth of the suburbs, though the nineties saw the rise of a new kind of suburbs, more affluent and more isolated, with larger and more expensive homes than the earlier suburban progenitors.

Urban growth was certainly nothing new, nor were the suburbs, but both took on a new character in the 1990s as urban growth seemed to speed up considerably. It is certainly worth considering just why such an acceleration may occur; however, the reasons are not simple. The beginning of urban sprawl and, indeed, of the suburbs, is generally thought to have been with the conclusion of World War II, as GIs, financed by government grants, moved away from the cities and into the newly developed suburbs, seeking a fresh start. The motivation then was not greatly different from that of the 1990s. Those moving to new housing developments typically sought to escape the older and, in many cases, declining areas, driven not only by the desire to have a fresh start, but also to improve their social status. Even as those who could afford to left older areas, those areas came to be increasingly inhabited by the lower class and largely ignored by policy makers. Estimates placed the number of such depleted suburban neighborhoods at eighty-seven in the Chicago area alone, in a pattern repeated by many other large citites.[1] As one book on the subject of suburbia has explained, "As the ring of suburbia grows around most of our cities, so grows the void at the center. Even while the struggle to revitalize deteriorated downtown neighborhoods and business districts continues, the inner ring of suburbs is already at risk, losing residents and businesses to fresher locations on a new suburban edge."[2]

As this implies, it is important to distinguish between the different kinds of suburbs. The earlier versions were largely designed as affordable housing, easily available to middle class families. But the newer suburbs were frequently of a different sort, both architecturally and demographically. Even at first glance, the suburban houses of the 1990s tended to appear larger than previous models, 3,000 square feet or more not being at all unusual. The single story or small bi-level dwellings of prior generations were transformed to multi-storied mini-mansions. Such houses, sometimes referred to by detractors as *McMansions*, in reference to the McDonalds' fast-food chain, were, in fact, frequently prefab, or modular, with parts largely built off-site and fitted together at the desired location. A study released by the federal Department of Housing and Urban Development reported that the number of prefab houses shipped in 1996 reached 363,000, more than double the number reported in a 1991 study.[3] While conformity had always been an aspect of the traditional suburbs, this seemed even more the case with the new version. An older suburban neighborhood might have houses that all conformed to the same basic floor plan and the same sized plot of land, but did not exhibit the same monochromatic nature of the new suburbs, wherein no house, either on account of structure or color, would stand out. Such could also be said of the inhabitants of said housing. Frequently, suburban housing developments would be divided into clusters, groupings of houses at given costs. A particular development, for instance, could have a cluster of houses costing $350,000, and a second cluster with $200,000 houses, and so on.

This kind of separation of housing helped to contribute to a segregation of the populace on the basis of wealth. Thus, the new suburbs, and especially the more affluent segments thereof, came to be sold not only on the basis of location and quality of construction, but also on the basis of exclusivity.[4] At the extreme, this exclusivity manifested itself in the form of gated communities, where residents needed special pass codes and approval to enter the neighborhood. A 1997 survey placed the number of gated communities at approximately 20,000.[5] Among the general populace, the idea of gated communities, designed to keep out all but an elite few, met with considerable disapproval. Yet the snobbishness with which gated communities were associated was less often associated with the new affluent suburbs, which were nonetheless virtually as exclusive, and protected from the masses by prohibitive costs and distance from urban areas. Even as there were class separations from one suburban cluster to another, the class distinction between those who could afford the new suburbs and those left to the old suburbs and inner cities was marked. This is not to suggest that all those who lived in the new suburbs were wealthy. Indeed, they tended to be middle class families using credit to purchase a house. That said, the ownership of such a house did much to improve a family's social status and self-image, placing them somehow above those forced to live in cities or in the old suburbs that had once upon a time offered the top-notch domiciles.

When this previous generation of suburbia had first sprung up in the postwar years, there had been justified concern about how their erection drew money out of the cities, and indeed this was also a concern in the 1990s. Many businesses left the cities to relocate nearer the new suburban areas, and the increased disposable income possessed by those living within. Likewise, government money that might be used in the cities was drained away to construct and maintain suburban infrastructure, from sewers and plumbing, to communication wiring, to roads. Vitally important was the establishment of roads from the suburbs to the cities, where many of the suburban inhabitants worked. New highways were constructed to connect the urban centers with the suburban fringes. In areas that already had highway access, the increased commuter traffic necessitated roadway development, particularly involving the widening of roads.

URBAN RENEWAL

With funds diverted elsewhere, urban decay was a very real threat. But this was not a new problem. Instead, the 1990s saw the taking on of this issue with a new vigor, as many cities attempted to revitalize downtowns and other urban areas that had come to be plagued by structural decay, poverty, and crime. The task, however, proved a challenging one, though it was not without some success.

New York provides a good example of revitalization in action. Although certain areas experienced some significant revitalization, there were still areas that remained in relative ruin. The problem lies in the fact that the decay of urban buildings was part of a larger problem. Aggressive city planning and architectural repair had limits if not supported by the social ser-

vices designed to combat poverty and crime. It was believed that the physical revitalization of an area, the refurbishing of buildings, and the substi-
tution of irreparably dilapidated structures with new ones, would draw
wealth, both in the form of consumers and businesses. By and large, this
proved to be true, but often led to a mere relocating of the negative social
elements of urban decay to neighborhoods still in a state of disrepair. In New
York, the poverty certainly did not vanish, and in fact, the revitalization appeared to have helped the rich and middle class more than those living
below the poverty line, about one-quarter of the city's population. Still, the
city saw some truly desperate neighborhoods brought back to life. In 1997,
President Clinton visited the South Bronx to celebrate its improvement. The
South Bronx had once been renowned for its state of decay and disarray, but
in the 1990s significant portions were rebuilt, with buildings that had once
been abandoned, or burned, or otherwise damaged, now reconstructed.[6]
Likewise, other areas of New York, including the downtown, were brought
out of their state of disrepair. New York is but one example of attempts at
urban renewal, but other cities experienced similar patterns.

Of vital importance to revitalization was the drawing of big business to
urban areas. But major corporations not only brought new wealth to urban
areas, but effected an architectural change in developing communities as
well. Even as the coming of chain retailers to an area brought an additional
economic boost to those areas, so too did it bring a growing homogeneity
across America's landscape. Smaller shops, like a Starbucks coffee shop or
a McDonald's restaurant, could slip their way into a community without
overtly altering its look, but this was not the case for larger stores. The subject of considerable controversy, Wal-Mart stores, for instance, could not,
given their enormous size, fit easily into a pre-established strip mall. Utili-
tarian in their design, the gigantic discount department stores frequently
gave the impression that an gargantuan cube had been dropped into the
middle of a community, a cube with few architectural frills and a vast spread
of parking spaces. Moreover, Wal-Mart was accused of contributing to urban
sprawl, since the stores were frequently constructed on the previously un-
broken ground at the edges of developing cities, and of contributing to
urban blight. Indeed, by having so many goods under one roof, such stores
took customers away from small businesses, including those located in
downtown areas. With less incentive to go downtown, patrons of such stores
dwindled, and small businesses vacated buildings, leaving them hollow and
subject to eventual dilapidation, and, in some cities, the eventual need for
yet more urban revitalization. As a result, in some communities, active efforts were made to keep Wal-Marts (or *Sprawl-Marts*) out.[7]

It is, however, unfair to single out Wal-Mart as the only cause of the changing landscape of American cities. The 1990s saw the spread of a multitude
of similar new buildings, including not only other department stores like
Target and Super Kmart, but also of specialty super-stores like Barnes and

Noble for books, Gart Sports for sporting equipment, and others. As a result, an aerial view of many cities at the end of the decade was considerably altered from what it had been ten years earlier, with the hub of consumer activity in a city looking very much the same as a warehouse district.

With growing homogeneity and growing reliance on pre-fab houses and other buildings, one might imagine that the 1990s was a difficult decade for architects, and a rather creatively stifling one as well. A quick glance can, however, be deceiving. If, for most Americans, the architecture of the nineties seemed little more than Wal-Marts and suburbs, further investigation reveals that the nineties were an exciting, if difficult, period for the *art* of architecture. A March 2000 article in *Architectural Record* asked the question, "Is there a place for architecture?" The answer provided by the article was, indeed, a resounding yes, but it was likewise quick to point out that the place for architects had changed and that architects would have to redefine what they did. William Gallis, a Charlotte, North Carolina architect who made efforts to change this role, considered how architects were generally regarded: "At best, we decorate the city with fascinating and interesting objects. At bottom, we are service providers, warehousing people."[8] He also suggested that if the profession were to thrive, architects would need to get themselves involved in urban and suburban issues, well beyond the design and construction of single buildings.

Cities grew in the 1990s largely without the influence of architects; growth was instead handled primarily by city planners, developers, and political leaders. But given the problems associated with such growth, the argument was made that those most versed in the "housing of humans and the activities they perform" could well have an ameliorating effect on such problems if included more closely in urban development. As Gallis suggested, "Large scale urbanization has had a hard time delivering environmental sustainability and quality of life, so we fear it. Cities are physical artifacts and they can be managed and designed."[9] Consequently, Gallis's firm involved itself increasingly in the planning and design of communities, in considering the forces of the natural environment, traffic patterns, and surrounding urban areas. Likewise, other firms specialized in the renovation and revitalization of older buildings and neighborhoods.

TECHNOLOGY AND NEW WORLDS OF ARCHITECTURE

For those who stuck to more traditional ground, the 1990s was a particularly challenging decade. New college graduates with architecture degrees often found the jobs to be scarce. The economic recession of the late 1980s and early 1990s made an already competitive employment market considerably more difficult. Many of those who found jobs were employed in the creatively stifling world of corporate projects. The general dissatisfaction with such projects seems to have manifested itself in the 1999 American Institute of Architects Honor Awards, which only recognized two corporate buildings (the K.J. McNitt Building in Oklahoma City, designed by Elliott + Associates Architects, and the FILA Corporate Headquarters in Maryland, whose award-winning interiors were designed by Shelton, Mindel & Associates), much in contrast to the 1980s, when such corporate works were the high-profile, high-prestige projects.[10] But, of course, corporate projects were exactly the kinds of projects on which newly graduated architectural interns—those who could find work—could expect to find themselves working.

Given the difficulties facing young architects, in a business climate that limited creative opportunities for all but the most established of architects, many turned to other avenues of self-expression. The entertainment world, especially the movie and electronic game industries, provided a new venue for some architects. As David Glenn, an architecture graduate from Virginia Polytechnic Institute, put it, "I could never have predicted this path...But it allows me to actualize what I enjoy about architecture without having to be a monkey in some big corporate machinery."[11] What Glenn was commenting upon was his work as a building and background designer for computer games, including the popular *Diablo II*. In fact, as computer game environments became more sophisticated, thousands of new architecture graduates pursued careers not in the building trades, but in computer technology. The draw of such a field is obvious: architects were allowed a creative freedom not stifled by corporate or fiscal concerns. Presumably, such *cyber-structures* could flout conventional rules of structural soundness as well. But one of the greatest draws was money. At the end of the century, the average pay for a newly graduated architecture firm intern was less the $40,000 a year. The architects working in the gaming field typically made $50,000. Moreover, as the movie industry came to use more and more computer graphics in film, the call to architects from Hollywood was even more alluring, with even greater pay opportunities.[12]

Part of the reason that so many young architects proved so adept in computer graphic design was that computers had, in fact, become an indispensable part of their education. Indeed, the computer became as vital a tool for real-world architecture as for the virtual worlds. Architectural software became central to design of all sorts, including city planning and building construction. More than simply a tool for illustrating plans, computers allowed architects and city planners to gauge structural integrity and manage space. Traffic flow, for instance, could be modeled in virtual cities before the expensive work of constructing roads actually began. And even as computers came to prominence in architectural design, architects also found themselves in a position where they had to accommodate the growing technological functions of those they housed. As a 1999 article suggested, "Technology may enable elements of disparate building programs to merge—for example, the computerized, self-service business centers in hotels and airports—in what William J. Mitchell, dean of architecture and planning at MIT, calls 'recombinant architecture.' Meanwhile, new building types, like university computer science centers, arise in response to technology-driven requirements."[13] Such developments required designers, particularly those working on business buildings, to think about new configurations for computer work spaces, the reduced amount of space needed for filing systems, and the wiring of a structure for inter-office computerized communications.

FRANK GEHRY

For all the utilitarianism of 1990s architecture, there was, as there always has been, room for some architects to experiment, to create structures that pushed the bounds of the imagination and redefined how Americans thought of their buildings. One of the general trends, started in earlier decades but further emphasized in the 1990s, was that towards a rather industrial, even incomplete look. Many newer buildings seemed to leave the very nature of their construction apparent. Glass work, for instance, allowed one to see through the walls to the very supports of a structure. Other buildings emphasized the steel and concrete instead of covering them, exposing the structural skeleton as well as the duct systems of a building. In short, much of the architecture of the 1990s seemed to celebrate the internal structures that had been previously hidden away. There was also a continuing move away from symmetry, toward a more fluid and chaotic look, as in the work of Frank Gehry (b. 1929).

Gehry, the recipient of many awards and honors over the course of the decade, was one of the 1990s most renowned architects. An adventurous designer—"I thought my work was weird," he claimed—Gehry had his start much earlier, establishing a name for himself until he won, in 1989, the Pritzker Prize for architecture.[14] This can be seen as something of a turning point in Gehry's career. Gehry had received a fair share of criticism from those who claimed his work was structurally impractical and unrealistic. Gehry felt ostracized by the architectural community, stating, "They didn't think I was [serious]—I don't know why...I wasn't welcome with them, and I couldn't talk to them. I found I could really talk with the artists. So I became more a part of their community."[15] With this strong artistic streak, Gehry continued to push the envelope with striking, expressionistic buildings, that he nonetheless took care to make structurally sound. By the end of the 1990s, Gehry had earned the respect of his peers and much of the general public. In 1998, he was awarded the National Medal of the Arts, and in 1999, he was named a Gold Medallist by the American Institute of Architects, taking his place amongst such previous recipients as Thomas Jefferson and Frank Lloyd Wright. More importantly, Gehry earned some high profile jobs. Erected in 1993, the Frederick R. Weisman Art Museum, on the campus of the University of Minnesota, almost defied description, with a look simultaneously industrial and organic, constructed of stainless steel and orange brick, and exhibiting various structural angles that seem to follow no form save that of the designer's imagination. Perhaps Gehry's greatest structure was the Guggenheim Museum in Bilbao, Spain, begun in 1991, completed in 1997, and exhibiting the same kind of expressionistic freedom of design demonstrated by the Weisman Museum. Gehry also designed significant portions of the Paris, France, Disneyland in the late 1980s and early 1990s, which led to his commission to design the Disney Concert Hall (1989–2001) to house the Los Angeles Philharmonic, described by one observer as "designed to leave passers-by in no doubt that here is a building of cultural importance, even if it is not wholly clear from the outside what goes where."[16]

I. M. PEI

The renowned architect I. M. (Ieoh Ming) Pei also had a place of importance in the 1990s. Perhaps best known for his glass pyramid addition to the Louvre in Paris, France, Pei was less widely visible in the 1990s as he was in the 1980s, but his firm of Pei Cobb Freed & Partners made a significant contribution to the American cultural landscape with the United States Holocaust Memorial Museum in Washington, D.C. The museum, completed in 1993, presented a considerable challenge. How could a mere building measure up to the historical importance, to the human tragedy of the Nazi concentration camps? Ultimately, a building could not, so the architects instead attempted to capture select elements of the Holocaust experience. The museum, while hanging together thematically, was of a modular kind of design, with different sections of the building hinting at different aspects of the concentration camp experience. The towers suggested the watchtowers of the camps, and gantry-bridges suggested the Warsaw ghetto. High walls and narrow hallways with sinister doorways gave one the impression of a prison walkway, made all the more claustrophobic by the photographs of victims of the Holocaust covering every surface of the walls.[17] The Holocaust Memorial Museum also included a central "Hall of Witness"—described by one critic as "a demonic space of brick and steel"[18]—lit by an overhead skylight, stark and haunting. Although principally overseen by partner James Ingo Freed, Pei's interest in order and geometrical shapes was clearly noticeable in the museum's design, particularly in the pyramidal towers and the glass work of the Hall of Witness skylight.

GLASS ARCHITECTURE

Pei's influence, however, extended well beyond his close peers. Particularly Pei's work with glass provided a model for architects across the world.

Smithsonian magazine, in fact, noting the almost uncountable number of major glass buildings in the works, proclaimed a new age of glass construction. Ultimately, this revived interest in glass was not merely aesthetic. There had always been risks when it came to building with such a fragile substance, but new technologies and building methods improved glass's standing considerably. As Martin Powell, of Design Alliance Architects, explained, "It's amazing the way glass has gone from being a material that was beautiful but difficult to work with to a material that's now one of the most versatile you can use."[19] Design Alliance Architects was responsible for the Alcoa Corporate Center, which opened in 1998 in Pittsburgh. The Alcoa Center appeared almost to be principally made of glass, with but a thin latticework of steel encaging it. The building was even more striking for its location, just alongside the Allegheny River. During the day, it would catch the lights reflected from the water and sparkle. During the night, it would reflect its otherworldly glow off the surface of the river.

Even more striking was the work begun on the Rose Center for Earth and Space at the American Museum of Natural History in Manhattan. The Rose Center, designed by the firm of Polshek Partnership Architects, appeared as a 95-foot high glass cube encasing an aluminum sphere, which itself encases the Hayden Planetarium. Like nothing else ever constructed, the building was indeed intended to draw attention. Particularly, it was designed to be quite clear in its purpose, strange though it might appear, or as James Polshek explained, "We wanted to build a structure that would say science."[20] And indeed it did. In fact, the building was itself a marvel of scientific engineering and, like the Alcoa center, hailed an age wherein glass could be used with at least as much freedom, if not more, than steel and masonry, an age wherein concerns about the structural soundness and energy efficiency of glass were overcome. But one of the many glass-heavy structures following hard on the heels of the Rose Center was the Sandra Day O'Connor U.S. Courthouse in Phoenix, Arizona, was likewise notable not only for the complex use of steel and glass in its 120-foot high structure, but also for its energy efficiency.

GREEN ARCHITECTURE

Another area of specialization that developed in the 1990s was *Green* architecture. As ecological concerns grew, so did they manifest themselves in architecture. These efforts sought not only to conserve resources, but to make structures an integral part of nature, organically co-existing with the environment, so as not to appear an environmental intrusion. At the extreme, there was architect Obie Bowman, who designed numerous buildings, like the Spring Lake Park Visitors Center in Sonoma County, California, which but barely peeked out of its environment. The Visitors Center, constructed to house information resources on the surrounding natural environment, was designed to blend harmoniously with the landscape. The 2,000-square-foot building was constructed in something of a pyramid shape, giving it an appearance rather like an additional small hill rising from the surrounding forest. Additionally, Bowman paid close attention to the effect of visitors at the site, as well as to the energy systems of the building, with solar collectors to provide warmth and suction ducts to draw cool air inside during the hot season.[21] But Green architecture was not merely restricted to parklands. Indeed, concerns about energy, the environment, and the physical and psychological well-being of citizens, led some cities to commission environmentally conscious architects with urban projects. For example, attempts were made to negotiate the established look of a city with environmental soundness by James Polshek in San Marcos, California, and in the Bronx, and Troy West in New Jersey and in Rhode Island.[22] Ultimately, for these and other environmentalist architects, the negotiation between nature and the costs of technology became paramount. Building construction, whatever precautions were taken, would necessarily have some kind of environmental cost, so technology had to be used with care, or as James Wines, in the conclusion of his book *Green Architecture,* wrote "A great part of the solution is technological, but filtered through a study of the way nature solves its own engineering problems and how resourcefully energy and materials are converted to function."[23]

One of the most notable ecologically conscious buildings to be erected in the 1990s was Birmingham, Alabama's Southern Progress Building, designed by Jova/Daniels/Busby, architects, with the assistance of landscape architect Robert E. Marvin. The Southern Progress Corporation, a book and magazine publisher, long held to the idea of "responsible and enlightened use of the land," and the building to house the company was designed with this well in mind. The building was erected in 1991 within a 27-acre suburban forest setting, yet care was taken in its placement and design so that few trees were cut and little smoothing of the hillside site was necessary. In fact, the site was cleared by hand, rather than by heavy equipment, in order to spare the environment as much as possible. The five-story Southern Progress Building was expanded in 1994, bringing it to 142,000 square meters, but remained so integrated with the environment as to be practically undetectable from the nearby highway.[24]

MUSEUMS

Where corporate structures were less well received in the 1990s than in the 1980s, museums seemed to become the new showcase for the imaginative architect. Indeed, in addition to Gehry's Guggenheim and Weisman museums, many other high-profile museums and exhibition halls went up. In addition to the exhibits within, the buildings themselves became showpieces. Among these was the Getty Center, one of influential architect

A group of reporters preview the new Getty Center on Dec. 9, 1997, in the Westwood area of Los Angeles. The center, designed by architect Richard Meier, is situated in six buildings on 110 acres and includes the J. Paul Getty Museum and research and educational institutes. The one-billion-dollar Getty Center was scheduled to open for the public Dec.16. © AP/Wide World Photos.

Richard Meier's most ambitious projects. Begun in 1984, the Getty Center was opened in Los Angeles in 1997. More than simply a museum, the Getty Center was an art complex, almost a small city in and of itself. This was further emphasized by its physical removal from L.A.'s more urban landscape. The center was perched upon a hill, an exclusive futuristic railway strung between it and the city. With its multiple massive buildings, including the J. Paul Getty Museum, and carefully landscaped and waterlined grounds, the Getty was touted as the first billion dollar construction project in the country. This cost was received with scorn by some critics, who also cast the structure as little more than another corporate building on Meier's résumé. One writer suggested that "The fact that it is wholly privately financed adds to its slightly sinister quality—as if some James Bond villain were seated in a control room at its center, preparing to bring ruin to the world."[25] Indeed, compared to the city below, the Getty Center did seem somewhat otherworldly, if not malevolent, and some accused it of being simply inappropriate for the locale, as if Meier had designed it without considering the environment, both urban and natural.

Other significant museums of the 1990s include the Seattle Art Museum (1991), the San Francisco Museum of Modern Art (1994), and the American Heritage Center and University Art Museum in Laramie, Wyoming (1992). The Seattle Museum, designed by Venturi, Scott Brown & Associates and located between Seattle's business district and the waterfront, stretched to a height of five stories, made all the more striking by a series of vertical lines running the length of the building. Architect Mario Botta's San Francisco Museum of Modern Art was notable for its striking geometry, especially the enormous circular skylight, angled at 45 degrees, looking much like a gigantic eye peering skyward. More unusual was the American Heritage Center, designed by New Mexico architect Antoine Predock. Predock had previously been involved in the design of the Las Vegas Library and Discovery Museum and the Nelson Fine Arts Center at Arizona State University, both of which had a distinct, if very modern, Southwestern feel. This tendency continued with the American Heritage Center, designed to resemble a Native American tepee, an appropriate design given the museum's devotion to American, and especially Western, history.

OTHER SIGNIFICANT BUILDINGS

A 2002 article in *USA Weekend* took the ambitious step of naming the five most important buildings of the twenty-first century, all of which were begun, and some finished, in the 1990s. The list included both the Rose Center and the O'Connor courthouse. Also included was the Quadracci Pavilion of the Milwaukee Art Museum, which increased gallery space from 90,000 to 117,000 feet, but also proved to be a draw in and of itself with its 250-foot-long suspension bridge and flapping sunscreen about which architect Carol Ross Barney commented, "It's so graceful...It's the illusion, a bird taking off, that's so romantic." Rolling Meadows, Illinois' 3Com Midwest Headquarters, opened in 1999, also made the list. This structure bore some resemblance to conventional office space, but took those conventions and literally tilted them. Walls tilted at varying angles flouted the boxiness of most office designs, lending considerable charm to the 3Com Headquarters. This list was rounded out by the Westside Light Rail corridor in Portland, Oregon, which, upon its opening in 1998, offered the deepest transit station in North America, reaching 260 feet below ground. The winner of the White House Presidential Award for Design Excellence, much care was put into making the corridor environmentally and aesthetically friendly. The careful combination of glass, stone, and organic materials made the corridor an inviting and comfortable environment for travellers.[26]

A discussion of 1990s architecture would not be complete without consideration of one of its largest architectural projects, the Denver International Airport Terminal Building, designed by Fentress Bradburn Architects, and erected in 1995. This massive structure stretched 900 feet long and 240 feet wide, and an Automated Ground Transportation System, a sort of self-contained subway, was designed to assist travelers with the distances between concourses. But more striking than its size was its external appearance. The roofing of the Terminal Building consisted of Teflon-coated fiberglass layers draped over steel masts placed 150 feet apart. The result was what appeared as a series of tents, lined up one after another, running the length of the terminal. Met by both praise and disdain, the terminal nonetheless was an impressive showcase of how the avant-garde could be incorporated into public buildings quite successfully.

Of course, these more experimental structures were exceptions, with most architects working on rather pedestrian projects, be they suburban developments or the latest link in a chain of boxy superstores. But it should be noted that the aesthetics of people like Pei and Gehry did manage to filter down to more pragmatic projects. Gehry's plastic fluidity found its way into the design of shopping malls, for instance, and Pei's glass work became an inspirational impetus to incorporate larger windows in both residences and business buildings. Ultimately, even with the sprawl and decay, even with the growing architectural homogeneity within and between communities, the boundaries of architectural creativity were being pushed, even as was architectural technology. The true adventures in architecture might require some searching out, but beyond the McMansions, 1990s architecture offered as much imagination as prior decades.

5

Fads, Games, Toys, Hobbies, and Sports

Studies have suggested that Americans spent more time working in the 1990s than ever before. But no matter how much time they spent at the office, they nonetheless seemed to have plenty of time for leisure activities. Indeed, the amount of time spent playing or watching spectator sports created several massive industries. Certainly, the market for toys seemed endless, with more toys being produced than ever before. Of course, there were fewer toys that had the lasting popularity of such classics as Lincoln Logs and Legos, but the average child also tended to have more toys than children of earlier generations. Likewise, the market for games boomed, especially that for computer games, which, in the nineties, developed astonishing sophistication. For adults with less interest in toys and games, sports provided plenty of opportunities to pass the time, either as participant or spectator. And they also provided plenty of opportunities for Americans to spend their hard-earned dollars.

TOYS

Toy sales were measured at about 15 billion dollars in 1993, and this continued increase in the toy market can in part be attributed to the increase in disposable income held not only by parents, but also by children themselves. Also important to the growth and stabilization of the toy market was the continued success of chain retail outlets, like Toys R Us, which accounted for about 20 percent of the retail toy market.

To a large extent, the toy market was driven by licensed properties. Rather than being focused on original toys, many children were most interested in toys based on characters and situations they had seen on TV or in movies, be they related to *Star Wars,* or the *Mighty Morphing Power Rangers,* or *Pokémon.* The classic Lego line of building toys saw a renovation along these lines. A *Star Wars* Lego series proved very popular, but also posed a problem for the company. Now that it had featured a licensed property in its toys, it had to follow up the *Star Wars* toys with something equally exciting. Previously Lego had been able to count on a child's own creativity for its popularity, but the company found itself increasingly having to rely on some kind of commercial hook. Ultimately, Lego toys became more action-, rather than creation-, oriented, leaving the company to compete even harder in the already overcrowded action-toy market.

Except for Barbie, most doll sales slumped in the 1990s. However, even as the retail doll market slumped, the collectors' market picked up considerably, becoming one of the 1990s fastest-growing hobbies, and perhaps suggesting a nostalgia on the part of adults for the days when toys were simpler, and perhaps even for the days when gender roles were less ambiguous. Just as she dominated the general doll market, Barbie also dominated the collectors' market. Increasingly, Mattel released Barbies that were too elaborate to be thought of as mere playthings. A series of international Barbies showed off meticulously-designed ethnic costuming. Barbie also appeared in movie-themed costumes, covering classic films like *The Wizard of Oz* and *Gone with the Wind.* It is difficult to imagine the average girl being excited about a Barbie designed after Vivien Leigh's Scarlett O'Hara, and, indeed, the appeal of this doll was with a decidedly older audience.

Another toy line that generated enormous consumer appeal and garnered massive collectors' interest in the 1990s was the Beanie Baby. This unlikely craze centered around a line of small stuffed animals produced by Ty Inc. Certainly this large line encompassing many different kinds of animals was cute, but its soaring popularity was much more than most would have expected. The competition to attain all of the Beanie Babies was fierce, especially among adult collectors, who would sometimes pay outlandish prices for certain dolls. Certainly, Ty stoked the fires of the collector's fury by releasing especially rare dolls, produced well under the demand level of the market.

Beanie Babies were one of the toys to stimulate a buyers frenzy, not unlike that seen for Cabbage Patch Dolls in the eighties. Another was Tickle-Me Elmo, a plush version of the character from the popular Sesame Street children's television program. Reaching the market in 1996, the Elmo doll was fairly simple in its conception. It was simply a doll that would laugh hysterically when tickled on its tummy. The doll's success led to numerous imitators, and *Sesame Street* licensed the creation of similar dolls of other characters from the show. Moreover, Tickle-Me Elmo evolved, with later models responding in different ways to being tickled or otherwise prodded on various parts of the body.

ACTION FIGURES

Along with Barbie, Beanie Babies, and others, action figures found a considerable market among adults. One might attribute this to the newfound adulthood of many who grew up during what might be considered the golden age of the action figure. Prior parallels like G.I. Joe notwithstanding, the action figure came into its own in the 1970s, particularly with the release of the *Star Wars* action figures line. In the 1990s, *Star Wars* experienced a new surge in popularity due to the release of several well-received *Star Wars* novels and anticipation of new films in the series. Naturally, the action figures also saw a rebirth. But this time, there were adults who had grown up on the movies and who fondly remembered playing with the toys. Therefore, the acquisition of the action figures, now no longer de-

Toy maker Hasbro rolled out a big line of merchandise linked to *Star Wars: Episode I—The Phantom Menace,* under an estimated $600 million licensing deal with director George Lucas. Among the products are the reissued *Star Wars* action figures Darth Vader, right, and Ben (Obi-Wan) Kenobi, left, displayed April 7, 1999, with Princess Leia Organa in her ceremonial dress in front of other packaged characters from the film. © AP/Wide World Photos.

Todd McFarlane poses with his creation, Spawn, at his office in Tempe, Ariz., April 22, 1999. McFarlane has turned Spawn into a $65 million comic book, movie, and action figure empire. Fans have responded well to *Spawn*, a dark, shadowy creature who works for the devil, and Spawn books consistently rank among the top-sellers. © AP/Wide World Photos.

pendent on allowances or parental kindness, served as a kind of nostalgic, reclamation of the past. Though central to the adult collectors' market, *Star Wars* figures were not the only ones to demand an audience. Indeed, *Star Trek* figures also flourished, as did many others tied to various movies and television programs. With the growth of the collectible toy market, the stigma of adults owning action figures was reduced, if not altogether eliminated, and this naturally spurred collectors even more. Noting the rise in action figure purchases by adults, manufacturers began catering more to this audience.

One of the groundbreaking companies in this field was McFarlane Toys, founded by Todd McFarlane, creator of the comic book series *Spawn*. McFarlane oversaw the production of figures based on his comic book designs. The result was the most meticulously-detailed, and decidedly gruesome, figures to ever hit toy stores. McFarlane's zombies, demons, and monstrosities introduced a new aesthetic to action figure production, such that many other properties, including the popular *X-Files* TV series, flocked to his company in order to have but the highest quality figures produced. These figures served as a clarion call for the adult collectors' market and many other companies, and by the end of the decade the number of figures produced with adults in mind was not far off the mark from the number being created for children. McFarlane Toys itself produced figures for such decidedly non-children-oriented properties as Shaft, Austin Powers, and SCTV's Bob and Doug McKenzie. The company even produced a popular line of figures based on the rock band KISS.[1] These changes in the market also ushered in a new era of sex in action figure production. McFarlane Toys had produced several figures of scantily-clad, well-endowed women, principally characters drawn from the comic books. And many other companies followed suit, creating figures, again mostly based on comic book characters, whose proportions made Barbie's look quite natural. These figures did merit some criticism, but the outcry was limited, given that the market for these figures was clearly not young children and given that few such figures were sold in toy stores, relegated instead to comic shops and stores specializing in collectibles.

VIRTUAL PETS

Virtual pets also became very popular, starting in 1996. First developed in Japan, the earliest virtual pet toys were small handheld electronic devices with a fairly primitive artificial intelligence (A.I.). The pets were egg-shaped (in fact, one of the early products was called Tamagotchi, which means "lovable egg"), and responded to how much they were played with. The owner had limited control over the pet—able to put it to bed, or wake it, or feed it—but the pet's response to its owner was partly a response to his or her activities and partly random. To make the pets more endearing, makers showed some kind of actual animal on an LCD display, whose expression made it quite clear when it was happy, angry, or sleeping. The typical pets, cats and dogs, were among the most popular pets depicted, but more exotic animals like the panda were also used. Some even utilized the altogether fictional creatures from the *Pokémon* card game and cartoons. From these origins, which included popular virtual pet makes such as GigaPets and NeoPets, came much more sophisticated models. A number of toys were created using the virtual pet style of A.I., but transcended the egg shape altogether. Several models of robot dogs were created, including the most popular Poo-Chi. In 1998, Dave Hampton, a freelance engineer who had worked on the Atari video games in the 1980s, introduced a new product called Furby, which combined the virtual pet with the plush doll. Furbies were equipped with seven sensors, which reacted to sound, touch, and other stimuli. They represented the most advanced virtual pet at the time, not only responding to immediate stimuli, but also appearing to learn. In fact, Furbies, who spoke their own *Furbish* language, were programmed to gradually learn English as they were played with. When new, they spoke about 20 percent English, but could learn to speak up to 80 percent. The toys were an immediate hit, not only among children, but also among adult collectors.

COMPUTER GAMES

Obviously, with the computer boom of the 1990s, the decade also saw an according rise in the popularity of video games. And the quality of the games increased significantly, as well. Advances in graphics, complexity, and sophistication of computer gaming engines far outpaced the advances for the entire pre-nineties history of computer gaming. Several major breakthroughs occurred in 1989 with the development of two 16-bit (a unit of memory) gaming consoles, NEC TurboGrafx 16 and Sega Genesis. Much more sophisticated than prior game systems created by companies like Amiga, Atari, and Coleco, these consoles immediately gained wide acceptance among consumers who could afford the price tag of nearly $250. Genesis sales generally outpaced those of the TurboGrafx 16, largely due to the wider selection of games available for the system, particularly those by Electronic Arts, a company which began by specializing in sports-related games, but which, in 1990 began a campaign of buying out other game publishers. Sega also benefited from the exclusive rights to its own widely popular line of arcade video games. One of the decade's biggest names in electronic gaming, Nintendo, made a late foray into the 16-bit market in 1991 with its Super NES system, but had previously made a name for itself as a software developer, particularly with the best-selling *Super Mario 3* game, and with its development of the Game Boy handheld video game console. In 1992, Sega released the first CD-driven console, an early step in technology that would revolutionize not only electronic games, but computer operations in general. The system was highly touted, but Sega failed to release the tools that would allow other companies to produce games. These protectionist tactics ultimately hurt Sega sales as they limited the number of games available to consumers. Nonetheless, other companies, including Sony and Nintendo, began creating their own CD systems. Before long, CDs would replace the software cartridges completely, except in handheld systems.

In 1993, Panasonic released the first 32-bit console, 3DO. The system was a limited success, held back by the $699 price, as well as by the looming release of Atari's Jaguar, a 64-bit gaming system. Although the Jaguar suffered from internal hardware limitations, it demonstrated the full force of game console competition, in which each company tried to keep technologically ahead of the competition. It also made clear how rapidly obsolescence could set in. Naturally, it didn't take long for other companies to leap into the 64-bit fray, though the 32-bit console still dominated, with particular success for Sony's 1995 release of a 32-bit PlayStation console. Sony also gained in the market by reducing the PlayStation price to $199 in 1996, making it far more affordable than any prior systems of similar grade. That year, Nintendo also released its first 64-bit system. In Japan, where it was first released, the Nintendo 64 sold 500,000 units in the first day, and the 350,000 shipment to the U.S. sold out in less than three days. Typically the capacity of the systems was larger than that exploited by the games themselves, but by the end of the decade, the games were catching up, using the systems to near full potential. The result was astonishingly sophisticated games with elaborate virtual environments. But the end of the decade by no means saw the end of technological advancements. In 1999, Sega announced plans to release a 128-bit system using CD-ROM technology and with built in modem play support. With systems such as this on the horizon, players looked with the greatest anticipation to the gaming experiences to come.

Nintendo's Game Boy system provided another major venue for electronic gaming, spawning numerous imitators in the handheld console market, including Atari's early competition, Lynx. In 1995, Nintendo released its Virtual Boy 32-bit portable system, which, along with continued advances in the Game Boy systems, left the company utterly dominant in this niche of electronic gaming for the duration of the nineties. Portable game systems naturally never reached the level of sophistication displayed by non-portable systems, but they still saw considerable advances in technology. The earliest games were quite simple, with the game *Tetris* at one time the cutting edge. But Nintendo continued to increase the memory and processing capacity of the systems, such that the games grew in complexity and graphic quality.

Of course, with the proliferation of video games in arcades, in homes, and in the palms of players' hands, concerns about their effects increased considerably. Worries about how much time children spent in front of television screens had plagued parents, educators, and child welfare experts for some decades. The growing popularity of video games seemed only to encourage more time in front of screens. Some experts worried that time spent in this way created stupid children, and most agreed that it contributed to a decrease in physical activity, thereby contributing to obesity and other physiological problems. Moreover, many were concerned about the kinds of games being played by children, many of which seemed to celebrate violence without showing the consequences of such violence. Shooting games were popular, as were hand-to-hand combat games.

Street Fighter II, introduced in 1991 in arcades and later for home systems, was one of the most popular video games ever. It involved one-on-one combat between colorful characters modeled on Japanese animation (*anime*). The goal of the game was to beat opponent after opponent into submission. The violence of the game was reasonably non-realistic, but flecks of blood and the fact that players were encouraged to hurt others in the game world troubled critics. But whatever the complaints might be, the success of *Street Fighter II*, produced by Capcom, was undeniable, and many similar games thrived in its wake. Parents shocked by *Street Fighter II*'s violence, however, were in for an even bigger shock with Midway Games' 1993 introduction of *Mortal Kombat*, which used photographic instead of cartoonish characters in similar combat situations. Furthermore, the violence became much more graphic. Blood flowed more freely, and players who had perfected the game controls could execute maneuvers such as yanking the hearts out of opponents' chests, beheading them, or stripping them of their spines. Outrage over the violence led to the creation of a rating system for video games, both in homes and arcades, but this did little to deter the flow of violence. Ultimately, despite criticisms, no definitive relationship between video game violence and real-world violent acts committed by youths was ever proven. Nonetheless, attacks on violence in games continued well into the new millennium, even as game manufacturers did little to reduce the electronic carnage.

One of the most significant names in the realm of personal computer gaming was id Software, founded in 1992 by John Romero, then still in his early twenties, with John Carmack, Adrian Carmack, and Todd Hall. The company's first big success was *Wolfenstein 3-D*, in which the player raced around various levels of an old castle shooting down aggressive Nazi soldiers. The game introduced the first-person shooter style of computer gaming, maze-oriented action combat gaming from a first-person point of view. *Wolfenstein 3-D* was followed by *Doom*, a similarly oriented game in which the player assumed the role of a space marine battling zombies and hellish monsters. The game was a resounding success and revolutionized the industry. Imitators leapt on the first-person shooter bandwagon until an almost uncountable number of such games filled the shelves of software retailers. Id itself soon released the sequel *Doom II*, and then *Quake*, which refined the Doom software engine, offering a greater flexibility of character movement. Each of these games, all released within the first five years of id's existence, was more successful than its predecessors, with *Quake* selling over 1.7 million copies in its first year (compared to sales of about 100,000 for most PC games.) These games were not without controversy, given their graphic violence and the fact that, to opponents, the storylines seemed little more than excuses for simulated killing. The games were accused of desensitizing youths and some went so far as to directly blame the games for the increase in suburban high-school shooting. The principal designer of these games, Romero, who had been called the Steven Spielberg of game design, would eventually break away from id and found his own company, called Ion Storm which publicly prized game design over technology, but was plagued by release date delays which hindered overall sales.[2]

Other significant names in PC game design were Richard Garriott, the man behind a series of games under the Ultima title, begun in the 1980s, and Shigeru Miyamoto, creator of *Super Mario.* Created by Robyn and Rand Miller in 1994 for the Broderbund software company, *Myst* offered a very different gaming experience from Romero-style shooting games. *Myst* involved an exquisitely rendered three-dimensional environment through which players roamed in search of puzzles to solve. With about four million units sold, *Myst* became the top selling computer game. *Myst* and similar games, including *The 7th Guest* and its sequel *The Eleventh Hour*, were primarily puzzle oriented, but the environments, along with the narrative structures of the games made them every bit as popular as most action games, especially with those who preferred their gaming leisurely paced and less gory.

Perhaps the ultimate computer game of the nineties, however, was more than mere entertainment, it was actually a contest between machine and the human mind. The game was chess, and the participants were the master of the game Garry Kasparov and the IBM RS/6000SP named Deep Blue. Kasparov was regarded by most not only as the top current player, but as very likely the best there had ever been, and he went into the match with Deep Blue having won the World Championship for 11 years running. The man and machine met in February 1996. The multi-game match began on a startling note, with Deep Blue defeating the world champion handily. But thereafter, Kasparov seemed to take the match more seriously and soundly defeated Deep Blue, winning four games to the computer's two. The opponents met for a rematch a year later. This time Kasparov won the first game, but the second, third, and fifth games ended in draws. The fourth was won by Deep Blue. Then, in the final game, Kasparov crumbled under an aggressive and unpredictable assault by Deep Blue, conceding the game and match to the computer after the loss of his queen. By the time the final game had commenced, the media had turned more attention to the match than it ever had to a chess game, aware that something truly remarkable was happening, and something rather frightening to even the slightest technophobe. Millions watched as man at his best was defeated by a synthetic mind. Kasparov defenders accused the programmers of designing Deep Blue to not play a fine chess match per se, but to defeat Kasparov's specific style of play. Kasparov himself had a different reaction: "I'm a human being. When I see something that is well beyond my understanding, I'm afraid."[3]

COLLECTIBLE CARD GAMES

Another important development in the game field was the rise of collectible card games. The creation of such games was quite savvy given that it tapped into two potential markets: game players and collectors. The first

A selection of *Pokémon* trading cards are displayed in Scituate, Mass., Sept. 8, 1999. Hasbro Inc., the world's second largest toy manufacturer, acquired Wizards of the Coast, maker of *Pokémon* trading cards, for $325 million. *Pokémon* trading cards were so hot that stores found it hard to keep them on the shelves. Hasbro cashed in on the craze with the purchase.© AP/Wide World Photos.

popular card game to hit the market was *Magic the Gathering*, a fantasy-oriented game. A fairly complex game, *Magic the Gathering* did not function like traditional card games, but featured cards representing characters or weapons, of events or powers. The basic unit of this and similar games was the *starter deck*, a set of cards that included everything that players needed to play the game. The real money for companies in this market, however, was in *booster* packs. The packs of, typically, 10 to 15 cards, gave the players the opportunity to supplement their starter deck with more powerful cards, which were also usually rare and highly collectible, as well. Detractors criticized the fact that the amount of money paid directly influenced the strength of a player's deck, but the booster cards had other advantages, as well. For one thing, they allowed players to customize their decks, and with the literally thousands of different cards available in the many types of booster packs available, a *Magic the Gathering* player could develop a seemingly infinite number of combinations. Such possibilities made for a game that was extremely unpredictable and therefore exciting.

Similar card games followed. Among the most successful were those tied in with other media. The *Star Trek* game cards snared both gamers and science fiction fans, who were delighted by the attention to detail shown by the cards, which depicted not only major characters and events from the shows, but also the minutia that added so much to their atmosphere. Similar sets featuring *Star Wars, Hercules: The Legendary Journeys, Babylon 5,* and *Xena, Warrior Princess,* also appeared, as did other independent collectible card games. With simpler rules, geared towards a younger audience, the *Pokémon* collectible card game became, for a time, the hottest such game on the market. Although started as a game, *Pokémon* quickly grew into an empire, manifesting itself in television programs and movies, as well as on sneakers, backpacks, food products, T-shirts, and, in short, anything on which a *Pokémon* image could be pasted. The commercial beauty of the game itself was that it had such a broad appeal. Children could enjoy the colorful creatures featured on the cards, yet also learn the game fairly quickly. The cards also found an audience among adult collectors, especially those interested in Japanese culture, out of which *Pokémon* was born. The game utilized very basic rules, but many of the rules could be bent based on text printed on the cards in play, which allowed for simplicity that could grow complex as play unfolded, and this made the game an ideal one to be played by both adults and children, across generational boundaries. Of course, despite its good points, the *Pokémon* empire had its critics, given its ravenous marketing program and the fact that for a time it seemed utterly impossible to escape from its ubiquity.

THE INTERNET

An important part of the collectors market was the development of online auctions. Indeed, the search for antiques and collectibles was once a laborious process, involving the scouring of thrift and antique stores, and communication with other collectors and sellers via phone and letter writing. With the rise of the Internet, however, and especially with the birth of the Internet's largest auction house, eBay, collecting took on an altogether different dynamic. Now collectors could search a wide database of items, and contact sellers by e-mail as easily as they could stroll into a local antique shop. The Internet also simplified the process of attaining information on a particular item by allowing sellers to post full information about an item, including photographs, online. EBay was founded in September 1995 as the only online marketplace of major significance, and its rapid growth guaranteed that it maintained its dominant status throughout the decade. By decade's end, eBay had over 40 million registered users, and in 2000, it facilitated over five billion dollars in merchandise transactions.

The Internet in general quickly became a kind of hobbyist paradise. Seemingly, no matter how obscure a hobby, at least one Web site could be found devoted to it, and in most cases, more than one. Sites devoted to various collectibles, from stamps to Beanie Babies, flourished as both dealers and collectors showed off their wares. Surfers could easily compare the completeness of their own collections to those of others, or even to definitive catalogues of a given collectible. Likewise, those more interested in craft hobbies could easily find tips and ideas online. Perhaps most importantly, the Internet provided a medium through which hobbyists could communicate with one another. Not only could they e-mail one another, but the development of real-time chat rooms allowed them to communicate with their fellows anywhere in the U.S. and even internationally.

In fact, the Internet itself became something of a hobby for many Americans. Chat rooms on a multitude of subjects, or no subjects at all, provided millions with a form of relatively inexpensive entertainment, and, in its way, revived the art of conversation. If some complained that the kind of discussion in chat rooms was frequently banal and that online conversations lacked the intimacy of personal or even telephone contact, others pointed out that some online relationships actually flourished, growing well beyond their electronic origins. Stories of romance born of online interaction became increasingly common as the decade progressed.

The Internet also provided a medium for game playing. Individuals could easily find simple games like card games and puzzles online from the earliest years of the Internet. But as technology advanced, many games became increasingly complex. Game players were also able to network their systems and thereby play multiplayer games of popular software titles, like *Doom*. But perhaps the biggest source of Internet amusement was the simple act of surfing. The increase in Internet users during the decade was utterly staggering. Largely made public in 1992, by 1994 about three million people went online regularly. By 1998 more than 100 million were online, with no end to the growth in sight. Many took to the online world without any specific goal in mind, instead simply typing topics of interest into search engines and following where they led. Most Web sites were elaborately linked up with other sites of similar interest, and by following these links, surfers could easily spend hours on end online. For some, the Internet became an even more compelling form of entertainment than television, and many were wrested from the TV screen to the computer screen. The lure of the Internet was, at least in part, the semblance of control. Television largely dictated what a viewer could watch and when. The choices on the Internet were seemingly infinite, and were typically available precisely when the consumer wanted to pursue them. Naturally, television networks and movie studios, as well as radio stations, noted this shifting audience and frequently implemented their own Web sites, complete with online broadcasts.

LEISURE SPORTS PASTIMES

A growing American population and increased concerns about health and fitness contributed to an overall growth in sports participation during the 1990s. There were other reasons for this increase, as well. A growing environmental impulse prompted an increase in the number of Americans seeking outdoor experiences, like hiking, camping, backpacking, and bicycling. With busier lives, many sought nearby, inexpensive vacations that accommodated these kinds of activities. Moreover, the appeal of sports was cultivated by the media and big business, as advertisers exploited the appeal of sports imagery in commercials. Additionally, the growth of sports supply superstore chains made sporting gear easily attainable, affordable, and fashionable. In fact, retail sales for sporting gear had the fastest growth ever in the nineties, as did spending on recreational team sports and gym memberships.

A survey for 1995 found that more than 24 million people participated in in-line skating that year. In-line skating, also called roller-blading, was a hybrid sport, combining roller-skating and ice-skating. In-line skates had wheels, like traditional roller skates, but the wheels were placed, quite literally, in a line, a single row that simulated the straight blade of an ice skate. The tremendous popularity of in-line skating was such that the sport became more popular than traditional roller-skating. It also overtook ice-skating in popularity, despite a boom in the ice-skating market, largely effected by increased media attention paid to the sport and its stars. One probable reason for this was expense. In-line skates tended to be less expensive than ice skates, but more importantly, people could in-line skate on any paved surface, saving the cost of ice rink admission. A 1997 survey found that in-line skating was the second fastest growing sport in the world, but as the decade closed, its growth began to even out. Still consistently popular, in-line skate sales hit a plateau, particularly as other vehicular fads, like the scooter craze of the early 2000s, cut into the demand for roller blades among the youths who had constituted 62 percent of skaters according to the 1995 study.[4]

Another athletic trend of the 1990s was an exercise program called Tae-Bo, which had a fairly limited pool of participants, at least compared to traditional programs like aerobics and weight training. But Tae-Bo nonetheless became something of a household word due to the tremendous publicity generated by the program and its energetic creator and spokesman, Billy Blanks. The program, a combination of martial arts and aerobics, was largely propelled by a series of TV ads and infomercials, and also by its reputation as a celebrity exercise program. Introduced publicly in 1989, Tae-Bo had, according to Blanks, evolved out of his own experimentation with the traditional martial art tae kwon do. He incorporated aerobics and boxing moves, and hit upon his own program. Experts were divided about whether or not Tae-Bo offered more than traditional aerobic and martial arts training, but the hyper kinetic activity of the program was certainly far from harmful, and was notable for the media blitz that brought knowledge of it into virtually every American home.

EXTREME SPORTS

Perhaps the most striking development in sports was the popularization of extreme sports. While traditional sports continued to enjoy widespread participation, a growing segment of the populace began looking for something new, something that stimulated an adrenaline rush well beyond that provided by traditional athletics. Many of these individuals turned to activities that had at least some semblance of danger, or sports that had previously enjoyed something of an underground following. Such was the case with skateboarding and snowboarding. Snowboarding, once a fringe hybrid of skiing and surfing, enjoyed widespread growth. A 1995 study found that there were about 2.3 million snowboarders in the country, a growth of 800,000 since 1990. The study also noted that most snowboarders were under the age of 18, suggesting that the sport was still very much in its growth stage.[5]

Extreme sports also frequently involved using traditional sporting equipment in a new and more exciting way. Traditional skiing was mutated into free-style and aerial skiing, wherein what a skier did while in the air, flung by jumping ramps, was at least as important as what he or she did in contact with the snow. Likewise, bicycling, particularly with BMX (bicycle motocross) bikes, became an extreme sport, as riders performed acrobatics while balanced on the bike frame, spinning the handlebars, or soaring off of ramps. The biggest star of this sport was Mat Hoffman, the nine-time world champion of BMX biking.

While many of these activities had existed in some form before the nineties, now they became a popular spectacle, flirting with mainstream success. Snowboarding and free-style skiing gained particular prestige by becoming official Olympic sports. White-water rafting, skateboarding, and bungee jumping, as well as other extreme sports appeared in many advertisements as companies tried to tap into a market of young people with disposable income. Many of these sports were brought together by an an-

Mat Hoffman, of Oklahoma City, practices prior to the Men's Bike Vert finals, June 28, 1997, in San Diego, at the X Games. The bike vert finals were the last competition at the 1997 X Games.
© AP/Wide World Photos.

nual tournament, the X Games, created by and broadcast on the cable network ESPN with great success. First held in 1995 as the Extreme Games, the X Games featured 350 competitors in 27 events, and both numbers increased every year thereafter. The growing extreme sports culture spawned its own celebrities, perhaps none as famed as skateboarder Tony Hawk, whose name transcended the niche market for his sport, entering American culture at large. Hawk appeared on numerous TV shows, was signed to advertising contracts on a par with other sports stars, and had his name pasted on a multitude of products, from clothing to Hot Wheels toy cars.

PROFESSIONAL WRESTLING

On February 9, 1989, the New Jersey Senate proclaimed that, for purposes of regulation, big-time professional wrestling was entertainment rather than a sport. The Senate's legislation removed some of the restrictions placed on wrestling matches, but it also acknowledged that the activity, which had so long worked to depict itself as an authentic athletic contest, was one in which matches were to some extent choreographed and participants trained to avoid serious injury. Other states followed New Jersey's legislative lead. But rather than stifling enthusiasm, this proclamation breathed new life into pro wrestling. In fact, the World Wrestling Foundation (WWF) had requested the legislation. The major wrestling organizations, the WWF, headed by Vince McMahon, who also started the ill-fated XFL football league in the early 2000s, and the smaller World Championship Wrestling (WCW), founded in 1994 by Ted Turner, became increasingly flamboyant. The competitors of the 1990s were as flashy as anything before them, as they engaged in larger than life (and thoroughly choreographed) combat. Moreover, the behind-the-scenes action became a major part of professional wrestling's appeal.

Wrestlers developed striking personas and acted out elaborate dramas of betrayal, of jealousy, and of revenge, both in the ring and in the locker rooms. There was frequently a kind of mythic quality to the dramas, with good being pitted against evil, and heroes fallen and redeemed. Many celebrities were born of pro wrestling, celebrities with names like "Stone Cold" Steve Austin, The Rock, and Mankind. There was also plenty of over-the-top action, often laced with an audacious sense of the absurd. In a September 1999 WWF bout, for instance, Austin beat up an opponent in the ring, then dragged him out of it, out into the wings, and threw him into the back of an ambulance. The absurdity was compounded when Austin climbed into a semi and drove it smashing into the ambulance. Few adults who saw such a spectacle could swallow it as a real fight, but worries abounded about the number of young people who watched these events. The WWF did, after all, market to youth at least as much as it did to adults, and even issued a line of WWF action figures for sale in toy stores. Desensitization to violence was the primary fear, but there was also concern about imitation. Among teenagers the popularity of backyard wrestling, in imitation of the WWF and the WCW, grew enormously. And whatever one's opinion of professional wrestling might be, there were few doubts about the danger posed to untrained teens, a number of whom suffered serious injuries as a result of their imitations.

The success of pro wrestling in the eighties and nineties spawned similar athletic entertainments, like *American Gladiators*, which was broadcast from 1989 to 1997. In this TV show, contestants, who were real athletes rather than trained performers, competed in odd events against each other and the Gladiators, muscle-bound men and women whose primary goal was to infringe on the contestants' successful execution of an event. The events included climbing rock walls with Gladiators in hot pursuit, or rolling around in giant cage-like balls resembling something a hamster might use. *Battle Dome*, which debuted in 1999, offered similar entertainment, increasing the amount of physical contact, as well as the flamboyancy of their costumed gladiators, called Warriors. However, the feuds between the Battle Dome Warriors bore a stronger resemblance to those of pro wrestling. With all the drama and violence, *Battle Dome* bridged the gap between wrestling and *American Gladiators*.

WOMEN'S SPORTS

In 1972, Title IX, guaranteeing gender equality in educational programs, was instituted. The legislation mandated that women be given the equal opportunity to participate in high school and college sports. Title IX was never without controversy, and many athletic directors and administrators continued to hold to the beliefs that sports were primarily the realm of men, and that women's sports just couldn't bring in the same kind of revenue that men's sports did. The Women's Sports Foundation conducted a study as late as 1998 which found these attitudes to be still strong, even as, in the same year, the Supreme Court declined to hear an appeal to overturn Title IX.[6]

Even as Title IX had been increasing the number of women taking part in amateur sports, professionally, women were making a name for themselves like never before. Moreover, they were making a name for themselves in sports that were not typically thought of as women's sports, like gymnastics and figure skating. Instead, they were playing basketball in the WNBA. The league was conceived in 1996, after U.S. women won Olympic gold earlier in the year, and the first WNBA tip-off took place on June 21, 1997. Women's soccer received a considerable boost in popularity as well. In 1991, the U.S. team won the first women's World's Cup, and this was only the start. While that first triumph received relatively little press, in 1999, more attention was being paid. The United States women's World Cup team took home the trophy again, much in contrast to the preceding men's World Cup tournament in 1998, in which the U.S. team was ranked dead last. The spectacular performance of the women's team created several minor celebrities, including Mia Hamm and Brandi Chastain. Chastain was widely publicized for kneeling on the field and pulling off her jersey, stripping to a sports bra, upon winning the tournament. Even hockey opened up to women in the 1990s. The first Women's World Hockey Championship, won by Canada, was held in 1990, and in 1998, the United States team won the first Olympic gold medal in women's hockey. Despite these inroads, however, and despite the growing popularity of women's sports, they continued to receive considerably less publicity than men's

Mia Hamm, forward on the U.S. National Women's Soccer Team,
gets ready to unleash a shot on net against the Russia National
during first half action in the Nike U.S. Women's Cup '98 at Frontier
Field in Rochester, N.Y. on Sept. 18, 1998. Hamm scored her 100th
and 101st career international goals as the United States toppled
Russia 4–0. © AP/Wide World Photos.

events, demonstrating a continued inequality in the world of professional
sports.

PROFESSIONAL SPORTS

Auto Racing

The 1990s were a golden age for auto racing, and particularly for the National Association for Stock Car Auto Racing (NASCAR). Directed in the

nineties by Bill France, Sr. and Bill France, Jr., NASCAR was the fastest-growing spectator sport of the decade. But the source of this growth can be found in the previous decade. Started in the late 1940s, NASCAR-sanctioned stock car racing experienced gradual growth, but in the 1980s, it nurtured a growing number of corporate sponsorships, and saw the rise of celebrity racers whose names began gaining recognition outside of the racing world. Sponsorship from major corporations and growing television coverage brought NASCAR to new audiences. Broadcast coverage began slow, featuring only the most important races, but high television ratings convinced the media that NASCAR was a goldmine, and with the increased number of broadcasts, so grew the fan base for the sport. From 1990 to 1998, attendance at Winston Cup races grew from 3.3 million to more than 6 million. Additionally, NASCAR-licensed merchandise, an $80 million industry in 1990, brought in over $950 million in 1998. Racers like Dale Earnhardt, Jeff Gordon, Dale Jarrett, and Sterling Marlin became celebrities on a par with those of football, basketball, and baseball. Of course, fame did not diminish the danger of high-speed racing. The 1990s saw the loss of several racers, including J. D. McDuffie, Clifford Allison, Rodney Orr, Neil Bonnett, and John Nemechek. Earnhardt, one of the sport's biggest stars in the 1990s, died in a crash in February 2001.

Basketball

Another sport whose popularity grew rapidly in the 1990s was basketball, propelled by fast-paced action and a marketing campaign designed to emphasize the sheer entertainment value of the sport. Certainly, basketball had no shortage of charming players who had tremendous appeal well beyond their skills on the court. First and foremost among these was Michael Jordan, a phenomenal player whose reputation was bolstered further by his charm and geniality. But other players—Earvin "Magic" Johnson, Charles Barkley, David Robinson, Karl Malone, Rick Fox, and Shaquille O'Neal among them—also attained celebrity status. Jordan proved to be the highest-profile player in what was unarguably the strongest team of the decade, the Chicago Bulls. Despite his short-lived retirement during the 1993–1994 season, Jordan was instrumental in leading the Bulls to six NBA championships (1991–1993, 1996–1998). But Jordan's skill was supplemented by a top-notch team, which included Scotty Pippen, Dennis Rodman, and European import Toni Kukoc.

Football

The National Football League literally grew in the nineties, adding three teams, the Carolina Panthers and the Jacksonville Jaguars in 1995, and the Baltimore Ravens in 1996. These teams increased the number to 31, making it the largest league in pro sports. Attendance at NFL games continued to rise, with the Super Bowl championships consistently rating as the most popular annual event in spectator sports. One of the top teams of the decade was the Dallas Cowboys, who won Super Bowls XXVI (1993), XXVIII (1994), and XXX (1996). But there were other champions, as well, including the San Francisco 49ers who were out to prove wrong those who claimed their glory days were behind them. San Francisco won the Super Bowl in 1990, and again in 1995, becoming the first team to win five Super Bowls. The Green Bay Packers won the Super Bowl for the first time in 29 years in 1997. They returned to the Bowl the next year, but were defeated by the Denver Broncos in their Super Bowl debut. In winning Super Bowl XXXII, Denver became the first AFC team to win in 13 years. Moreover, they proved that their victory was no fluke by winning their second consecutive Super Bowl in 1999.

Hockey

The 1990s were a particularly good decade for American hockey, though it must be acknowledged that American teams were heavily stocked with players from other countries, especially Canada. Nonetheless, never before had teams based in the United States earned such good standing in the Staley Cup hockey championships. The Pittsburgh Penguins won back-to-back Cups in 1991 and 1992, and so too did the Detroit Red Wings in 1997 and 1998. Other American teams winning the cup in the nineties were the New York Rangers in 1994, the New Jersey Devils in 1995 (who again won in 2000), the Colorado Avalanche (formerly the Quebec Nordiques) in 1996, and the Dallas Stars (formerly the Minnesota North Stars) in 1999. These championships certainly contributed to the growing popularity of hockey in the U.S., despite a 1994 labor dispute which resulted in a 103-day lockout of National Hockey League players. Also adding to the popularity was the growing number of American teams in the NHL. In the course of the decade, professional hockey welcomed the San Jose Sharks, the Tampa Bay Lightning, the Florida Panthers, the Anaheim Mighty Ducks, and the Nashville Predators.

Despite the successes of these teams and individual players, none stood so high as Wayne Gretzky, justifiably referred to as "The Great One." Indeed, the affable Gretzky represented hockey to the world like no other player. Over 19 seasons, beginning in 1979, Gretzky had proven himself to be one of the finest athletes to ever play the game. He won virtually every award given to hockey players, playing for the Edmonton Oilers, the Los Angeles Kings, the St. Louis Blues, and the New York Rangers. The end of the decade, however, also marked the end of Gretzky's career in the National Hockey League. On April 25, 1999, Gretzky played his last NHL match, retiring at the top of his game.

Baseball

Baseball reached highs and lows during the 1990s. Even as it suffered from scandal and controversy (see below), the sport also showed itself at its best. Several longstanding records fell during the decade, including that for the most consecutive games played. The 56-year-old record, set by New York Yankee Lou Gehrig, fell on September 6, 1995, when Baltimore Orioles shortstop Cal Ripken stepped onto the field for his 2,131st game. And to confirm his place as a quality player, Ripken hit home runs in both the record tying and breaking games.

Later in the decade, however, an even more sacred baseball record came under fire. In the 1998 season, not just one, but two players were poised to break New York Yankee Roger Maris's long-standing homerun record, set in 1961. As St. Louis Cardinal Mark McGwire and Chicago Cub Sammy Sosa came closer to the mark, so did game attendance and television ratings rise. In the end, McGwire would break the record and hold it for the season, though Sosa would also exceed Maris's record. Although there was grumbling on some fronts that steroid use—which many believed was rampant in pro sports in general and in baseball in particular—had played a role in the fall of Maris's record, for most fans this was a welcome return to the glory days of the sport.

Although two long-standing Yankee-held records fell, the New York team had little to feel bad about in the nineties. The team reached the World Series three times, and won each, in 1996, 1998, and 1999. Atlanta had less luck. Although the Braves played in five of the nine 1990s Series, they only won it in 1995. The Toronto Blue Jays proved themselves by taking the pennant in 1992 and 1993, while the Cincinnati Reds, Minnesota Twins, and Florida Marlins rounded out the list of champions for 1990, 1991, and 1997, respectively.

SCANDAL AND CONTROVERSY IN PRO SPORTS

During the nineties, it seemed as if professional sports was continuously rocked by scandal. Misbehaving sports stars, current and former, appeared to get as much, if not more, press than box scores. Of course, the most high-profile case was that of retired football great O. J. Simpson, but his was far from the only name to drag the reputation of professional sports through the mud. Drugs and violence infected nearly every major pro sport, and while it's fair to say that the guilty players were in the minority, the sports scandal sheets seemed to grow longer with each passing season. Scandal even infected the most gentile of sports in 1994, when Olympic figure skater Nancy Kerrigan was attacked, her knee severely beaten after a practice session, in a conspiracy that involved Kerrigan's rival Tonya Harding.

Boxing came under particular fire. Never a gentle sport, boxing had long suffered the slings and arrows of critics, for its violence and its exploitation of athletes. But in the 1990s, the accusations of barbarity focused principally on one man: Mike Tyson. Tyson, the heavy-weight champion, had developed a well-deserved reputation as a strong and ferocious fighter, but his antics outside the ring drew considerable publicity as well. High-profile accusations of abuse by his wife, actress Robin Givens, and conviction of rape charges destroyed the fighter's reputation. But upon his release from prison, Tyson was swiftly swept back into the ring. Returning in 1996, Tyson fought Evander Holyfield, then current heavy-weight champ. The fight was stopped by the referee after Holyfield clearly had Tyson at a disadvantage. But a rematch was soon scheduled, and it was in this fight that Tyson showed himself at his most savage. The fight was cut short by referee Mills Lane, a Nevada judge who would gain considerable fame with his own courtroom TV show, after Tyson twice bit his opponent, literally tearing off part of Holyfield's ear with his teeth. The spectacle drew renewed criticism of boxing, with some claiming that Tyson, as wife beater, as rapist, as mutilator, was simply what an inherently violent sport had made him. But though Tyson was barred from the sport (only to eventually return in 2002), the criticisms of boxing continued to be largely ignored. Boxing remained big business, bringing large revenues to the host cities and proving extraordinarily popular on pay-per-view cable TV.

The nation's great pastime of baseball also suffered, morally if not commercially, in the nineties, with numerous player run-ins with the law. Most of these cases were drug-related, a fact that particularly tarnished the image of a game that traditionally had great family appeal. The image was also damaged by Atlanta Braves pitcher John Rocker, who let loose in a *Sports Illustrated* interview with a tirade of racist and bigoted slurs. The league did not take kindly to Rocker's outbursts, nor did the many non-white players, but the fine and short suspension of Rocker ultimately seemed a mere slap on the hand, his prowess on the field clearly ranking as more important than his ethical conduct as a citizen. Despite these cases, however, what hurt baseball the most was probably a player strike in the 1994–1995 season. For many fans, the suspension of the season seemed an affront, particularly since the cause was already highly paid players demanding still higher pay. The players came across as spoiled children demanding more than their fair share, and this left a bad taste in the mouth of even the most ardent fan. Defenders of the strike noted that professional baseball made ungodly amounts of money, and that the money not going to the players was only going to already wealthy executives and owners. But combined with the ever increasing cost of game tickets, the strike signaled that baseball was no longer about tradition and history, and that the nobility of a game well-played had been buried under the mounting commercialism of the sport. In short, baseball suffered a crisis of confidence among fans, and the popular PBS TV series, *Baseball,* produced by Ken Burns and aired in 1994, seemed to many to only signal what baseball had once been and how far it had fallen.

Sports also suffered some major losses due to AIDS and the HIV virus. In 1991, basketball superstar Earvin "Magic" Johnson announced that he had contracted HIV and was consequently retiring from the game (although he would have a brief return to the court later in the decade). In 1993, tennis legend Arthur Ashe died of AIDS. In 1996, boxer Tommy Morrison was barred from the sport upon revelation that he was HIV-positive. As unfortunate as these cases were, they woke many athletes and young people to the risks of sexual promiscuity, and also drew national attention to the cause of AIDS, which could no longer been seen as a fringe disease if it was affecting the country's sports heroes.

SPORTS AND MONEY

The crises in sports ethics were only a partial contributor to the tarnished image of professional sports. It also suffered as a result of spiraling costs. The inflating cost of attending sports events became prohibitive for many Americans. This was especially true of newly constructed sports arenas, many of which devoted part of their space to catering to wealthy spectators and corporate interests, with private clubs and luxurious boxes rentable for between $75,000 and $300,000. Even the less glamorous seats became increasingly expensive. This was particularly due to the widespread introduction of permanent seat licenses, which consumers would have to purchase just to acquire the right to buy tickets to an event. Therefore, the additional license fee charged by stadium owners could jack up the price of a forty-dollar ticket to several hundred dollars. Stadiums also continued to rely on corporate sponsorship. Advertising became omnipresent within stadiums, and arenas forged special arrangements to only serve a particular brand of beer, or hotdog, or soda.[7] San Francisco's historic Candlestick Park even changed its name to demonstrate its corporate allegiance. In 1995, rights were purchased to its name, and Candlestick became, officially, 3Com Park. Most San Franciscans continued to call the stadium Candlestick, and in 2002, 3Com's rights expired and the stadium officially reverted to its original designation.

As ticket prices and advertising increased, many sports fans also looked with disdain towards the increasing wealth of players. Few fans would deny that players deserved high compensation, since they did in fact entertain millions and brought in high revenues, but to many, salaries seemed to skyrocket to ridiculous levels. NBA players in 1995, for instance negotiated a rising salary cap, from the $15.9 million per team in 1994 to $32 million in 2001.[8]

Distressing as the rising player pay rate was, however, there was no denying that players were bringing in lots of money for others, as well. Besides ticket prices, sports leagues charged an ever increasing rate for broadcast rights. The amount of money circulating for the sake of professional sports broadcasts was truly staggering. In 1993, the NBA negotiated four-year deals with NBC for $750 million and with cable's TNT for $352 million. In 1994, the NFL entered into deals with ABC, NBC, Fox, and ESPN, which garnered the league $4.4 billion (approximately $39.2 million per team). And yet, despite the amounts they were frequently willing to pay, many television broadcasters actually lost money on sports broadcasts. But they still kept buying. There was certainly prestige connected with sports broadcasts, especially such events as the Olympics, the Super Bowl, and the World Series, but the monetary payoff sometimes fell quite short of expectations. Networks were spending a great deal of money to acquire broadcast rights, but they had also to make back their money, and the primary source of revenue was advertising. Getting advertisers to buy airtime at a high enough cost to cover the acquisition expenses, however, was a challenge. CBS had some of the greatest losses, particularly early in the decade, with the 1992 Winter Olympic broadcast and a $1.06 billion arrangement with Major League Baseball from 1990 to 1994. Even as the networks were struggling to afford broadcast rights for sports, cable providers were exploiting the pay-per-view system of subscription television. Pay-per-view had considerable success with broadcasting relatively inexpensive, and typically regional, sporting events, like hockey and college football. But the service's greatest success came with boxing and professional wrestling matches. A 1993 fight between Evander Holyfield and Riddick Bowe, for instance, brought in $33 million dollars for pay-per-view broadcasters.[9]

Top athletes themselves made a good deal of money on endorsements. In some cases, product sponsorship even outpaced their salaries. In 1997, for instance, basketball star Michael Jordan made $31.3 million on salary, but $47 million on product sponsorships, making him the highest-paid athlete of the year. For athletes with a lower salary rate, the gap between salary and sponsorship earnings was even more astounding. Tiger Woods, who earned a salary of $2.1 million in 1997, earned $24 million in sponsorships. Dale Earnardt made $15.5 million in sponsorships to his $3.6 million salary.[10]

CELEBRITY ATHLETES

Sports celebrities became major commercial assets for anyone who could get hold of them. Basketball spawned perhaps more superstars than any other sport in the 1990s, none more popular than Michael Jordan. His skill and clean image, as compared to far too many other sports figures, made Jordan an ideal role model, and consequently an ideal product spokesman. He became the most sought after basketball player by advertisers, making

Tiger Woods, right, and his father, Earl Woods, left, wait for their agent Hughes Norton to tee off on the 10th tee of the Spyglass Hill Golf Course during a practice round in Pebble Beach, Calif., Jan. 27, 1998. Tiger and his father would be playing together as a team in the AT&T Pebble Beach National Pro-Am. © AP/Wide World Photos.

commercials for Hanes underwear and Nike shoes, which produced the basketball shoe called the Air Jordan. After the murder of his father, Jordan retired, temporarily, from basketball to play minor league baseball, but during this hiatus, his popularity seemed undiminished. He also appeared on the large screen in 1996, playing basketball with the Warner Brothers cartoon characters in the blockbuster *Space Jam.* Jordan, however, was hardly alone in his commercial success. Basketball players seemed to appear as much in TV commercials as they did on the court, and others also made it to the big screen. Shaquille O'Neal starred in *Kazaam* (1996) and *Steel* (1997), and Dennis Rodman appeared in *Double Team* (1997) and a short-lived TV series, *Soldier of Fortune, Inc.*, in 1998. As well behaved and mannered as

Jordan was, Rodman was rambunctious and truculent. The author of a biography called *Bad As I Wanna Be,* Rodman's reputation was largely built on flamboyant manner of dress, from brightly-died hair to dressing in drag, and his propensity for violence, especially a highly-publicized kick at a courtside photographer. For these things he was much better known than for his not inconsiderable talent on court, but the shock value of his conduct ultimately made less of a lasting impact than did Jordan's composure.

Another major sports celebrity was the unlikely golf hero, Tiger Woods. Young, charming, handsome, and black, Woods was not the kind of person typically associated with the game of golf. Highly touted as an amateur, Woods hit the professional circuit with a vengeance, winning the Master's Tournament in 1997, the youngest player to do so, at 21 years. In 1999, he ranked first five times in the PGA tour. Woods broke major ground in a sport that had long been regarded as the elite realm of white men. He was not only the first African American to win a major tournament, but also, since his mother was Thai, the first Asian-American to do so. Tiger Woods as a result became another highly sought after advertising property, and subsequently made ads for Titleist golf gear, Nike, American Express, Rolex, and others. Clearly, he was the most widely-recognized celebrity ever to emerge from the game of golf.

No one would deny that professional sports in the nineties evoked all the emotions with which it had always been associated, the proverbial thrill of victory and agony of defeat. They allowed people to see human beings performing at their full physical potential, frequently executing awe-inspiring feats of athleticism. Still, like all areas of culture, including hobbies and pastimes, pro sports became big business. And commerce certainly helped to shape them at the end of the millennium. Some certainly felt that the money tainted the athleticism, that commerce corrupted the purity of the sport. Yet even those who grumbled frequently, found themselves wrapped up in the excitement of the competition, suggesting that very likely, underneath the marketing and politics, true athleticism still shone bright.

6
Fashion

GENERAL TRENDS

Fashion has never existed in isolation. In fact, it has always been greatly influenced by current events and by other areas of popular culture. This certainly was the case as the 1990s came to a close, with fashion choices, as much as ever, making a statement, frequently overt, sometimes unconscious, but always resounding. The 1990s saw considerable variation in fashion, particularly as previously fringe elements of popular culture came into the mainstream. Thus, while a certain kind of *high fashion* might have been in vogue at any given time, alternative fashions constituted a strong impulse against these modes. American media came to depict a much wider range of people, both within and outside of the mainstream. And with this variety came a diversity of competing and complementary in-vogue fashions. As one writer suggested, "while the marketing and consumption of clothing, especially women's clothing, may still fall into recognizable patterns, fashion is no longer able to impose an annual 'Look' to which there are no or few alternatives."[1] The 1990s have been referred to as the decade of anti-fashion, but this is not altogether an accurate descriptor. In fact, fashion was as important as ever before, but the interest turned increasingly to how fashion could serve the individual, and the notion of the "slave to fashion" waned in the nineties.

In general, simplicity reigned over the world of fashion in the 1990s. The nineties were described by many as a decade of minimalism, and many designers suggested that this was the result of a significant change in concepts of fashion. Fashion design seemed to be increasingly dictated by consumers rather than by designers, who instead found that consumers were less interested in the flash of the 1980s; so designers implemented simple, elegant lines to their clothing. Black, which famed designer Giorgio Armani went so far as to call the most "elegant and intellectual" color in 1995, became the dominant color for women's clothing, and combined with a trend towards longer skirts. In this, many saw subtle dress as a statement about the role of women in general. One designer, Martine Sitbon, argued "Women don't have to show they're very strong in the '90s compared to the '80s . . . They feel very comfortable with themselves."[2] In other words, women did not have the same need to attract attention, or the need to attract the same kind of attention, as seen in the 1980s. Additionally, as women became a stronger force in public life, so were fashions sought that, while retaining femininity, provided no undue distraction from a woman's substantial role.

In general, youths had more money of their own in the nineties and a surprising amount of this money went towards clothing. The industry for children's clothing garnered almost $700 million in 1992, and most of this was the children's own money, given by parents and relatives as allowance, gifts, and pay for tasks performed. As a consequence, manufacturers of children's apparel catered increasingly to children's tastes, rather than to the tastes of parents. Thus, the fashions worn by high school students could be just as easily found in elementary school classrooms.

In all its dimensions, fashion was big business in the nineties, netting over $100 billion a year every year. By the late nineties, sales were topping $170 billion. But the industry was also an extremely competitive one, with companies having to fight to stay in fashion. The growth of the industry itself consumed much of the profit, as the natural metamorphosis of fashion trends seemed to accelerate. One estimate placed the average fashion trend at the end of the decade as lasting about six to twelve weeks.

FORMAL AND BUSINESS ATTIRE

Formal wear strove for simplicity and elegance. The ruffles and garnishes of the 1980s were largely eliminated, as long, sleek dresses took their place. Again, black seemed the preferred color, though other colors were also popular, particularly neutral or earthy colors. More flamboyant colors, red and blues, for instance, still enjoyed some popularity. The important distinction here was that colors tended to be strong colors, solid red and blues, instead of the washed out or pastel colors of the eighties.

Business suits stayed largely the same, with relatively minor variation, throughout the century, but the nineties actually saw some decline in the popularity of the business suit. This has been attributed, at least in part, to the growth of the computer industry. This industry was dominated by a relatively young workforce, and young management, as well. This youth certainly fed the desire to break from the traditional business attire, as did the fact that many workers at such companies did not need to interact so much with the world at large. That this was a new industry also encouraged a more casual approach to dress, since these companies were not competing against old, venerable institutions. But even the classically formal industries found themselves becoming increasingly casual. An article in *The Atlantic Monthly* quoted a New York law firm partner who explained the way formality had suffered: "We went casual in the nineties…We had to compete with the dot-coms for the best and the brightest new talent, and not just with money. The dot-coms didn't wear suits. No ties. Comfortable cottons. They looked like a new way to do business." This development largely began with the implementation of casual Fridays, in which employees could give their suits and ties a pass. But for many companies, a single day of dressing down seemed insufficient, resulting in the adaptation of a looser, more casual overall dress code. In 1992, about 7 percent of U.S. companies had a casual dress code, but by 1998, this number had increased to 53 percent.[3]

HIGH FASHION

The world of haut couture, of high fashion, seemed to grow continually more flamboyant in the eighties and also in the nineties, perhaps as an adverse response to the booming market for casual, comfortable clothes. Fashion designers seemingly had two choices in the 1990s. They could either seek to cash in on the casual looks that were popular, as indeed some did. Or they could swing to the opposite extreme. Colin McDowell, writing for *The Guardian* in 1998, clearly stated his objections to this trend, stating that "traditionally the fashion designers role has been to create clothes which make ordinary woman feel beautiful and therefore confident. Today's alternatives propose looks which no woman of sane mind would ever dream of wearing, being offered the choice of baring the breasts, exposing their buttocks, looking as if they had been violated, or posing as prepubescent children. Naturally many have rejected such suggestions, so who are women to trust to create clothes for them that are not only new and exciting, but are actually capable of being worn?"[4] In fact, those designers that worked on such clothes were clearly working on designs that were not really meant to be worn anywhere but on the catwalk, and in that respect, their work came closer to the arts of painting, sculpture, or even music, than fashion typically had in the past. But the sentiment of the general populace, as always, did have a distinct effect on high fashion. Many designers moved away from the flamboyantly unwearable, and away from the overly casual, and instead tapped into the desire for an uncomplicated but graceful, even classical, style of dress. Channel and Yohji Yamamoto significantly championed a revival of the black dress and classical lines. By the end of the decade, even guests at that bastion of fashion on display, the Academy Awards, were opting for elegant simplicity over audacious flash.

Gianni Versace reached new heights in popularity in the early 1990s, with among others, a line of clothing influenced by underground fetish-wear. The kinkiness of the look gained wide popularity in some circles, though naturally the average American shied away from the leather and latex of such designs. Versace didn't stick solely to this kind of fashion, but it did serve to make him a considerable celebrity, and his name became a household word, in part because of his friendships with other celebrities, like Elton John, who championed his work. Consequently, his murder in July 1997 in Miami, Florida, created quite a sensation. His company continued with his sister, Donatella, at the helm, if anything propelled by the publicity garnered by his tragic death.

Other important designers of the decade included Anna Sui, Alexander McQueen, Isaac Mizrahi, Gucci, Donna Karan, and Miuccia Prada. Japanese designers, especially Yohji Yamamoto and Rei Kawakubo, also began having significant influence on worldwide high fashion.

CASUAL WEAR

For everyday wear, T-shirts and jeans continued to be popular, just as they had been in preceding decades. The outfit provided a perfect means to fit in with a dominant look, while still providing a forum for self expression. T-shirts, of course, could express any number of things about the wearer, from what bands they liked, to what school they attended, to what products they consumed. In fact, many, perhaps even a majority, of the T-shirts being produced in the country served the dual purpose of clothing and advertising. A less obvious means of self-expression, jeans nonetheless suggested much about their wearers. More than any other decade since their introduction, a variety of jean designs were simultaneously in vogue, depending on with which crowd the wearer wanted to be identified. Of course, with the coming of grunge style it became fashionable to have jeans that were worn out, with tears riddling the knees or upper thighs, thereby revealing boxer shorts, intimate apparel become publicly fashionable. Some designers even went so far as to market pre-tattered jeans. The display of boxers was also associated with the trend of wearing large, ill-fitting pants, jeans and otherwise, which hung at the lowest part of the hips, whereas the shorts still clung to the waist. Boot cut jeans had long been popular among certain segments of the populace, especially in rural and semi-rural areas, but in the mid-nineties, they also became popular among urban women because of how they highlighted footwear, especially high heeled boots. In 1998, hard jeans became quite popular. Quite in contrast to the well-worn jeans that were popular among some, wearers of these pants treasured the new, untouched look, and frequently took to ironing tight creases into the front of the legs, held well by the stiffness of the denim. Denim overalls, considered rather unfashionable a decade before, also became popular, especially with girls.

Two teenagers dressed in grunge fashion. © Image Source/
elektraVision/ PictureQuest.

Clothing made of khaki became increasingly popular into the 1990s. Certainly, part of the popularity was the very nature of the fabric, which was
light and comfortable. Not as casual as T-shirts and jeans, khaki clothing
could be worn in a variety of situations. In fact, by the end of the decade,
entire suits made of khaki hit the market. But part of khaki's revival was
certainly due to a series of advertisements that depicted khaki as hip and
exciting. The most popular line of TV ads, produced by The Gap, involved
young, handsome dancers. The first in this line, which debuted in 1998,
showcased khaki clothes in an elaborate dance to Louis Prima's swing classic "Jump, Jive, an' Wail." The ad was such a success that it was followed
by similar displays to techno, hip hop, and other musical styles.

In the mid-1980s, there was considerable growth in sport-related fashion, and this trend reached a peak in the 1990s. Of course, clothing with
professional sports team logos continued to be very popular, from T-shirts,
to shorts, to jackets, to socks. In addition, sports stars were hired, with great
success, to publicize certain lines of clothing. Perhaps no company bene-
fited more from ties to professional sports than the shoe company Nike,

which associated itself with two of the highest profiles sportsmen of the decade, Tiger Woods and Michael Jordan. Jordan proved especially profitable for Nike, which created a shoe called the Air Jordan. In its first year, the Air Jordan brought in $130 million for Nike.

CONTEMPORARY CASUAL RETAIL

The turn towards more casual modes of dress breathed new life into some retail establishments. Most notably Gap Inc., which owned The Gap, Old Navy, and Banana Republic stores, had its strongest decade ever, ranking as the country's largest apparel retailer. The company earned about $1.93 billion in 1990, but by the end of the decade, profits were up to $11.64 billion. The company's secret was to market simple, comfortable, casual, but also good-looking clothes. It did so with a line of khaki clothes, polo shirts, and even quality T-shirts and jeans. The Old Navy stores particularly grabbed consumer attention, with a line of kitschy television commercials and a semi-retro look. But perhaps due to the dying down of the retro fad, profits began dropping significantly for Gap Inc. just as the 1990s were winding down. The company's hesitancy to change the general look of its clothes, in contrast to changing public tastes, led to an widespread abandonment of The Gap, as well as Old Navy and Banana Republic, in late 1999 and the early 2000s.[5]

Target department stores also gained considerably in reputation in the 1990s. The stores had initially been started as a competitor to Kmart and other discount department stores, but as the 1990s started, Target strove to develop its own unique image. Like The Gap stores, Target exploited the somewhat retro look, emphasizing casual but fashionable apparel. As the decade waned though, Target avoided the pitfalls of Gap Inc., successfully keeping its image fresh with a line of sharp, stylized TV commercials, and continued innovation in its clothing lines. In the early 2000s, Target hired famed designer Todd Oldham to design a new line, thereby demonstrating that Target was not sitting on its laurels, and that even fashion makers like Oldham still found Target a vital outlet.

HIP-HOP

Hip-hop fashion took tenacious hold in the 1990s, and found its largest market not in the ghettos where it originated, but among middle-American suburban youth. Hip-hop fashion displayed a considerable amount of variety, even if it was clearly identifiable as hip-hop. In short, it provided individual expression within an identifiable framework. Common elements included baggy denim pants and overalls, wool and baseball-style caps, and sports-style jerseys and jackets. Likewise, shoes were vital to the hip-hop look, with Nike being the most popular brand.

One label, Fubu, was formed by four men, all under thirty years of age, who came from a lower-middle-class background in Hollis, Queens, New York. Formed in 1992, Fubu, an acronym for "for us by us," quickly gained popularity, partly due to well-placed publicity. Fubu clothes were being worn by rappers like LL Cool J and Busta Rhymes and pop stars like Mariah Carey. They also appeared on television programs. But in addition to this publicity, the company flourished due to the work of the four who founded it, Carl Brown, Daymond John, J. Alexander Martin, and Keith Perrin. Many consumers of hip-hop clothing found an honesty in the founders who attempted to bridge street style with mainstream style. That these men believed enough in their clothes to wear them regularly, rather than suits and ties, also added to the mystique. Their efforts paid off and in 1998, the company's men's line made around $200 million. The founders of Fubu had intended to reach an African-American consumer base that had largely been ignored by most clothing manufacturers, so were themselves surprised when their line of clothes found such an enthusiastic reception among white youth.

Naturally, Fubu was not the only success in the field of hip-hop fashion. Other companies, including Ecko Unlimited, Enyce, Mecca, Pelle Pelle, and Phat Farm also thrived. Most of these companies enjoyed similar credentials to Fubu. In fact, Phat Farm was founded by Russell Simmons, who had been instrumental in the creation of the major hip-hop record label Def Jam. Another line, Sean John, was started by rapper Sean "P. Diddy" Combs. In all, hip-hop fashions, sometimes called urban sportswear, was bringing in an estimated $5 billion a year by the end of the decade.

The Tommy Hilfiger brand also became associated with hip-hop fashion, though through very different means. Hilfiger, rather than being born out of a hip-hop culture, had started in the 1980s with a line of preppy designs; but in 1992, these clothes were mentioned in a Grand Puba rap, and found new life in urban neighborhoods. So, too, did Ralph Lauren and Fila. But in finding a new audience, these clothes also found a new aesthetic, which led to the clothes being worn in a different way than they traditionally had been (most commonly in oversize), or mixed with more common street-level urban clothing.[6]

GRUNGE, SKATE, RAVE, AND GOTHIC FASHION

Hip-hop design was a perfect example of the growing trend in the eighties and nineties of developing street style into major markets. Next to hip hop, the most popular adapted street style was grunge. The grunge look was at its most popular in the early years of the decade, though it held significant sway well into the new millennium. The look was taken primarily from that of musicians of the so-called grunge movement, originally out of the Seattle region. In addition to the low-riding, tattered jeans, flannel shirts were a major part of this look. Flannel as a whole experienced a consider-able surge in popularity, driven almost exclusively by the grunge trend. Flannel shirts were rarely buttoned up, instead worn loose over T-shirts, or tied around the waist. The grunge look persisted through the end of the de-cade largely because of its simplicity. The original emissaries of grunge style were trying less to make a fashion statement than they were altogether ig-noring fashion, wearing the shirts and pants that provided the most com-fort. Among those who went grunge in the name of keeping up with fashion, however, the trend began dying down mid-decade. In a way, the grunge look started dying out the day it was adapted into high couture. Designers like Marc Jacobs took the look, a casual street style, and brought it to the high fashion catwalks. Jacobs was working for Perry Ellis designers at the time, but was dismissed as head designer shortly thereafter, only to be picked by Louis Vuitton. Whatever initial enthusiasm grunge's introduc-tion to high fashion might have evoked, many reacted negatively, finding the grunge look altogether out of place in the world of high fashion.

Bearing similarities to both the grunge look and hip-hop fashion, the skater look was also popular with young people. One of the most signifi-cant companies exploiting this look, which had the bagginess of hip hop but the also the T-shirt and jeans look of grunge, was X-Large. In addition to offering a description of how its oversized clothes fit, the name X-Large was a merging of the phrases *Gen-X* and *Living Large*. The line started in 1991 with the opening of a Los Angeles X-Large store, which sold the com-pany's own clothing, as well as other brands. The line quickly became pop-ular among skaters, but it also got significant publicity from other celebrities. Particularly, Mike D of the rap-rock group The Beastie Boys was an early investor in the company and helped bring it to nationwide atten-tion. The company spread quickly. It opened a store in Tokyo in 1992, and one in New York in 1993. In 1994, it introduced the x-girl line of similar fashions, specifically designed for women.

The raver look, named after the culture of underground, after-hours dance parties, had started in England, but began waning in popularity in the early 1990s. In the U.S., its popularity lasted somewhat longer. But its influence on fashion stayed strong throughout the decade. Most influen-tial was the rave tendency towards loose-fitting clothing, from oversized T-shirts to baggy trousers worn low on the hips. The rave look was, in fact, quite mercurial, especially at the start of the nineties, but this emphasis on looseness, intended so as not to restrict one's dancing, was a constant. A great deal of rave clothing emphasized bright colors, which matched well the spirit of fun and high-energy that raves represented, and the look also frequently drew from 1970s club fashions.

Gothic, or Goth, clothing also got considerable attention as youth fash-ion. However, the Goth style, which originated in the early eighties among the cult following of bands like Bauhaus and the Sisters of Mercy, was not especially widespread. Rather, the attention came as a result of the spate of high school shootings in the late nineties. It was revealed that several of the youths who had committed the violence were fans of bands like Marilyn Manson, who bore some similarities to the Gothic bands of the eighties. In addition, the youths seemed to have a kind of common uniform, consisting of black clothes and dark trench coats. Media and parents, looking for some kind of explanation for the violence frequently found a scapegoat in the music and fashion culture inhabited by these youths. As a consequence, nearly any youth who listened to dark, aggressive music or wore black clothes or a trench coat, came under suspicion, despite the fact that few who did so entertained vicious thoughts of the magnitude of the shooters'. Moreover, this look was decidedly different from the eighties Goth look, still embraced by a small segment of youths, a fact which proved irrelevant to frightened parents and school officials. Although the fervor over Goth style died down as school shootings diminished, it nonetheless added considerable energy to an ongoing debate about school uniforms.

SCHOOL UNIFORMS

Fears of a growing gang problem among American youths led many to endorse the idea of traditional school uniforms in the 1980s. Clothing, they feared, might well be a sign of gang affiliation, and uniformity would reduce the potential for school violence. Additionally, it was believed that uniforms would diminish class distinctions, and keep students, particularly young girls, from wearing inappropriately revealing clothes, which became a growing issue in American schools in the 1990s, especially with the popularization of scantily clad singers like Britney Spears and Christina Aguilera. It was argued that uniforms would create a less distracting environment, that students would relate to each other on more legitimate grounds than fashion sense, and that they would have an easier time concentrating on academic pursuits. The trend towards school uniforms gained a considerable boost in 1996, when President Clinton announced his support for it, proclaiming, "If it means that the school rooms will be more orderly and disciplined, and that our young people will learn to evaluate themselves by what they are on the inside, instead of what they're wearing on the outside, then our public schools should be able to require their students to wear uniforms."[7] It did seem that the application of uniform policies to schools produced a greater sense of order in them. But school uniform critics noted that they also reduced children's ability to make their own choices, which itself was a part of the learning process. Others argued that uniform guidelines smacked of constitutionally unsound oppression and that they stripped students of a vital sense of individuality and identity. Given the controversy, uniforms were most widely adopted by private schools. While a growing number of public schools adopted uniforms in the 1990s, most continued without, though even these almost always maintained some sort of dress code.[8]

RECYCLED CLOTHING

Clothing with an ecological bent also became popular, especially in the early part of the decade, when it dovetailed nicely with the retro-sixties look. One important designer was Sarah Jenkins, who had been employed in T-shirt design in the late eighties. Many of her designs had found a strong following among ravers and the New Age crowd, so her name had considerable cachet when she turned to designing recycled clothes. Her company, Conscious Earthwear, recycled jumpers and other pre-used clothing into hats, jackets, skirts, and other articles. The radically altered clothing was embraced by the high-end fashion world in the 1994–1995 season. Conscious Earthwear was not the only company to make good with recycled clothing. So, too, did companies like Killogram, Vegetarian Shoes, and Eggplant. Among the same crowd, one of the most prized shoe companies was the more traditional Birkenstocks.

The clothing created by these designers was often rather unusual, and not what most Americans would be likely to wear in public. Still, the populace did find its own way to recycle clothes. While thrift stores had previously been where financially struggling consumers might shop, in the 1990s, they became much more popular among the middle class, as well. Ecological concerns may had been part of the drive for some consumers, but it seems likely that interest in various retro styles—from the sixties in the early 1990s, and the seventies and eighties later—was the primary driving force behind the second-hand clothing craze.

TECHNOLOGY

Fashion was also affected by technological developments in fabrics. Gore-Tex®, a synthetic material designed to be breathable and water and windproof, was introduced in 1989 by W. L. Gore & Associates, and became very popular in the nineties. Also in 1989, microfibers were introduced by I.E. duPont de Nemours & Company. This revolutionary development of fibers about one one-hundredth of the thickness of human hair, finer that the finest silk threads, served to refine polyester, nylon, acrylic and other synthetic materials. Another important development was Lyocell, released under the trade name Tencel®. Lyocell was developed as an environmentally safe fiber made from the pulp of trees grown specifically for this purpose.

Although the advances in actual clothing materials was tremendous, perhaps a greater technological advancement could be found in the fashion industry's relationship to ever-advancing computer technology. The apparel industry only began fully exploiting computer technology in the mid-

1990s, largely due to the complications inherent in such a rapidly changing industry. But ultimately the technology improved the distribution of goods. Computers also proved invaluable for keeping track of shifting inventories. An important name in this dimension of the industry was SAP, a software developer which modified its existing systems to suit the needs of major companies, including footwear company Reebok and the VF Corporation, the force behind the Wrangler, Lee, JanSport, and Vanity Fair lines of apparel. The installation of the system increased both companies' revenues by streamlining their sales and distribution. Designers also used the Internet as a showroom and sales floor for their goods. At decade's end, virtually every major designer had a Web site on which consumers could browse products, and order to size.[9]

Naturally, fashion design schools, including major institutions like the Parsons School of Design and the Fashion Institute of Technology, increasingly taught computer use to students. Computers became instrumental to the very process of designing clothes. While some stuck to traditional methods, increasingly clothing designers used CAD computer systems to design. Gap, Banana Republic, Polo Ralph Lauren, Tommy Hilfiger, and numerous others all used CAD to a great extent. Even Calvin Klein began using the system extensively in 1995.

JEWELRY

With the turn towards simplicity in dress came a new emphasis on accessorizing. Jewelry played an extremely important role in the world of couture, as it was the place where individuals could truly express themselves. An anything goes attitude seemed to take hold during the decade when it came to jewelry, and consequently, the variety to be seen was vast. A great deal of modern jewelry borrowed its look from the jewelry of the past, but no specific era dominated. Brooches and chokers echoed the jewelry of the nineteenth and early twentieth centuries, while jewelry of the 1960s also influenced nineties design. Peace signs, for instance, made something of a comeback. So, too, did jewelry utilizing hemp twine and wooden beads. Christian iconography was also popular in nineties jewelry, but so, too, were images from other religions and cultures, from African, to Asian, to Celtic. There was an increased use of synthetic material, especially polymer clays, like Das and Fimo, which could easily be formed and hardened into virtually any desired shape.

There was also considerable growth in home manufacturing of jewelry. Many Americans found home-made jewelry to be the ultimate way of expressing oneself. Furthermore, it was easier than ever before to make one's own jewelry, given not only a number of home-jewelry kits on the market, but also the availability of home kilns, stationary torches, and low-temperature soldering torches. These devices made it easier for the home jeweler to go beyond the traditional work with beads and bobbles, and into the realm of metal work, in creating necklaces, earrings, bracelets, and any other form of jewelry.

COSMETICS

As fashion drifted towards simplicity, and muted colors dominated, so, too, did the cosmetic industry exploit earthier tones. For many women, naturalistic tones were the preference when it came to lipstick and nail polish. But there were many times when women wished to use makeup as a way to cut loose, to express themselves and to fly in the face of convention. And so there arose an important counter impulse in the cosmetic industry. Several women became makeup entrepreneurs in the 1990s, largely driven by their dissatisfaction with the limited palette of cosmetics available to them. Dineh Mohajer started her company, Hard Candy, as a 22-year-old pre-med student. Her inability to find the nail polish colors she wanted led her to start mixing her own. She developed four bright pastels, called Lime, Sky, Sunshine, and Violet, which she sold first to one store, then to another. Her customer base grew quickly as the line expanded and continued to experiment. By the end of the decade, Hard Candy was a million dollar company. Although it was naturally less popular, in the same sense of fun that she started Hard Candy, Mohajer started a men's line of nail polish called Candy Man.[10] The same kind of dissatisfaction prompted Sandy Lerner, who had co-founded the high tech company Cisco Systems, and Wende Zomnir to launch their own company, Urban Decay. Started in 1996, Urban Decay's philosophy was to create colors with an urban, industrial edge, including greens, purples, and grays. It began with 10 lipstick colors, 12 nail polishes, and an advertising slogan, "Does Pink Make You Puke?" The company also selected caustic names for its colors: Acid Rain, Frostbite, Oil Slick, Ozone, Shattered, Smog, Rust, Roach, and the like. Urban Decay also expanded into other cosmetics.[11] The success of these companies led even venerable cosmetic lines, like Channel and Revlon, to experiment with edgier colors.

In part due to these companies which sought to make cosmetics interesting and fun again, the industry as a whole grew a great deal in the 1990s, which also gave rise to many stores dedicated solely to cosmetics and fragrances. Department stores had been the dominant retailer of such items prior to the nineties, but now the industry was strong enough to support specialized outlets. Sephora was one of the first to enter the market, and remained the most popular throughout the decade. The first Sephora store was opened in France in 1993, and was later acquired by the company Louis Vuitton Moet Hennessy (LVMH), which looked to overseas expansion. The first American store was opened in New York City in 1998. Sephora's success was driven by their emphasis on wide selection,

knowledgeable staff, and customers' ability to try products before purchasing them. By decade's end, there were over 70 Sephora stores in the
U.S. and over 400 internationally.[12]

HAIR

Naturally, what people did with their hair also provided an outlet for self-
expression. Hair extensions increased in popularity, particularly with
African American women. Elaborate hair pieces, straight or braided, were
weaved into the natural hair of many women. Not new to the decade, extensions nonetheless experienced growth in popularity, in part driven by
their use by a number of African America singers, including Patti LaBelle
and Queen Latifah.

Hair coloring continued to be popular as well, with use increasing about
70 percent over the course of the decade. This growth was in part attributed to aging baby boomers, but growth was also considerable among
younger groups who were not yet in a position to worry about graying.
The growth was also considerable among Hispanics, due to the general
growth in the size of this demographic, and also to the fact that an estimated 55 percent of the Hispanic population was buying hair coloring
products by 2000.[13] For some time women had turned to hair color to cover
gray, but increasingly men turned to hair color as well. While gray hair
might have been considered distinguished in certain circles, a growing
number of men reacted negatively to the thought of going gray, and the
market for men's hair color correspondingly surged. On television, advertisements for products to color men's hair, including facial hair, aired nearly
as often as similar ads for women's hair color products.

But hair coloring was not used only to battle the natural effects of aging.
It was also popular for those simply seeking to change their look, either sub-
tly or radically. While some sought to keep changes subtle enough so none
would notice that they were using hair color, coloring one's hair was not
necessarily something to be ashamed of in the nineties, so dramatic change
was not only possible, but even an object of pride. A popular hair color
choice for women in the 1990s was red, which may also have been driven
in part by figures in the media, especially models and actresses. Actress
Gillian Anderson of the TV show *The X-Files* alone contributed to an increase
in the amount of brassy red hair adorning women's heads. Blonde was also
a color of choice, particularly among teen and pre-teen girls. This was par-
tially driven by the styles of Britney Spears and a cadre of young blonde
pop singers. It is notable that many of these singers, and their fashion followers among the general public, didn't hide the fact that their hair was
dyed, frequently allowing their darker roots to show freely. There was less
of a tendency toward dramatic change among men, though younger men
and boys frequently turned to coloring or bleaching their hair. The surf-bum

Punk rocker, age 24, looking thoughtful at a Bastille Day Festival in Minneapolis. © Skjold Photographs.

bleaching of longish hair filtered into the 1990s. In the early nineties, this took hold with followers of the grunge movement, but by the end of the decade it was more popular to wear bleached hair short. The ideal seemed to be peroxide-bleached, lightly spiked hair with very apparent dark roots. The look was very popular among skaters and other extreme sports athletes, and also among musicians. It could be seen on the head of punk and hard rock musicians, and also in more mainstream music, sported by such top acts as Ricky Martin and members of the singing group 'N Sync.

The number of celebrities mentioned in relation to hair should not be overlooked. Fashion has always been influenced by how celebrities dressed, but in the nineties this was far more true of hair. The average hair-styling magazine was filled with photos of celebrities, or models sporting styles deliberately copied from celebrities. Each new season of the sitcom *Friends* drew as much comment about actress Jennifer Aniston's hairstyle as about the storylines. Indeed, Aniston was something of a darling of the hairstyle magazines, the issue not featuring a model for Aniston hair being a very rare thing indeed.

TATTOOS, PIERCING, AND SCARRING

Another important component of 1990s fashion was body scarring and adornment. Pierced ears had long been popular in the U.S., but piercing of the nose or navel were considered fringe practices. But in the 1990s, these kinds of piercing became increasingly popular. Young people embraced nose and navel piercing rather quickly, but the practice also grew among adults, becoming no longer a cause for scandal. More extreme piercings, like the impaling of the tongue with a small bar, were less widely embraced, but still grew in popularity. Tattooing also became a mainstream practice. Once largely thought the realm of convicts, sailors, and bikers, tattooing became commonplace throughout most of the nation. The proliferation of the tattoo was in part encouraged by a growing number of celebrities, from sports stars to movie and TV actors, sporting tattoos. Though many chose to be tattooed to express their individuality, to be "edgy," for an increasing number of Americans tattoos lost their rebel connotations. Instead they became just another means of self-expression and adornment. Tattoos became largely acceptable in virtually all tiers of society. Of course, young Americans most frequently sported tattoos, but the practice even took hold among middle-class, suburban professional men and women. More extreme forms of bodily mutilation, like body scarring, remained rare, but nonetheless experienced small growth, largely among those who saw the mainstreaming of tattooing and piercing and sought new forms of cultural rebellion. And if pierced noses and tattoos could become, for all intents and purposes, mainstream, perhaps these forms of bodily alteration might one day become so as well.

THE BREAST ENHANCEMENT INDUSTRY

A multi-billion dollar industry developed in the 1990s, all centered around the size of women's breasts. The media over the past decades had certainly emphasized large breasts as a sign of sexual desirability, and as a consequence products and procedures to make breasts look larger soared. The Wonderbra, designed to lift and pad a woman's breasts, was introduced in the U.S. in 1994 by Bali Brassiere Company, and spawned numerous copies and imitations. In 1998, retail sales of the Wonderbra and other makes exceeded $100 million. A *falsie*, a silicone bra insertion, called Curvec, also spawned numerous imitations, and this industry collected $50 million in retail sales.[14]

But, of course, these products merely created the illusion of size. Surgical breast augmentation provided for the actual increase in size that many women desired. Silicone pouches surgically implanted in breasts became enormously popular, even with the hefty $3,000 price tag. To some detractors, the implants made breasts look unrealistic, with comparison's to the doll Barbie's figure not uncommon. In addition, serious health concerns were raised about the implants. Frequently, implants resulted in the hardening of the breast, making it difficult for a recipient to lie down or raise her arms. The surgery carried the additional risk of reduced sensitivity, and the biological creation of fibrous tissue around the implant's foreign body. Furthermore, the fear of silicone leakage into breast tissue became very real to many in the health community. In all, health experts estimated the chance of developing serious health risks from breast augmentation at between 30 percent and 50 percent. But despite these concerns, the demand for enlarged breasts continued, not at all surprising considering the continuing portrait of women perpetrated by the TV and film industries, and both men's magazines and women's fashion periodicals. In 1999, over 167,000 breast implants were performed, more than 50 percent more than just three years before.[15]

COSMETIC SURGERY

Cosmetic surgery, not new to the nineties, certainly saw a surge in popularity at the end of the decade. In some circles, it even became acceptable to discuss one's surgical alterations. With such surgery being so common, and even something that celebrities frequently spoke about openly, the stigma of the surgical pursuit of youth was reduced. A survey by the American Association of Plastic Surgeons suggested that as much as 57 percent of women and 58 percent of men approved of plastic surgery.[16] But for many, the numbers were shocking and disturbing in their revelation of the number of women who felt that they fell too far short of the ideal and needed surgery to improve their appearance. In 1999, about 2.2 million cosmetic surgery procedures were performed, an increase of 44 percent from just 1996, and a phenomenal 153 percent increase from 1992. The most common procedure was liposuction, the literal sucking of fat out of the body, which was performed 230,865 times in 1999, an increase of 264 percent from 1992. The second most popular procedure was breast augmentation, and the third was surgery on the eyelids, called blepharoplasty. Also popular were face-lifts, the surgical tightening of facial skin, and chemical peels, which stripped the top layers of facial skin away altogether. Perhaps part of the reason why cosmetic surgery was not looked down upon was that it was a sign of affluence. All of these procedures were quite expensive, with a facelift commonly costing more than $5,000, and a chemical peel, the simplest of these procedures, costing around $1,300.[17] There was also growing interest in Botox. Botox was actually a form of botulism injected into women's faces with the intention of paralyzing the muscles, thereby reducing the appearance of wrinkles. While the treatment did indeed lessen wrinkling, it also limited facial expressions.

BODY IMAGE

The 1980s saw the rise of the supermodel, which continued throughout the 1990s, setting an ideal to which women aspired. A few noted that, in fact, there were very few supermodels, and that there were few women who even had the potential to look like them. Supermodels provided an utterly unrealistic model for most women, especially as the new supermodels seemed to get thinner and thinner, with a much lighter natural bone structure. The extreme case of thinning models came in a trend towards advertising with emaciated, almost skeletal models. A series of Calvin Klein print ads was credited with starting what came to be known as the "heroin chic" look. In these ads, the models were so thin and drawn as to look like extremely unhealthy drug addicts. Calvin Klein's intention had been to counter conventional ideals of beauty, as suggested by the campaign slogan, "Just Be." But the response was, by and large, not especially positive. Many Americans were repulsed by the ads, but they nonetheless had an impact. These were, after all, fashion models, and if sickly thin appeared in a fashion magazine ad, then some readers would certainly take sickly thin as fashionable.

In 1990, the average fashion model weighed 23 percent less than the average American woman, compared to a mere 8 percent difference from a quarter-century earlier.[18] The reason for this was two-fold. First, the eighties and nineties saw an increase in obesity. The fact was that by 1990, the average American woman weighed more than she did twenty-five years earlier. But at the same time that this was happening, the average fashion model was also getting lighter. The curves on fashion models of the 1950s, for instance, fell to the wayside in favor of a much narrower, sleeker look. The result was that in the nineties a greater number of women than ever before fell short of the ideal being depicted in fashion magazines, and also in movies, television broadcasts, and the world of pop music. As a response to this, there was an increased emphasis placed on accepting one's body for what it was, and for acknowledging that the media image was only one standard of beauty, which could, in fact, take many forms. This was especially geared towards teenaged girls, among which there were skyrocketing rates of anorexia and bulimia. There was a flood of articles and books published examining the beauty industry and its effects on the psychology of women and girls, most notably Naomi Wolf's *The Beauty Myth: How Images of Beauty are Used Against Women* (1991). But all of this seemed mere palaver next to the power of the media to define the most desired look, both in terms of fashion and in terms of body shape.

New to the last decades of the century was a similar infection of men and boys. The number of cases of boys becoming similarly obsessed with body image increased greatly in the eighties and nineties. The hyper-masculine men of action films and pro wrestling created as much of a gap between the ideal and the average male body as there was for women. As a result, many men, especially young men in their teens and early twenties, turned to bodybuilding. More disturbingly, more men turned to the use of supplements and steroids. Some experts in youth psychology suggested that boys who failed to live up to the masculine image were more likely to see themselves as outcasts, and that this may well have contributed to the rise in suburban teen violence during the nineties.

Ultimately, for both men and women, body image became a much greater concern than ever before. Ironically, those who pursued dramatic means of matching the supermodel or muscle man ideal did not necessarily see these as ideal. Instead, many sought not to be extraordinary, but to match the image which was not, in their eyes, exceptional, but was normal. The actually normal bodies possessed by many of these individuals were regarded as inferior to the norm, because the norm had been redefined by the carefully photographed, meticulously lighted, and sometimes airbrushed or otherwise altered images on magazine pages and TV and movie screens.

The very youngest of children were frequently exposed to exceptional ideals of beauty. They were exposed to this partly in the media, but parents also played a part, conveying their own sense of what was ideal to their children. Perhaps the most notable example of this was the growing world of children's beauty pageants. Pageants of this sort were quite popular at the beginning of the 1990s, and the popularity continued to grow until there were approximately 3,000 being held in the United States annually, with around 100,000 participants. The pageant business became a billion-dollar-a-year industry.[19] Children's beauty pageants suffered a sudden sharp decline in 1997, however, largely due to the JonBenet Ramsey murder case. Six-year-old Ramsey was murdered in late 1996 in a case that was sensational enough for its brutality and mysteriousness. But contributing to the sensation was the fact that Ramsey had been a child beauty queen. The wide media coverage repeatedly showed footage of Ramsey strutting across stages, wearing garish makeup and scanty outfits, exuding sex appeal that seemed altogether inappropriate for a six-year-old girl. Almost overnight, the growing fad of children's beauty pageants became something that many Americans regarded with distaste.

This obsession with body image, then, came under a great deal of criticism in the 1990s, but so, too, did fashion in general. Even as a greater variety of trends allowed for more creativity in dress than ever before, worries developed, especially in respect to young people, about how fashionability might be prioritized over more substantive measures of character, morals and talents. While there may be some truth to this, it should be noted that despite changes in fashion, the impulse to follow fashion remained little changed from earlier times. One's desire to fit in to a select group or to the dominant culture was nothing new in the 1990s, and for most, this was enough. For those seeking to match the celebrated ideal of the media, however, a greater problem was posed, as that ideal became more and more exceptional.

7

Food

GENERAL TRENDS

When it comes to food, what was put on the plates of Americans in the 1990s was probably less important than what was erected in their shopping centers. The franchise, though not new to the decade, certainly ruled, as traditional fast-food chains continued to expand their influence and new higher class chain restaurants found their way into cities from coast to coast. Even the great chefs, people like Wolfgang Puck and Emeril Lagasse, for instance, got into the franchise game, not only with restaurants, but also with packaged foods in major supermarket chains.

The decade also saw seemingly contradictory movements in nutrition. Greater than ever before seemed the interest in healthy eating. A flood of low-fat, low-calorie packaged goods reached the supermarket shelves, restaurants paid more attention to the nutritional value of their offerings, and diet books and videos experienced a swell in sales. Yet this was also a decade that saw notable increases in nutrition-related health risks and growing obesity in all demographics.

The trend away from meals prepared from scratch had started long before the 1990s, but continued unabated as the century came to a close. The nineties were a period when many Americans were working longer hours and had a greater number of commitments. Moreover, fewer Americans seemed interested in investing their preciously limited leisure time in preparing elaborate meals. As a consequence, anything that could ease the trouble of preparing meals seemed to flourish. Processed and packaged foods certainly proved popular. About 90 percent of the money spent by Americans on food in the nineties went to processed goods, canned, frozen, and dehydrated. This was true not only of supermarket goods, but also of the processed food found in fast-food and other restaurants employing pre-prepared goods. In general, Americans seemed to be eating out of the house much more, and as a consequence the restaurant industry expanded considerably. Restaurants remained among the hardest small businesses to make succeed, but with the growth of chain restaurants and the change in Americans' dining patterns, the industry nonetheless found itself the largest employer of the 1990s. A 1998 report released by the National Restaurant Association projected total sales for the food service industry at $336.4 billion. This was an increase of almost 5 percent over 1997. By the end of the decade, the industry employed over nine million people.[1]

Consumption of sugar skyrocketed in the 1990s, particularly in the latter half of the decade. A study by the Department of Agriculture estimated that by decade's end, the average American was consuming about 150 pounds of sugar a year, an increase of nearly 30 pounds from two decades earlier. As the American public became increasingly diet-conscious, so increased the number of fat-free foods on the market. But in many cases, as fat was removed, manufacturers replaced it with sugar, and dieters looking for low-fat foods tended to overlook the bloated sugar content. Many sweet products had their sugar content amplified by manufacturers. In 1998, for instance, Nabisco increased the amount of sugar added to its low-fat Snack-well cookies in order to boost sales. But this sugar increase was not merely the result of increased consumption of sweets. In fact, sugar was a common additive to many different kinds of food. Potato chips (and other potato products), meats, and even packaged vegetables saw sugar becoming a more and more common additive. A best-selling diet book called *Sugar Busters!,* published in 1998, brought considerable attention to this, but it is questionable how much the book truly countered the convincing food labels proclaiming products' healthiness. Nonetheless, with increased notice to sugar content, the craze for fat-free food seemed to become somewhat tempered as the new millennium began.[2] Even Nabisco created a sugar-free version of its Snackwell cookies as awareness of sugar content increased.

SUPERMARKET GOODS

Supermarket sales declined during the 1990s. The percentage of food bought at supermarkets—as opposed to specialty stores, warehouse clubs, or chain stores like Wal-Mart—measured at 61.5 percent in 1990, and reached a peak of 65.9 percent in 1993. But by 2000, that number had slipped to 55.8 percent. With more than 9,000 new food products being introduced per year by the end of the decade, one might think this was a boom period for supermarkets, but as the number of new outlets for products grew, the once unbeatable supermarket chains were forced into fiercer competition.[3]

The trend towards consumption of pre-packaged and pre-prepared food started in earnest mid-century, and continued to accelerate with each passing decade. The nineties certainly continued this acceleration with no end in sight. A 2000 survey conducted by the Food Marketing Institute found that 62 percent of shoppers bought precut and ready-to-eat packaged vegetables once a month or more. Thirty-nine percent bought frozen side dishes and 26 percent purchased pre-cooked or marinated, pre-seasoned ready-to-cook meat.[4]

One important development in the packaging of food was a new packing method sometimes called modified atmosphere packaging. This technique was instrumental in the increased prevalence of packaged salad mixes. The pre-washed and prepared mixes ranged from simple iceberg lettuce varieties to more exotic mixes including such lettuces as radicchio and endive. Many of these kits even went so far as to included dressing, croutons, and seed or crushed nut garnishes, thereby giving consumers everything they would need to prepare an elaborate salad. The Food Marketing Institute survey found that nearly half of all shoppers bought packaged salad mixes at least once a month.

A popular item for children was the Oscar Mayer Lunchable. For many parents across the country, these became a substitute for the traditional parent-made lunch sent off to school with the kids. Lunchables offered a boxed lunch of cracker and cold cuts, cold burgers or hotdogs with buns, cold pizza, or nachos, with the inclusion of a drink (soda or juice), a dessert (cookies, chocolate bars, etc.), and frequently a small, cheap toy. The actual cost of putting together the various components of a Lunchable was negligible, but the company was able to charge considerably more than it would cost a parent to put together the same meal. In creating these simple food packages, Oscar Mayer exploited both the tastes of children and also the increasingly busy schedule of parents. More than simply a desire for the food enclosed, children came to demand Lunchables because marketing had trained them to respond to the trademark.

Frozen diet foods saw a surge in popularity as well, with brand names like Lean Cuisine, Smart Ones, and Healthy Choice offering relatively healthy variations on the classic TV dinner. Even vegetarian foods found a solid niche in supermarket freezers. Frozen vegetarian burgers, like top brands Garden Burger and Boca, reached a wider audience, with products made of grain and vegetables, tofu, and texturized vegetable protein or TVP. In fact, these products demonstrated a growing trend in food production and service in general. With the ground swell of vegetarians and vegans in the U.S., many in the food industry sought to diversify so that they could cater to vegetarians as well as to meat eaters. Many restaurants added vegetarian entrees to their menus, and the number of supermarket food products directed specifically to the non-meat-eating consumer increased, as well. Even McDonald's got into the act. In 1990, McDonald's changed the way it cooked its french fries, switching from a high beef-tal-low cooking oil to a pure vegetable oil, and using additives to simulate the flavor that had long made McDonald's fries so popular.[5] In addition to frozen veggie burgers, consumers could find vegetarian hot dogs, sausage, faux-chicken nuggets, and other goods.

But while frozen foods continued to sell well, by 1999 their sales were overtaken by ready-made meals, prepared by supermarket delis and kept chilled and ready for reheating. These ready-made meals typically ap-proximated a home-cooked meal better than did frozen foods, yet required no more work in the kitchen than they did. Many could be microwaved, but there were also goods that called for very basic use of ovens or stove-tops. Although these products were all but finished, they gave consumers the impression that they were actually cooking, which reduced the guilt of instant foods. Moreover, consumers tended to think of these as fresher than frozen meals, though top quality frozen foods were flash-frozen using a process that kept them just about as fresh as prior to freezing.

The nineties also were a golden age for that most portable of foods, the bar. Bars were certainly nothing new, given the long-lived popularity of chocolate and other candy bars. But consumption of various bar-shaped foods increased notably in the nineties, as did the variety. Cereal bars were among the most popular, catering to those who missed breakfast, and also those who simply wanted a sweet snack that provided a healthy alterna-tive to the traditional candy bar. The bars were frequently modeled on the flavors and ingredients of traditional cereals, particularly those consisting of oats, nuts, and honey. Indeed, many cereal bars were different from the classic granola bar more in marketing strategy than in terms of content. The Kellogg's company, largely due to name recognition, was one of the strongest competitors in this market, particularly with their Nutri-Grain line of bars. But it was far from the only company to exploit the cereal bar market, facing strong competition from General Mills and Quaker, well-established makers of traditional granola bars. Also popular were diet bars, such as Slimfast and 30–40–30 bars, which were typically designed to sim-ulate the sweetness of a candy bar, thereby satiating the urge without im-parting the caloric content. Moreover, these bars were often marketed as a high-nutrition meal substitute. Similarly, energy bars found a considerable audience, especially among athletes and would-be athletes. These were seen as an excellent supplement to a high-protein diet. Central to this mar-ket were Power Bars and Balance bars.

The nineties also saw a notable increase in the popularity of energy drinks. Traditional sports drinks like Gatorade continued to find a strong market, but so, too, did products like Red Bull and KMX. These energy drinks typically came in cans that were much smaller than a traditional soda can, at usually twice or more the price. But rather than simply offer-ing a refreshing beverage, they promised to "vitalize the body and stimulate the mind," as the Red Bull marketing campaign would have it. Red Bull, originally from Austria, topped the energy drink market, due in part to a highly successful line of animated commercials praising Red Bull for "giving you wings" with its formula of high caffeine and taurine, an amino acid touted as a metabolic transmitter and detoxifier.[6]

Bottled iced teas also experienced a growth in popularity, largely due to an aggressive marketing campaign by the leading brand in the field, Snapple. Snapple iced teas were more than the traditional iced tea, incorporating a great variety of fruity and sweet flavors to make the tea palatable to an entirely new type of tea drinker. Moreover, Snapple packaging and advertising downplayed the old-fashioned image of iced tea, and for the first time in many years, the beverage became chic. Snapple and other companies were, of course, helped by the growing desire on the part of many Americans to develop healthier eating habits. Tea was seen as far less offensive than sodas or even coffee, particularly green tea, which was praised for its high level of antioxidants. In fact, hot teas, traditional and herbal, also experienced considerable market growth, with Lipton, Bigelow, and Celestial Seasonings dominating, though smaller companies also held their own. Many tea manufacturers exploited the rising interest in herbal supplements. Celestial Seasoning developed a line of special Wellness Teas using increased amounts of ginseng, echinacea, valerian root, and other herbal additives. One company of growing popularity even called itself Traditional Medicinals and marketed teas designed to assist in everything from stress reduction to weight loss to respiratory improvement. The claims made by these teas, and other herbal remedies had not, by the end of the decade, been evaluated by the Food and Drug Administration, but this lack seemed to have little effect on consumers, many of whom swore by the claims printed on the packaging and continued to purchase the products.

FAST FOOD

By the end of the 1990s, Americans were spending about $110 billion dollars on fast food. In his book, *Fast Food Nation: The Dark Side of the All-American Meal,* Eric Schlosser suggested that "Americans now spend more money on fast food than on higher education, personal computers, computer software, or new cars. They spend more on fast food than on movies, books, magazines, newspapers, videos, and recorded music—combined."[7]

Children had long been a prime target for fast-food chain marketing. And this was certainly true in the 1990s. Advertisers realized that the ability to coax a child into a restaurant meant not only a sale of food to that child, but also to one or more parents, and spared no effort in their marketing. Certainly, McDonald's, through the use of their clown mascot Ronald McDonald and the erection of restaurants which included playgrounds, appealed to children. McDonald's further encouraged visits to the restaurants with Happy Meals, complete with toys. In the 1990s, however, the Happy Meals seemed to experience unprecedented popularity, in part due to the nature of the toys included. More than simply including traditional toys featuring the McDonald's cast of characters—Ronald, the Hamburglar, Grimace, and others—the company joined with major toy manufacturers in the 1990s, tapping into already established markets to boost their sales. McDonald's association with Disney certainly proved successful, as movie-related toys in Happy Meals not only boosted McDonald's sales, but also served as vital promotion of Disney movie productions. In 1996, McDonald's and the Walt Disney Company forged a 10-year agreement, according to which the fast-food chain received exclusive rights to Disney film characters for the purpose of promotions like Happy Meal toys. With these and other toys, McDonald's emphasized the "collect them all" mentality, thereby tapping not only into children's interests, but also into a collectors' market. Indeed, the collectors' market for McDonald's toys grew enormously in the 1990s, as evidenced by the publication of at least five different price guides devoted to McDonald's paraphernalia. Even adults were buying Happy Meals in the interest of completing a collection. This was certainly true when in 1999, McDonald's offered eight different kinds of Furby dolls in the meals. In 1997, McDonald's Happy Meals featured highly collectible Beanie Babies, and during this promotion Happy Meal sales leapt. Whereas McDonald's typically sold about 10 million Happy Meals a week, a 10-day period in April 1997 measured about 100 million Happy Meal sales.[8]

The importance of a corporate liaison for the fast-food industry cannot be overemphasized. As much as competing fast-food chains were fighting for market shares, they were also fighting to have exclusive rights to tie their products to the latest blockbuster movie, or popular television show, or latest toy craze. Taco Bell introduced several new food items in the 1990s, but none of these came close to being the marketing boon that was the chain's association with the long-awaited new *Star Wars* movie. Television ads for Taco Bell, as well as for KFC (Kentucky Fried Chicken) and Pizza Hut (all three owned by Tricon Global Restaurants, Inc.), looked very much like ads for the movie, and indeed, they served the same purpose. Taco Bell sales increased not because of their food, but because of the various *Star Wars* goodies that could be attained at the restaurants. Likewise, Taco Bell associated itself with the new American-made *Godzilla* movie, coupling the giant lizard with the fast-food chain's extremely popular line of Chihuahua commercials. When it became clear that the movie was failing to live up to commercial expectations, Taco Bell quickly ended the promotion and pulled its TV commercials, which nevertheless ran a for a long duration before the movie's release, and probably made a much greater impression than did the film. This only hints at how strongly ties were formed between the entertainment industry and the fast-food industry. McDonald's also forged ties with the Fox Kids Network and Klasky-Cuspo, the producer of *Rugrats* and *The Simpsons*, and Burger King became linked with Nickelodeon and *Pokémon*. Restaurant chains also allied themselves with sports leagues and events: McDonald's with the National Basketball Association and the Olympics, Wendy's with the National Hockey League, Denny's with Major League Baseball, and the triumvirate of KFC, Pizza Hut, and Taco Bell with the National Collegiate Athletic Association.[9]

Of course, restaurants were not the only sector of the food industry to build a fruitful association with non-food businesses. This was also very true of products sold in grocery stores. Products from chips to cereal to sodas attempted to gain an additional edge in the market by proudly displaying, for instance, sports stars or movie characters on their packaging. As in the case with the Happy Meal, traditional cereal box toys increasingly had some larger association, and many products offered some kind of mail-in offer, in which toys or other goods would be rewarded with a given number of proofs-of-purchase.

It was clear by the start of the decade that fast food had for all intents and purposes conquered the United States; now it was time to conquer the world. American fast-food chains expanded internationally like never before. In 1993, McDonald's opened 193 new restaurants, but of these only 50 were opened within the U.S. Taco Bell even successfully opened locations in Mexico. Ultimately, the fast-food restaurant became an international symbol of America, as prevalent as American movies and music had been in earlier times.

With the continued growth in fast food production and consumption, the 1990s saw a comparable rise in the demand for materials, from potatoes to meat. The meat industry, particularly, saw an acceleration and relative deregulation, which left many wondering if it was time for a new exposé in the vein of Upton Sinclair's classic novel *The Jungle*. As Eric Schlosser noted, "These changes have made meatpacking—once a highly skilled, highly paid occupation—into the most dangerous job in the United States, performed by armies of poor, transient immigrants whose injuries often go unrecorded and uncompensated."[10]

OTHER CHAINS

The growth of the market for chain restaurants was not limited to fast food, however. Other major chains grew considerably in the 1990s. Increasingly, diverse cities across the country came to have the same restaurants, much as they came to have the same department stores, the same hardware stores, and the same book and record stores. Many of these chains came about in earlier decades, but the 1990s saw an unprecedented acceleration in their growth. T.G.I. Friday's®, the first location of which opened in 1965, serves as a perfect example. The restaurant opened its second location in 1970, and gradually increased its numbers until, in 1990, it opened its 169th restaurant, including several international locations. In 1991 alone, the chain opened another twenty restaurants. In 1994, T.G.I. Friday's® reached 300 locations, and in 1998, it opened its 500th restaurant, more than tripling its 1990 total.[11]

T.G.I. Friday's® is just one example of a much larger pattern which saw an explosion in the number of Red Lobsters and Olive Gardens, and Outback Steakhouses, and other chain restaurants. A great deal of the success of these restaurants has to do with the quality of the food and atmospheres, which was a large step beyond anything available at fast food restaurants, or even the coffee-shop style of Denny's and the like. These restaurants provided a casual sit-down atmosphere, with menus that were both varied and familiar to diners. Moreover, visitors to a given town might not know about the quality of the local restaurants, but could walk into an Olive Garden with, if they had ever visited another chain location, a good idea of both quality and selection. Of course, not all were happy with the proliferation of chain restaurants. To some, the pervasiveness of these restaurants diminished the individuality of a given locale, effecting a kind of culinary homogeneity across the country. Naturally, local restaurant owners also resented the coming of the chains, which made it harder to entice diners into trying something new when established flavors awaited them at the chains. Clearly, the chains had a competitive advantage, aided by the fact that, given the volume of their business, they could offer large meals at very affordable prices. The larger portions served at these restaurants contributed to a trend throughout the restaurant business. Even independent restaurants were forced to resort to larger portions in order to appear competitive with the chains.

Many of the restaurant chains were part of a much larger package, with several operating under a single parent company, much as KFC, Pizza Hut, and Taco Bell all fell under the auspices of Tricon Global. Brinker International, known as Chili's, Inc. until a name change in 1991, owned not only the Chili's restaurant chain, but also Romano's Macaroni Grill, On The Border, and others. Consequently, it was not uncommon to find two or more of the restaurants in this mega-chain located right next to one another on the same plot of land. By the end of the nineties, Brinker owned more than 1,000 restaurants, over 700 of which were Chili's restaurants. Likewise, Darden Restaurants owned Red Lobster, The Olive Garden, and others. By 1994, Darden was making over $1 billion in sales, and at the end of the century had a growing assemblage of more than 1,000 restaurants.

The largest non-fast food restaurant group, however, was the Advantica Restaurant Group. Advantica acquired the Denny's restaurant chain in 1987. At the time, Denny's was suffering a serious image problem, plagued by high-profile charges of racism, which only became worse in the early 1990s. In 1993, these charges reached a peak when six black men accused an Annapolis Denny's of discrimination. Worse still was the fact that these six men were Secret Service officers who were to be protecting the president later that day. The publicity from the case was a public relations disaster, affecting not only the Annapolis location, but the entire company. In the following years, Denny's instituted high-profile efforts to clean up their tarnished image, including the hiring of a greater number of minorities both in individual restaurants, and in all levels of company management. Denny's also instituted a program of sensitivity training for all employees. Ultimately, the strategies seemed to have worked. By the end of the decade the racism charges were largely forgotten and Denny's was netting record-breaking revenues.[12] Denny's was already one of the largest such chains when acquired by Advantica, but upon cleaning up the Denny's image, the corporation increased the number of restaurants considerably. In 1996, Advantica acquired the Carrows and Coco's chain. In purchasing two major chains in the coffee-house restaurant niche also occupied by Denny's, Advantica essentially cornered that niche's market. By the end of the decade, Advantica owned literally thousands of restaurants across the U.S. and internationally.

CELEBRITY CHEFS

Chefs frequently became celebrities starting in the 1980s and the trend continued strongly into the 1990s. Certainly, there had been famous chefs before—Julia Child is a prime example—but a new culinary cult of personality developed at the end of the century, as chefs had unprecedented access to mass media. The cultivation of a flamboyant public persona also helped. Emeril Lagasse, for instance, attracted viewers to his cooking show not only through his culinary skills, but also by his boisterous presentation, punctuated with shouts of "Bam!," a catchphrase of sorts that would become more inextricably associated with Lagasse than any of his signature dishes. Lagasse was arguably the most famous chef of the 1990s. His popularity grew rapidly just in the 10 years that followed the opening of Emeril's Restaurant in March 1990. He opened his second restaurant only two and a half years later, and in 1993, he published his first cookbook, *New New Orleans Cooking.* That year, he was also asked to host his own cooking show, *The Essence of Emeril,* on the new cable Television Food Network. In the years that followed, Lagasse opened several new restaurants and published numerous books, and his television show gained unrivalled popularity for a cooking show, with *Time* magazine calling it one of the 10 best shows in 1996. In 2001, Lagasse was the first chef ever to be given his own television sitcom. The NBC show *Emeril* flopped, but the fact that executives thought it worth producing in the first place demonstrated just how popular Lagasse had become, and also served as notice to the new status of the celebrity chef going into the new millennium.[13]

Chef Emeril Lagasse poses on the set of his cooking show in
New York, April 17, 1998. *Emeril Live* is shown on the cable
Television Food Network (TVFN). © AP/Wide World Photos.

Celebrity chefs also found new outlets for their wares. In addition to running their own restaurants and appearing on their own television shows,
they marketed products through supermarket outlets. Wolfgang Puck was
a pioneering figure in this movement. The chef behind the famed restaurant Spago used his celebrity to push a line of frozen pizzas in the late 1980s,
and later branched out considerably, also selling a popular line of canned
soups. Others followed suit. Emeril Lagasse found supermarket success
with his jarred pasta sauces, as did Paul Prudhomme with his line of Cajun
spices and seasoning blends. Other restaurateurs also got into the supermarket game. California Pizza Kitchen, for instance, brought something
new to the world of frozen pizzas. In a market that seemed already overcrowded, the small company, originally started as a Southern California
restaurant, thought to market pizzas that were markedly different in their
toppings: Thai Chicken, Portobello Mixed Mushroom, BBQ Chicken, and
others. In so doing, California Pizza Kitchen may not have derailed the
major frozen pizza manufacturers, but they did carve themselves a sound
niche, aided by a major distributor, Kraft Foods.

Some fast-food companies even got into the supermarket business. Taco Bell, for instance, took to selling its own brands of hot sauce and taco shells in major American supermarkets. These products were immediate successes, due to brand familiarity. Consumers knew exactly what they were getting when they purchased a bottle of Taco Bell brand sauce, and lesser known brands simply could not compete with that level of name recognition.

COFFEE CULTURE AND STARBUCKS

One of the greatest culinary forces in the 1990s was a coffee company started in Seattle, Washington, that spread like wildfire across the country. The company, Starbucks Coffee, opened its first location in 1971 and started a gradual expansion in the 1980s, changing its approach in the hopes of nurturing a coffee bar culture similar to that in Europe. Indeed, in the late 1980s and the 1990s, many had the same idea as the number of independent coffee shops seemed to grow exponentially. But Starbucks would quickly become the real powerhouse in the market, becoming, as the company mission statement would have it, "the premier purveyor of the finest coffee in the world while maintaining our uncompromising principles as we grow." At the end of the 1980s, the company had 55 locations. In the next year, that number would grow to 84, and that was only the beginning. In 1991, Starbucks opened its first airport location in Seattle, starting a trend that would prove very profitable for the company. In 1993, it received enormous assistance in its climb to become far and away the most successful coffee house chain in the nation's history, through its alliance with Barnes & Noble bookstores. Barnes & Noble was likewise erecting numerous chain bookstores in the 1990s, and with their emphasis as much on atmosphere as on product, the stores frequently included a café serving Starbucks drinks. Partnerships with other corporations were a significant key in Starbucks' success, as it teamed with Dreyer's Grand Ice Cream, Inc. to produce what would quickly become the number one brand of coffee-flavored ice cream in the nation, with the Pepsi-Cola Company to market a bottled version of Starbucks' Frappuccino beverage, and with other companies, including Kraft Foods and Albertson's grocery stores. Starbuck's also expanded overseas, establishing locations not only in Europe, but in such unlikely places as the Philippines, Thailand, Kuwait, and Lebanon, among others. By the end of the decade, Starbucks would have 2,135 locations, a number that would more than double in the first two years of the new millennium. Thus were Americans in every major American city introduced to the coffee company, which dominated the market with bookstore distribution, airport vending stands, and self-standing coffee shops.[14] Starbucks coffee also appeared in many grocery stores. Of course, despite its claims to "uncompromising principles," Starbucks was the target of the same sort of criticism leveled against most major chain retailers, that it forced independent coffee houses out of business, and that it contributed to an unhealthy national homogeneity.

CRAFT BEER

The late eighties and early nineties were an era of beer connoisseurship, as reflected by the number of microbreweries spreading across the country. Indeed, in the 1990s, the usual major beer sellers—Coors, Budweiser, Miller—continued to dominate, but not without a surge in the market for lesser known brands of beer, coming from every corner of the country. Some microbreweries proved so successful that they could no longer really consider themselves micro-, the term craft beer proving much more suitable. The largest of these was the Boston Brewing Company, makers of Samuel Adams Lager. Brewer Jim Koch once suggested that the cutoff for being considered a microbrewery should be 15,000 barrels a year, believing that "Sam Adams will never get that big." But as the new millennium began, about 1.2 million barrels were being produced by the Boston Brewing Company.[15]

Other companies that surged to the top of the craft brew market were Sierra Nevada Brewing Company, New Belgium Brewing Company, Deschutes Brewery, Alaskan Brewing Company, Redhook Ale Brewery, and Harpoon Brewery.[16] While many craft brewers had their start in the 1980s, it is worth noting that some of the strongest had much earlier origins, including Jacob Leinenkugel and FX Matt, which started in the late nineteenth century, and Spoetzel Brewing Company, born in 1915. The popularity of craft beer in the eighties and nineties gave these long constant companies an additional market boost. The late 1990s, however, saw a significant slowdown in the popularity of microbreweries. Many small brewers folded, but a good number persevered, largely because microbrewers were frequently not people who got into the business to make a quick profit, but because of love of beer and brewing. Still, a 2000 survey by the Institute for Brewing Studies in Boulder, Colorado, found that 21 new microbreweries opened that year, while 31 folded. As a result of this trend, many microbreweries returned to an older strategy of catering to a regional customer base, slowing coast-to-coast distribution of their beer.

SODA

Soda consumption continued to grow in the 1990s, reaching an estimated annual rate of 56 gallons a person at the end of the decade. Fast-food chains provided a considerable outlet for soda companies, giving them exclusive rights to their restaurants. Such arrangements were extremely profitable to both the restaurant chains and the soda companies, as soft drinks offered the highest profit margin of all goods sold. Soft drink companies also amplified their advertising efforts, targeting every outlet possible, even some elementary and high school campuses. Ultimately, with all of the exclusive contracts in the offering, the soft drink market became a fiercely competitive one, and an actively hostile one for smaller soda producers. By decade's end, more than 90 percent of the market for soda was being controlled by three companies, Coca-Cola, Pepsi, and Cadbury-Schweppes.[17] According to nutritionists, this increased soda consumption marked a disturbing trend, especially among the nation's youth. A 1997 study showed that sodas constituted over 27 percent of Americans' beverage consumption, averaging out to the equivalent of more than 576 cans of soda a year per person. Consumers spent $54 billion dollars on soda in that year alone. Males 12- to 24-years old were the greatest consumers of sodas, averaging two and a half cans a day each. This was particularly alarming when it came to children and young teens. As soda consumption increased, so did consumption of other more nutritious beverages decrease. Milk and juice consumption by children fell considerably, with far more soda being consumed in its place. Soda's high sugar and calorie intake, and low nutrients, led many to raise warnings about the poor dietary habits of American youths.[18]

DIET AND NUTRITION

Indeed, nutrition in general seemed under siege in the 1990s, as more and more Americans consumed not only lots of soda, but also a great deal of fast food and high-fat snacks and packaged foods. Warnings abounded about the accelerating trend of obesity in Americans—a rate far outpacing that of Europeans—and especially in American children. But poor diet did more than stimulate weight gain. It also affected health in other ways, with increases in heart disease, bone loss, dental deficiencies, and other health problems frequently attributed to eating habits. A 1996 survey of American youth found that they fell well short of measuring up to government diet recommendations. Only 36 percent of boys and 14 percent of girls, for instance, consumed the recommended daily allowance of calcium. Only 34 percent of boys and 33 percent of girls ate the recommended amount of vegetables. And these stats were representative of the insufficient diet of most youths. Again and again, be it in the consumption of fruit, dairy, grains, or important vitamins and minerals, they fell short of the recommended consumption.[19] Poor diet combined with a decrease in the amount of physical exercise, as well as the increasingly sedentary lifestyle of most Americans, produced an embarrassingly unhealthy state for the wealthiest nation in the world.

For many, it became simply more difficult to maintain a sufficient diet in the 1990s. Certainly, it became far easier for many Americans to pay the small price of purchasing fast food or packaged microwavable meals than to prepare a full meal from raw materials. This was particularly true in the increasing number of households where all adults had to work. Additionally, some argued that much of that raw foodstuff simply lacked the nutrients that it once held. With acceleration in food production, new efforts were being made to stimulate the yield of crops and livestock. With mass-grown vegetables, efforts were made to shorten the growing season, thereby increasing the total amounts grown. But serious concerns arose about just how nutritious crops that had had reduced contact with the earth might really be. This is one reason why many Americans turned to dietary and vitamin supplements. The sale of vitamins skyrocketed in the 1990s. More than simple daily vitamins, the industry also produced special packets, advertised as giving energy or boosting mental prowess. Sold seemingly everywhere, these packaged pill cocktails frequently consisted not only of vitamins and minerals, but also of herbal compounds. Dietary supplements were frequently geared towards athletes, marketed as a healthy alternative to steroid use. And they also found a huge following among dieters.

As were the eighties, the nineties were a period of fad dieting. If anything, the popularity of fad diets grew considerably in the decade. The growing rate of obesity in the nation not withstanding, Americans put themselves on diets in unprecedented numbers. Certainly, this can be in part attributed to the images of both men and women in the media. Thin fashion models and actresses had long provided a perhaps unrealistic exemplar of beauty and health. Increasingly at the end of the century, this was also true of the depiction of men.

As indicated by how so much food was packaged and labeled, the 1990s began as a time of anti-fat paranoia. The most popular diets were those that called for a dramatic reduction in fat intake. This in part explains how, in 1992, consumption of chicken surpassed beef consumption, stimulating profits for chicken processors, the largest of which was Tyson Foods. Consumption of chicken and other fowl increased as health concerns did, largely due to the lower fat content than that measured in beef and other red meats.[20] However, a small but growing number of diet books argued that fat-free diets were problematic and that they ultimately didn't work very well. Rather, these diets proposed that carbohydrates were the real source of a fattening public, and called for a reduction in their consumption, along with increased protein consumption. Among these books were Robert C. Atkins's *New Diet Revolution* (actually introduced in a somewhat different form in the 1970s), Barry Sears's *The Zone*, Rachael F. Heller and Richard F. Heller's *The Carbohydrate Addict's Diet*, and Michael R. Eades and Mary Dan Eades's *Protein Power*.

The market for dietary drugs boomed during this period, but there were considerable concerns about the safety of these drugs. Few felt that they provided as beneficial weight-reduction as adjustments in diet and exercise, and some diet drugs were proven actively harmful to their consumers. It is true that they encouraged weight loss, but several were linked to liver disease, kidney disease, respiratory and coronary damage, and other problems. One of the more notorious dietary drugs "Fen-Phen," a cocktail of Pondimin and Redux (which individually were targeted for health risks), was found to result in high blood pressure, irregularities in heart rate, insomnia, tremors, nervousness, headaches, seizures, heart attacks, strokes, and other symptoms in certain consumers. First introduced in 1996, Fen-Phen later became the subject of several major class-action suits. So, too, did the diet drug Meridia which was introduced in 1998 and soon came under suspicion of causing, in combination with other factors, many deaths. Despite warnings, consumption of these drugs continued, the obsession with thinness on the part of consumers, and the lure of profit on the part of suppliers overriding the health concerns.

BIOENGINEERING

Food production was greatly affected by technological developments, as well. Obviously, computers came to play a major role in food information and distribution, with numerous companies establishing Web sites to peddle their wares and generally raise awareness of their brand names. But an even more significant development shook the world of food production, and may well serve as a harbinger of things to come. As important as information technology might have been, it was the advent of bioengineering that altered the way people thought about food and nutrition. The most significant name in bioengineering in the 1990s was the Monsanto corporation, which, under the auspices of CEO Bob Shapiro, took pioneering steps in the genetic manipulation of crops. Essentially, Monsanto began to look into how foreign DNA could be introduced into crop species, thereby altering such species to various effects. With the growing world population, there was considerable interest in how food could be produced at a greater rate. Moreover, geneticists hoped that their efforts could not only increase food production, but also make engineered vegetables more nutritious. Or perhaps crops could be engineered so that their growth and harvest would not strip soil of its nutrients, or so that they could grow in otherwise hostile environments, thereby using farm land more efficiently. Crops could also potentially be made extra-resistant to harsh weather or insects. Or perhaps different subspecies could be engineered based on the eventual uses of a crop. There could be a subspecies of corn, for instance, engineered for human consumption, another for animal feed, and another for processed foods like corn syrup. In short, the possibilities for bioengineered food were staggering. And these possibilities prompted Monsanto to deemphasize their role as a simple chemical business, and invest the whole of the company's assets in biotechnology, investing $8 billion dollars in seed processing.

But the road ahead was not an easy one for Monsanto. Principally, the company's efforts were met with ideological opposition, not unlike the opposition also facing the advances in animal cloning during the 1990s, particularly the 1996 cloning of Dolly the sheep. Many were worried about the risks of "playing God" that they saw as inherent in tampering with nature. Fears likewise arose about the as yet unassessed damage that altered plant life might have on the natural environment, on other plants and animals and on entire ecosystems. More than one commentator compared genetic engineering to the creation of the Frankenstein monster, painting pictures of uncontrollable mutant strains of not only plants, but of insects, and toxic biological agents, genetically engineered super-diseases. These fears were amplified as evidence mounted that some bioengineered corn produced a natural pesticide harmful to monarch butterflies and other beneficial insect populations. Thus, opposition to bioengineering came from religious fundamentalists and from radical environmentalists. And opposition also came from certain nations. Japan ruled that genetically altered foodstuff would have to be labeled as such, and several corporations, such as brewers Kirin and Sapporo, announced that they would not use genetically engineered materials. This was also true of several Mexican companies that traditionally imported corn from the United States. Within the U.S., companies like Gerber and H. J. Heinz, producers of baby food, also waived off of genetically engineered corn or soy. Kraft taco shells containing modified corn that had not been approved for human consumption were part of a high-profile, high-publicity recall. And worst of all for the bioengineering business was the European Union's decision to stop importing any American corn, coming on the heels of its ban on American beef raised using growth hormones.

These events ultimately resulted in the dissipation of Monsanto. Its resulting financial troubles forced it to merge with Phamacia & Upjohn, a major drug company which rendered Monsanto and Shapiro relatively impotent, selling off much of the company's agricultural assets. But Monsanto's stagnation was by no means the end of the story. With mounting concerns about the growing global population, and with the continuing advances in bioengineering, by the end of the decade the debate about genetically altered food looked to be only beginning.[21]

Ever popular as one of the healthiest of foods, milk also came under unusual scrutiny in the 1990s, even as it hit upon its most popular advertising campaign ever. Print advertising showing various celebrities sporting a milk moustache spurred consumption of milk, but many were in fact questioning just how healthy milk actually was. Monsanto had developed a hormone (IGF-1) to increase milk production in cows. Some claimed that the hormone brought with it increased risks of breast and prostate cancer. These claims were disputed, especially by Monsanto, but they still carried enough weight that many other nations, including Canada, refused to allow for its use, making the U.S. the only major developed nation to allow it. Consequently, many consumers turned to organically produced milk, but even this raised worries. Even without the hormone, milk was attacked for its high fat content. A study by the Center for Science in the Public Interest claimed that one cup of whole milk in fact carried as much detrimental fat as five strips of bacon, and a glass of 2 percent milk as much as three strips. Those who criticized milk made a case for calcium intake through the consumption of green vegetables.[22] Still, the long-held health benefits of milk continued to hold sway over the American public, as debates continued about its pluses and minuses. And certainly, most experts held to the notion that, whatever its flaws, milk consumption was better for the individual than heavy soda consumption.

Across the globe, American eating habits were increasingly seen to be rather opulent. This was a notion that was driven by the increasing weight of the American populace. Yet at the same time, more and more people throughout the world were being exposed to American-style dining, as American foods, in the form of restaurants and packaged goods, spread internationally. Thus did the debates about American eating habits become international. Concerns about the healthiness of Europeans regularly consuming McDonald's food grew, and so too did concerns about cultural homogenization. The food of a place, be it a foreign country or an American city, has long been a defining characteristic of a locale. The nationalization and internationalization of foods certainly added a great deal of variety to some people's diets, but the debate continues on what the cost might be.

The 1990s

8

Literature

Perhaps more significant than the actual literary production of the 1990s were the tremendous changes occurring in the way literature was distributed. Even as alarmists continued bemoaning the decline in literacy in the United States, the book business experienced an unprecedented boom.[1] This boom has largely been attributed to three factors. First, was the changing image of the book store, particularly with the development of superstores, led by Borders and Barnes & Noble booksellers. Second, as in seemingly all areas of American culture, the Internet stimulated growth of the book industry as online bookstores, spearheaded by Amazon.com, provided the option of purchasing books from the comfort of one's own home. The third factor was an increased attention to literature in the mass media, best exemplified by Oprah Winfrey's televised reading group.

SUPERSTORES

Given the large scale of their operations, both as individually large stores and as part of large corporations, superstores gained several advantages in the marketplace. First off, given their purchasing power with book distributors, the superstore chains could regularly provide discounts that smaller stores could not hope to match. Moreover, the volume of sales, along with their large stock, allowed these stores to carry prestige items. The philosophy section of a Barnes & Noble superstore, for instance, might provide little revenue, but the presence of a well-stocked philosophy section certainly added to the intellectual image of the store. This was another edge the superstores had over smaller stores that would have to take care to preserve their display space for items likely to sell well. The superstores provided much more than simply a place to buy books, however. Much of their appeal was atmospheric. Besides the large, diverse book selections, as well as book-related merchandise like bookends, book lights, writing materials, etc., the superstores also offered spaciousness and comfort. Liberally scattered chairs and sofas, along with low-pressure salesmanship were intended to create a comfortable shopping (and browsing) environment, one that encouraged the idea of reading as a leisure activity, as one of the finer things in life. Moreover, Borders and Barnes & Noble superstores dealt with more than simply books. Some stores extended their reach into software and music as well. Even more importantly, the stores sold coffee. Common to these stores, were cafés where patrons could purchase any of a large number of coffee concoctions, as well as pastries and light lunch foods. Barnes & Noble formed a partnership with Starbucks coffee. The cafés, originally intended as just a supplement to the bookstores, quickly became a significant draw in and of themselves. They became a place for friends to meet one another, and sometimes a place for people to meet new friends. Some stores, in fact, ventured so far as to have regular singles nights at their cafés.

Of course with the rise of these superstores, smaller booksellers suffered. The struggle to keep up with the superstores' competitive prices and large selections, and ultimately to continue drawing a clientele sizable enough to continue operations, eventually forced many bookstores to close their doors permanently. Those independent booksellers that survived generally sought out a new niche which could not so easily be matched by the large corporate bookstores, particularly focusing in on local affairs, emphasizing books and literary (and otherwise artistic) events of regional interest.

ONLINE BOOK BUYING

But even as Barnes & Noble and Borders laid claim to a large segment of book buyers via their physical sights, a new avenue of sales debuted in cyberspace. In July 1995, Jeffrey P. Bezos launched an Internet site called Amazon.com with the stated mission "to use the Internet to transform book buying into the fastest, easiest, and most enjoyable shopping experience possible."[2] The service was an immediate success, or so it first appeared. Retail bookstores felt the crunch as consumers took advantage of Amazon.com's convenience. From home, they could browse book titles and conduct their own book searches at their leisure, and could purchase books without having to brave crowded bookstores and without having to dig through packed shelves for a title that may or may not be in stock. Sales success led to a intense interest in Amazon.com's stock, which skyrocketed in the first few years of the company's existence. With all this excitement about the company, it might be thought that its founders were becoming exceedingly wealthy, but the truth was that even as others were profiting exceptionally from the company's artificially inflated stock, Amazon.com itself was struggling, its expenses virtually dissipating its profits.

Despite its early difficulties, however, Amazon.com continued to experience astonishing growth. In 1999, for instance, Amazon.com's net sales were a full 169 percent higher than they had been for 1998. Moreover, in 1999, Amazon.com at its peak shipped some $16 million worth of merchandise in a single day, more than for the entire year of 1996. Generally, Amazon.com managed to gain a degree of financial stability due to this growth, as well as its extension into other areas of service. As with the physical superstores, Amazon.com offered music, software, video cassettes and DVDs, toys and games, and more. In addition, the company also offered access to auctions and other distributors of out-of-print and rare books, thereby providing a service not available from most book retailers. Amazon.com also forged partnerships with several other non-book Internet companies, including pets.com, HomeGrocer.com, drugstore.com, and Gear.com (specializing in sporting goods.)

Naturally, the success of Amazon.com led other book retailers to exploit the Internet. Most importantly, Barnes & Noble launched its own Web-based business in March of 1997. Although it never quite reached the online success of Amazon.com, barnesandnoble.com, bolstered by name recognition and a lucrative alliance with America Online, certainly gave its predecessor some competition, easily becoming the second largest online book distributor. Like Amazon.com, barnesandnoble.com did not limit itself to books. It also featured live online author chats and an archive of interviews with writers in an attempt to "add to the experience of a personal literary community online."[3]

ONLINE PUBLISHING

The 1990s also saw tentative forays into online publishing. Online journals and 'zines flourished as the Internet provided a new and inexpensive way for publishers, editors, and writers to reach a wide audience. But for such publications, profit was generally not the goal. Indeed, the obstacles to money-making were numerous. Perhaps most insurmountable was the struggle against the sheer mass of material on the Web, which made it difficult for a "small-press" online magazine to stand out. In some cases, an access fee would be charged by an online publisher, but the cost that most readers were willing to pay to read words off a screen certainly limited the amount that online publishers were able to charge. This combined with the fact that many of these publications were geared towards a rather select audience largely limited Web publishing to a hobby or academic resource.

As a result of this, major publishers only took minor steps into the field, while still recognizing that the Internet was indeed an important new resource. In 1999, at the 21st annual meeting of International Distribution and

Supply Chain Specialists, the keynote speaker, publishing consultant Mike Shatzkin, suggested that by 2020 the printed book would become "an artifact of a rich person's toy," and that electronic publications (e-books) would displace the more expensive bound products. Of course, even Shatzkin noted the obstacles that lay ahead, including the cost of digitizing existing texts and developing new technologies for e-book distribution, as well as the as yet undetermined method of handling e-book pricing and rights.[4]

THE OPRAH EFFECT

Yet even as talk of the new electronic age of publishing heated up, the physical book flourished in new ways. In addition to the increase of sales brought about by the superstores both online and off, the media helped to send hoards of shoppers into the bookstores seeking titles. Ironically, television, long regarded as the greatest of threats to literacy, promoted titles of which the public could not seem to get enough. Of all the television personalities recommending and promoting books, none held close to the influence held by Oprah Winfrey. *The Oprah Winfrey Show* had long featured guests who used the show as an opportunity to publicize their books, but prior to 1996 these were generally non-fiction titles, frequently with a spiritual bent, like Sarah Ban Breathnach's *Simple Abundance* and Gary Zukov's *Seat of the Soul*. As the show continued its relentless climb in the ratings, it became quite clear to booksellers, and to producers of the show, that sales on such titles experienced a notable, even phenomenal, growth, in some cases exhausting distributor supply of a title and sending the publisher quickly back to the presses. *Simple Abundance* climbed to the top spot of the *New York Time*s Nonfiction Best-Seller list within weeks of its appearance on the show. In July 1993, Winfrey hosted a week's worth of shows featuring fiction writers she admired (or, as she phrased it, writers she would like to have dinner with). Included were Deepak Chopra, Maya Angelou, M. Scott Peck, Elie Weisel, and Andrew Vachss. But while the authors did garner increased sales, the show itself sunk in the ratings. The drop was attributed to the fact that viewers were not necessarily familiar with the work of the writers in question, and consequently had no emotional investment in the interviews. The solution to the problem would come several years down the line. In September of 1996, Winfrey started her on-the-air fiction book club with *The Deep End of the Ocean,* Jacquelyn Mitchard's debut novel. In this new format, Winfrey would announce the title of a novel far enough in advance that viewers could acquire and read it before the broadcast of the discussion, commonly held over a nice dinner attended by lucky viewers (invited on the basis of their letters to Oprah regarding the book) as well as by the author and the host.[5]

The ratings for the book club discussions proved to be steady, even improving as the club gained exposure and momentum. But the real repercussions of "Oprah's Book Club" were felt in the literary marketplace. It soon became clear that such an endorsement would not only improve a book's sales figures considerably, but would, in fact, invariably guarantee it a spot, usually the top spot, on the best-seller lists. *The Deep End of the Ocean* achieved the number one spot on the *New York Times* best-seller list almost immediately after mention on Winfrey's show, and this performance was repeated book after book as the club continued. Many of the books promoted by the club were new novels by first-time writers, like *White Oleander* by Janet Fitch and *Mother of Pearl* by Melinda Haynes, both of which were among the best-selling novels of 1999, riding the lists for 19 and 14 weeks respectively.[6] However, the club was also able to breathe new life into old books. Toni Morrison's 1977 novel, *Song of Solomon*, climbed up the paperback best-seller list when it was selected for the club in 1997, achieving sales numbers that dwarfed any the author had previously gotten, even after she was awarded the Pulitzer (for *Beloved*) in 1988 or the Nobel Prize for literature in 1993.

Of course, Oprah's Book Club did suffer its fair share of criticism. Her selection of books clearly favored female authors, for instance, and while Winfrey made efforts to include more male writers, she did so not without keeping well in mind the largely female demographic of her viewership. Also, her audience complained that her selections tended to be too depressing. Winfrey's response to this was that life itself was, indeed, difficult, but that the way the protagonists of these novels dealt with such hardships was in fact uplifting. Both of these criticisms were ameliorated somewhat by the selection of Wally Lamb's *She's Come Undone*, announced as her club selection in January 1997. *She's Come Undone* proved that the "Oprah Effect" driving books up the best-seller lists was neither bound by gender nor narrative tone. In fact, *She's Come Undone*, a coming-of-age novel about a young woman who grows to 257 pounds in weight as she grows up, was such a popular choice that when Lamb published his second novel, *I Know This Much is True* (1998), Winfrey was quick to choose it as a book club selection. Perhaps a more serious criticism of the club came from booksellers and publishers, who were regularly overrun immediately after the announcement of the latest books. Copies quickly sold out and irate customers were regularly left with no recourse but to place special orders, which were themselves delayed as publishers worked frantically to reprint the books. *Song of Solomon* publisher Plume, for instance, went back to press with that novel more than ten times after its announcement on *Oprah*. To counter these problems, Oprah Winfrey made arrangements with publishers and booksellers to give them an early heads-up on forthcoming selections.[7]

Despite these criticisms, there was more good than bad to say about Oprah's Book Club. It was credited not only with giving the book industry a shot in the arm, but also with increasing the market for literary fiction, with a nice mixture of both challenging and more accessible works. Moreover, the club deserved praise for its infectious emphasis on the joys of reading, which likely brought previous non-readers out to the bookstores. As one bookseller stated, "She really does seem to be bringing in new people, and they're people who specifically said they wouldn't otherwise have bought a book at all."[8] *The Oprah Winfrey Show* also contributed to the increase of literary discussion groups throughout the decade, though surely the rise of the superstores had some effect on this, as well. Oprah Winfrey was certainly not the only celebrity to endorse books in the 1990s. Even politicians got into the act, as was the case during Newt Gingrich's brief reign, during which he spurred sales on such titles as *The Federalist Papers* and *Democracy in America*. But no others ever came close to achieving the same clout in the book industry as Oprah Winfrey.

VETERAN BEST-SELLING AUTHORS

Winfrey and the superstores were not the only things to influence the best-seller lists. As always, the greatest selling point for books was name recognition, and while some new writers made inroads during the 1990s, the old literary stalwarts—Stephen King, Mary Higgins Clark, Tom Clancy, Danielle Steel, Anne Rice, Sidney Sheldon, and others—continued to reign. The 1993 list of the top 10 longest-running best-sellers, for instance, featured three novels by John Grisham and four by Michael Crichton.[9] Stephen King had by now accumulated such a following and such clout in the publishing industry that he could easily sway his publisher into allowing for format experimentation. One of King's novels, *The Green Mile*, was published in six installments, short mass-market (pocket book) paperbacks, once a month in 1996, in an effort to capture the excitement of, for instance, the episodic publication of Charles Dickens' novels in magazines. Although the cost of six paperbacks was as much as the price of most of King's hardcover novels, *The Green Mile* was a tremendous success, inspiring other attempts at the same format by others, like John Saul, whose own serial novel, *The Blackstone Chronicles*, though not as successful as King's, still garnered no small readership. Although King initially claimed that *The Green Mile* would not be published as a single volume, this decision was reversed and the novel enjoyed a new life as a single item (bolstered further by the Academy Award–nominated film adaptation.) Another King experiment involved the simultaneous publication in 1997 of two novels, *The Regulators* and *Desperation*, one written under his early pen-name Richard Bachman and one under his own name, respectively. While each stood as a self-contained narrative, each also served as a kind of twisted mirror image of the other. Moreover, as the 1990s reached its end, plans were effected to release a Stephen King novella, *Riding the Bullet*, exclusively over the Internet.

When it came to best-selling authors, however, King was unusual in his experimentation. Most other best-selling authors largely stayed with the kind of material which had won them their acclaim. Tom Clancy, for instance, continued to write the kind of political military techno thriller which may have seemed more appropriate to the Cold War era, but continued to find a strong audience in the 1990s, with titles such as *The Sum of All Fears* (1991), *Without Remorse* (1993), *Debt of Honor* (1994), *Executive Orders* (1996), and *Rainbow Six* (1998). Meanwhile, Clancy also took the time to oversee the publication of several series, featuring his name prominently displayed on the covers, though written by other authors (in a manner not unlike Don Pendleton's *The Executioner* and *Mack Bolan* series).

FILM, TELEVISION, AND LITERATURE

Also important to the shaping of the best-seller lists were ties with other media. Naturally, many books were boosted in sales by the release of cinematic adaptations. In truth, as was the case with *The Green Mile,* books adapted to the screen were already successful, but there's no denying that the films added further to the sales of Patricia Highsmith's *The Talented Mr. Ripley,* John Irving's *The Cider House Rules,* and Susanna Kaysen's *Girl, Interrupted.* Moreover, the enormous popularity of the James Cameron directed movie *Titanic* not only spurred sales of official movie books and merchandise, but of virtually any books related to the sinking of the famed ocean liner. Walter Lord's account of the Titanic, *A Night to Remember,* climbed back onto the best-seller list some 40 years after its original 1955 publication.

Perhaps on no other genre did the relationship with media have quite such an impact as it did on science fiction and fantasy. For many science fiction fans, the event of the decade was the release of a new *Star Wars* movie. But the literary fervor started earlier, with Bantam's release of Timothy Zahn's *Heir to the Empire,* the first in a trilogy and the first new *Star Wars* novel to see print since 1983. The success of Zahn's novels, each of which rode the weekly best-seller lists for strong double-digit runs, proved that although it had been some time since the last *Star Wars* movie, interest in this universe and cast of characters was far from gone, so more books were released, in increasing numbers as anticipation built for the new movie. Ultimately, the *Star Wars* publishing franchise became a force on the scale of the ever-popular *Star Trek* franchise. Both franchises increased their popularity during the 1990s, so that it was not in the least uncommon for books from the series to crack the bestseller lists. Although none were able to match these powerhouses, other movies and television shows found success on the science fiction shelves. Among them were *Stargate, Babylon Five,* and *The X-Files.* And, unlike the prior experiences of the *Star Trek* series, publishers now realized that these movie and TV tie-ins had a serious audience, a readership that would willingly pay hardcover prices for materials that it was previously believed could only be sold successfully as mass market.

SCIENCE FICTION AND FANTASY

In addition to the ties which science fiction literature shared with science fiction television and film, the genre was also given a boost by the game industry. For instance, TSR, the company best known for creating the Dungeons & Dragons role-playing game, started several lines of fantasy novels. Though related to their role-playing games, TSR novels also stood on their own, accessible to readers with no gaming experience. The novels featured a variety of stories occurring in several shared fantasy universes, delineated by the given line, the most successful of which were the *Forgotten Realms* and *Dragonlance* series. What is most remarkable about these books is that what may at one time have been considered disposable, escapist literature had now found an unprecedented popularity. The books experienced an extraordinary shelf life, all books in the *Forgotten Realms* and *Dragonlance* series remaining in print throughout the decade. Moreover, the line helped to develop some fantasy fiction stars, reader favorites like R. A. Salvatore and the writing team of Margaret Weis and Tracy Hickman, whose work for TSR also boosted sales of their non-TSR titles. Although most of the novels were first published in paperback, the success of the lines led TSR to release a growing number of hardcover editions, including Weis and Hickman's *Dragons of Summer Flame,* a *Dragonlance* novel which had an impressive 200,000- copy first printing. Although the most successful, role-playing games were not the only games to spawn novels. There was also growth in computer-game-based literature, including books based on *The Dig, The 7th Guest,* and several titles based on both of the very popular CD-ROM games, *Doom* and *Myst.* And Bantam arranged a double-coup with the publication of a series of novels based on the *Star Wars: X-wing* computer game.[10]

Of course, the science fiction and fantasy market was not all about licensed universes, and found itself well represented in the 1990s, even without the help of other media. The market for fantasy and science fiction had been growing consistently at least since the release of *Star Wars* in 1977, and in the 1990s, this translated to unprecedented opportunities for new writers. Science fiction publisher Tor, for instance, was publishing approximately one first novel per month in 1996. Other publishers followed suit, and many authors enjoyed a level of promotion from their publishers that would have been far less likely for earlier generations of first-time science fiction and fantasy novelists. Although some major names in these genres, like Isaac Asimov and Roger Zelazny, were lost during the decade, the 1990s proved to be quite beneficial to established writers, as well. Sequels and series did particularly well, with particular success for Kim Stanley Robinson's *Mars* trilogy, Terry Pratchett's *Discworld* series, Marion Zimmer-Bradley's *Darkover* series, and others. But arguably the most successful fantasy series of the decade was Robert Jordan's *Wheel of Time* series. Begun in 1990, the projected 10-volume series of high fantasy novels struck a chord with readers, whose anticipation for each coming volume has perhaps never been paralleled in the fantasy genre.[11]

With the broadening of the audience for these genres, publishers began to market their books in a way that downplayed the traditional ideas about fantasy and science fiction. Cover art moved away from the typical images of spaceships and dragons towards a more sophisticated type-driven look, akin to that of much mainstream fiction. Certainly, works of science fiction and fantasy had proven to be potential best-seller material. Michael Crichton's *Jurassic Park,* a novel about the genetic recreation of Cretaceous dinosaurs in the modern world, was certainly science fiction, but it was written by an author known for less fantastic works of fiction, and it was clearly marketed as mainstream fiction. Its success as a novel (well over a year on the best-seller lists) as well as its success as a series of films, clearly suggested that there was an audience for such stories. Understandably, then, many publishers who had largely devoted themselves to fantasy and science fiction began to market their wares as simply "fiction." Longtime science fiction publisher DAW launched such a line in 1996 with *Killjoy* by Elizabeth Forrest, and then published the first in a four-book series (*Otherland*) by its most popular author, Tad Williams, under this imprint as well.[12]

But science fiction and fantasy were not the only kinds of literature to explore the potential crossover between genre and mainstream fiction. Particularly, romance and mystery publishers began to experiment with new kinds of fiction and, perhaps more importantly, new methods of marketing their wares. Like science fiction, these genres released a greater number of books that downplayed the traditional imagery. The romance genre, for instance, often inclined away from the bodice-ripper covers traditionally associated with the genre, in favor of type-based design, often accompanied by more restrained imagery: flower bouquets or draped velvet and silk. Both romance and mystery likewise experimented with format, publishing a greater number of works in hardcover and trade-size paperback. And, like science fiction, other genres also saw a number of star writers rise from the heap and firmly establish themselves on the best-seller list. But all of this should not go to suggest that the various genres abandoned their roots and the audiences that they had cultivated for years. Indeed, science fiction still had its share of space opera, fantasy its sword and sorcery, mystery its hardboiled detectives, and romance its bodice-rippers. But the genres had grown so much broader, so much more inclusive. Along with this came the common reader claim that what they were reading was not really of any of these genres, that it somehow transcended the baseness associated with the genres, which in many people's eyes were something less than *real* literature.

MYSTERY AND CRIME FICTION

This was certainly the case when it came to mystery, which spread out into many sub-genres (and, some might argue, related non-mystery genres.) Certainly, there had long been books that, while lumped in with mystery, were something rather different from the traditional Victorian tales of crime investigation as puzzle solving. Police procedurals and hard-boiled crime fiction of the sort written by Raymond Chandler and James M. Cain had established a niche for themselves as early as the 1920s. But later in the century, the debate about what actually constituted a mystery novel intensified, with many readers, critics, and publishers claiming that there was a distinct difference between mysteries and what might be called "thrillers."[13]

Perhaps most notable of these related genres is the legal thriller. This was not a new genre in the 1990s—certainly, one can't forget the popularity of Erle Stanley Gardner's Perry Mason—but its successes are significant in examining the literary landscape. Two authors in particular propelled the genre to new heights: Scott Turow and John Grisham. Both authors, trained lawyers, began their fiction writing careers in the late 1980s and quickly became major players on the best-seller lists. Turow published numerous novels, the first, *Presumed Innocent* in 1987, followed by *Burden of Proof* (1990), *Pleading Guilty* (1993), and *The Laws of Our Fathers* (1996). The moral character of the protagonists of these novels varied, from devious and manipulative to decent and dedicated to justice. But Turow always emphasized the psychological elements of their individual strengths and weaknesses over the actual details of any mystery.

John Grisham's first novel, *A Time to Kill,* was published, after numerous rejections from publishers, in 1989 with a first run of 5,000 copies. The book got Grisham's foot in the door, but it was his second novel, *The Firm* (1991), that made him a literary powerhouse, landing him at the top of best-seller lists. In fact, every Grisham book published thereafter—nine in the 1990s alone—won long runs on the best-seller lists. Moreover, Grisham's books made for easy cinematic adaptation, resulting in the filming of no less than five of his books: *The Pelican Brief* (1992), *The Firm* (1993), *The Client* (1993), *The Rainmaker* (1995), and *A Time to Kill* (1996), and actually billed as *John Grisham's The Rainmaker,* confirming his place as a literary superstar.[14] Detractors claimed that Grisham's books were formulaic, always dealing with a young idealistic lawyer fighting against corruption in giant corporations, government, and the legal profession—in short, a kind of legal David and Goliath story. Yet none can argue that this formula, along with Grisham's accessible style, kept readers away. Moreover, the success of Grisham and Turow inspired the publication of many other legal thrillers by Richard North Patterson, Philip Friedman, Jay Brandon, Steve Martini, and others.

Women writers were particularly well represented in the mystery genre during the 1990s. It is true that they had long dominated the sub genre of cozy mysteries, perhaps best represented by the Miss Marple mysteries of Agatha Christie, in which, despite the frequent murder at the center of the plots, an atmosphere of ease and friendliness is established and cynicism and violence are downplayed. Related to this sub genre was the culinary mystery which also experienced considerable popularity during the decade, with titles like Lou Jane Temple's *Death by Rhubarb* (1996) and Diane Mott Davidson's *The Main Corpse* (1997), and utilized a generally domestic setting and printed usable recipes mixed into the crime solving. Likewise, animal mysteries continued the popularity they had been cultivating in earlier years. The cat was an especially popular sleuth, with a seemingly endless supply of novels, including those by Carole Nelson Douglas, Lydia Adamson, and Lilian Jackson Braun, whose long-running *The Cat Who…* (i.e., *The Cat Who Said Cheese, The Cat Who Blew the Whistle,* etc.) series continued unabated.

While these gentler sub genres continued to flourish, however, women writers were also making inroads into the darker side of the field. Patricia Cornwell had repeated best-seller success with sometimes gruesome novels, including *The Body Farm* (1994) and *Cause of Death* (1996), about a fictional medical examiner. Sara Paretsky had continued success with her hard-boiled detective, V. I. Warshawski. And then there was Sue Grafton and her alphabetic series about a tough, bitter private investigator named Kinsey Millhone. The series began in 1984 with *A is for Alibi*, with an expected conclusion around 2015 with *Z is for Zero*. The 1990s saw the publication of *G is for Gumshoe* through *O is for Outlaw*. They, and the seven novels between, experienced growing popularity, with each new volume climbing higher on the best-seller lists and garnering larger print runs, with *N is for Noose* breaking the one-million-copy first print mark for Grafton.[15]

One novel that was more of a clear-cut mystery (as opposed to crime fiction or a thriller) was David Guterson's first novel (after a collection of short stories and a non-fiction book on home schooling), *Snow Falling on Cedars,* an interesting case study in market crossovers. The plot of this 1995 novel involved the trial of a Japanese American man for the murder of a fellow fisherman near Puget Sound in 1954, and the investigation surrounding the death, which raises many questions about the accused's guilt. Despite this rather classical murder-mystery set up, the novel was not marketed as a mystery novel. Indeed, there was much more to it than the mystery at its center, including an inter-racial romance, lush treatments of the landscape, and, perhaps most importantly, significant historical detail, specifically involving the defendant's time spent in an American internment camp during World War II. Although not marketed as a straight mystery, however, *Snow Falling on Cedars* managed to draw a considerable audience among mystery readers. Moreover, it drew readers of historical fiction. And, of course, it drew a sizable mainstream audience as well, especially after its win of the PEN/Faulkner award. The hardcover sold quite well, but the paperback edition shattered all expectations, surpassing the 2.5 million sales mark by the end of the decade.[16]

ROMANCE

The romance genre also saw the steady continued success of traditional styles—from demure period pieces to steamy contemporary works—even as the bounds of what could be done changed. As a result, the lines between romance and what has typically been called *women's fiction* by publishers and retailers began to blur. Authors like the always popular Danielle Steel and Eileen Goudge could be considered either romance or mainstream, and bookstores might shelve them in either section. And even in those books whose label might be less disputable, changes were taking place.[17]

For a 1990s audience, the stereotypical virginal romance protagonist who swoons into the arms of her lover often proved problematic. Many modern women found the naiveté of these characters cloying and unrealistic. Consequently, many authors had the courage to push the confines of what had generally been fairly strict categorical bounds. Catherine Coulter, for instance, developed protagonists who were smart and self-sufficient, and not dependent on a male hero. Likewise, Diana Gabaldon developed a large and fanatical following with her *Outlander* series. Gabaldon's protagonist was anything but traditional. She was a strong, tough-minded woman who was not above reversing romantic conventions by playing the part of the seducer of the young virginal man. Moreover, Gabaldon's books—*Outlander* (1991), *Dragonfly in Amber* (1992), *Voyager* (1994), and *Drums of Autumn* (1997)—introduced a level of fantasy largely unknown to the genre prior to the *Outlander* series. The protagonist of Gabaldon's novels began the series during World War II, but time-traveled to eighteenth century Scotland. The series might well be considered romantic adventure, rather than strict romance, but the combination of genres proved nothing if not successful, making Gabaldon one of the most popular writers to be shelved in bookstore romance sections. Her successes inspired no small number of imitators—with a number, including Lynn Kurland and Arnette Lamb, even exploiting the same olden Scottish locale—and encouraged romance writers to incorporate an increased amount of adventure into their books, or to utilize devices traditionally found in science fiction or horror novels: time travel, magic, ghosts, and more. Leisure Publishing even started an imprint called Lovespells to capitalize on fantasy in romance, and Berkley started its Haunting Hearts and Time Passages lines.

Both Coulter and Gabaldon became best-selling authors, but they were far from the only romance writers to achieve mainstream popularity. Others like Sandra Brown, Jane Ann Krentz, Johanna Lindsey, and Fern Michaels also found a crossover audience. Also reaching the best-sellers lists was the 1992 novel, *Scarlett,* a sequel to *Gone with the Wind,* which had more in common with author Alexandra Ripley's roots in the romance genre than with Margaret Mitchell's original novel. In 1992, Krentz edited a collection of essays entitled *Dangerous Men and Adventurous Women: Romance Writers on the Appeal of the Romance,* which sought to defend the production and consumption of romance writing, long accused of training women to assume a submissive place in our culture. The book was well-received, particularly by feminists and academic organizations, and helped cultivate a greater acceptance of romance writing. But arguably, the most significant move on the part of romance publishers was to realize the growing diversity of its audience, and to offer a comparable diversity of literature, producing plenty of traditional romance, while broadening the scope to include African American and Hispanic audiences, and engaging modern issues in a romantic context. This broadening successfully drew in new readers to the point that, at the end of the 1990s, an estimated 45–50 percent of mass market paperbacks were romances.

At least one best-seller, however, walked the line between romance and mainstream. Robert James Waller's 1992 novel, *The Bridges of Madison County,* was indeed a romance, but had a rural setting in which a Idaho farmer's wife met and fell in love with a *National Geographic* photographer, sent to document the title landmarks. Part of the appeal of the book, written in a strange mixture of spare and purple prose, was that the romance involved not the twenty-somethings so common in most romances, but an older couple (played by the aging Meryl Streep and Clint Eastwood in the inevitable movie version directed by Eastwood in 1995.) The novel quickly became the fastest-selling hardcover up to that point, selling in excess of four million copies in a year, and claiming a spot on the best-sellers list for a year and a half. Moreover, his second novel, *Slow Waltz at Cedar Bend,* made Waller the first author to hold both the first and second slots on the hardcover best-sellers lists simultaneously. Waller also opened the door to a new popularity for mainstream romances, books that covered similar ground as traditional genre romances, but were shelved with general fiction instead, such as Nicholas Sparks's *Message in a Bottle* (1998) and Nicholas Evans's *The Horse Whisperer* (1995).[18]

LITERARY FICTION

Lest it be thought that there was only room on the best-sellers list for genre titles and those lionized by Oprah Winfrey, it should be noted that several established literary authors also made a stir. Thus, it was not unusual to see, among the Stephen King and John Grisham titles, such works as Don DeLillo's *Underworld* (1997), Edward Rutherford's *London* (1997), Salman Rushdie's *The Moor's Last Sigh* (1995), and Thomas Pynchon's long-awaited *Mason & Dixon* (1997). No easy reads, these titles belied a continued interest in high literary fiction. Certainly, name recognition made for stronger sales than had by similar fiction by relative unknowns, the very legacy of the name Pynchon, for instance, drawing a large chunk of the audience for such challenging literature.

There were some new writers who nonetheless created a stir. Amongst them were writers coming out of Generation X. Picking up on the heels of an earlier batch of similar writers from the 1980s, though leaving behind the gimmicky hipness associated with authors like Bret Easton Ellis, Jay McInerney, and Douglas Coupland, a new breed of Gen X writers created considerable critical stir. *The Secret History* (1992), Donna Tartt's debut novel took many of the ideas of her predecessors (like Ellis, to whom Tartt dedicated the book) about identity and morality for this generation, and infused them with extensive allusions to classical literature. The plot, in fact, dealt with a group of classics students who reenact a Greek Bacchanal, and, under the influence of drugs and alleged Dionysian frenzy, murder a farmer. What follows is a fairly straightforward story of crime and secrets, but conveyed with almost overwhelming classicisms. Other writers in some ways reinvented the post-modernism of earlier generations. David Foster Wallace was often compared to Thomas Pynchon, especially upon the publication of his enormous novel *Infinite Jest* (1996), a 1,000-plus page chronicle of drug abuse and tennis. Likewise, Rick Moody published three novels in the 1990s, *Garden State* (1992), *The Ice Storm* (1994), and *Purple America* (1997), which demonstrated skillful experimentation with narrative forms and points of view. *The Ice Storm*, for instance told the story of family strife from a first person perspective, a perspective that was not actually revealed until the final page. But more than simple narrative gamesmanship, Wallace and Moody demonstrated a sharp streak of humanity, their experimentations used not strictly to draw attention to storytelling techniques, but to the psychology underlying the characters manipulated by techniques.

POETRY AND MEMOIR

It has been reported that there were over 1,700 magazines in America that published poetry, but lest this number suggest an enormous number of poetry readers, it should be noted that most of these publications did not, in fact, exceed a thousand issues in circulation. Moreover, in this decade, a large portion of the audience for poetry was, in fact, the poets themselves.[19] Truthfully, this was not the friendliest decade for poetry, but then neither were those which preceded it. By 1990, poetry had become something of a marginal art form, quite limited in its audience, to small-press journals, and the occasional performance. *Cowboy poetry,* both live and in print, garnered some attention, though such attention was usually regional, not widespread. Likewise, poetry slams, a kind of high-energy recitation contest, proliferated, though this too was confined, particularly to college campuses and clubs catering to artistic patrons. The most successful book of poetry of the 1990s was not by an established poet, but by singer-song-writer Jewel Kilcher. In 1995, PBS broadcast *The Language of Life with Bill Moyers,* an eight-episode series featuring 18 poets. The program was critically praised and well-received by those who saw it. But the show inspired no one to follow suit and it remains the only one of its kind to be produced in the 1990s. Yet despite this, more poetry books were being published than ever before, suggesting that, small as the audience might be, it was a committed one. Notably, publication of traditionally marginalized groups— African Americans, Latinos, homosexuals—increased, bolstered by small presses devoted entirely to such groups.[20]

Many poets also delved into other genres to express themselves, a strategy that often opened them up to larger audiences, all the while stirring up interest in their verse. Memoir writing grew significantly during the 1990s and proved to be the genre most inviting to many poets, including Mary Karr whose memoir, *The Liar's Club,* was widely read and well-received. In all, memoirs shot to a new popularity, with several titles amongst the best-selling non-fiction books of the decade. Two of the most successful were Mitch Albom's *Tuesdays with Morrie* (1998), detailing the author's interaction with an elderly man who served as a kind of life advisor, which sold about a million copies in its first year, and Frank McCourt's *Angela's Ashes* (1996), about the author's childhood in a Irish ghetto, which spent more than one hundred weeks on the best-sellers list.

SELF-HELP

Of course, there was more to the literary world of the 1990s than fiction, poetry, and memoir; many other non-fiction genres experienced notable success as well. Self-help books enjoyed continued popularity. Besides the Oprah-assisted *Simple Abundance,* a number of self help books made it to the best-seller lists. Of these, most were of the relationship sub-genre, and the most popular of these was John Gray's *Men Are From Mars, Women Are From Venus,* which argued that men and women had very different psychological make-ups (as implied by the Roman god and goddess of the title), and that the genders needed to accept this difference in order to make their relationships work. The book claimed a spot on the non-fiction lists for more than 200 weeks. A more fleeting best-seller was *The Rules* (1996) by Ellen Fein and Sherrie Schneider, a book characterized by its detractors as little more than a guide to manipulating men into marriage. Perhaps the biggest success of the self-help category, however, was no single book so much as it was the self-help series. Long-lasted as the best-seller status of *Men Are from Mars, Women Are from Venus* may have been, it was finite, but Gray was savvy enough to hit the public with numerous variations and elaborations of this blockbuster, like *Mars and Venus in the Bedroom* (1995) and *Mars and Venus Starting Over* (1998). Then there were the books in Richard Canfield's series starting with the volume *Chicken Soup for the Soul.* These collections of inspiring stories were geared to virtually every possible audience: *Chicken Soup for the Woman's Soul, Chicken Soup for the Teenager's Soul, Chicken Soup for the Pet Lover's Soul, Chicken Soup for the Veteran's Soul,* etcetera. A similar, though decidedly more limited series was spawned from William Bennett's *The Book of Virtues* (1993), followed by *The Moral Compass* (1995) and *The Book of Virtue for Kids* (1995).

Another series encompassed the material generally treated in self-help books, plus much more. Begun particularly as a series of books to assist individuals with the varying aspects of computer technology, the *for Dummies* series soon expanded beyond its initial confines. Even as books like *Windows 98 for Dummies* continued to dominate the computer book market, publisher IDG successfully introduced titles like *Success for Dummies* (1997) by Zig Ziglar. Macmillan/QUE publishers followed suit with their *The Complete Idiot's Guide to...* series, and between them and IDG, an astonishing number of topics were covered, from *Diabetes for Dummies* to *The Complete Idiot's Guide to Hypnosis.*

The self-help market as a whole was frequently criticized, however. Even Harriet Lerner, author of the popular *The Dance of Deception: Pretending and Truth-Telling in Women's Lives* (1993), itself generally categorized as a self-help book, accused many books of the genre as "simplify[ing] human experience with platitudes, inspirational messages, recipes for success, self evaluation quizzes, and explain-everything guides to personal empowerment, self-esteem, and relational bliss."[21] Meanwhile, Wendy Kaminer published *I'm Dysfunctional, You're Dysfunctional* (1992), a scathing critique of self-help books and the industry that produced them, which allegedly encouraged more guilt in readers in the interest of selling more product.

RELIGIOUS LITERATURE

The 1990s also saw a resurgence in books on religion and spirituality. Not surprisingly, some titles were assisted on their way to the top by mentions on Oprah Winfrey's show, such as Gary Zukov's *Seat of the Soul* (1998) and Neale Donald Walsch's *Conversations with God* and its sequels. Then there was Deepak Chopra whose books walked the line between spirituality, self-help, and health (and who even published a novel, *The Return of Merlin,* in 1995.) His books, which expounded the ideas of "mind-body medicine" included best-sellers *Ageless Body, Timeless Mind* (1994) and *The Seven Spiritual*

Laws of Success, just two of more than a dozen books published by the pro-lific author starting in 1987.[22]

Also experiencing tremendous growth in the decade was the market for books about angels, ranging from art books, to inspirational story collec-tions, to canonical guides to angels in religion. A 1993 report estimated that since 1990 some 200 books about angels had been published.[23] The rise of angel imagery, both in publishing and elsewhere (as on the popular tele-vision show *Touched by an Angel*), and, indeed, the growth of the religious book market as a whole, may be attributable to fears about the end of the millennium, a claim supported by a large number of books that engaged the topic directly, books like *The Y2K Bug* and *The Y2K Personal Survival Guide* by Michael Hyatt, and Edward and Jennifer Yourdon's *Time Bomb 2000.*[24]

The same might have had some bearing on the popularity of a series of religious novels by Jerry B. Jenkins and Tim LaHaye. While religious fiction had always enjoyed a reasonably strong niche success, this series, begun with *Left Behind* (1995), mustered more and more popularity with each vol-ume, until it competed with mainstream literature on the best-seller lists. The books detailed the coming of the end times, beginning with the rapture, in which those in God's good graces are taken away. Thereafter, some of those left behind form a "tribulation force" (the title of the second novel, published in 1996) to battle the devil. Besides espousing a religious philos-ophy, the novels also provided exciting supernatural adventure stories, which garnered them readership not only among the devoutly religious, but through a much larger segment of the American Christian population.

CHILDREN'S BOOKS

Unlike so many other areas of publishing, children's book publishers, by and large, were not treated quite so kindly by the 1990s. Certainly, sales stayed consistent, but they failed to achieve the growth of other areas of the book industry. This is particularly notable in light of the significant growth of children's publishing in the latter half of the eighties and the early years of the 1990s. Part of the slump may have been due to natural market slowing as the children's book market settled and matured, but also of account are the distractions of other media.[25] While television had long been identified as an enemy of children's reading, the 1990s presented yet a new media challenge as the computer, as well as electronic game systems like Playstation, rose to greater prominence. Though other media might have hurt children's sales in general, book tie-ins also helped to maintain stability in the market. Of course, tie-ins to Disney films were as popular as ever, with books published in every format, for every reading level, from every one of its feature films. Likewise, books featuring television and video game characters, as well as characters from the *Pokémon* collectible card game, had a strong reception, even if books from entirely original concepts struggled.

Despite the slowdown, however, there were great success stories to report from the children's market. In the first half of the 1990s, one of the greatest of these successes was R. L. Stine and his *Goosebumps* series. This series of horror novels aimed at young readers started in 1989 and continued steadily into the 1990s. The series became an immediate success with readers, largely due to a deft combination of safe scares and humor, and continued to grow in popularity until 1996 when it experienced a marked decline in sales, contributing largely to an overall 25% sales slump for publisher Scholastic.[26] Still the success of the series cannot be denied, as more than 160 million copies of *Goosebumps* books were printed, with more than a hundred different novels printed. Stine also made a successful foray into young adult literature with his Fear Street line, and inspired numerous, if less successful, imitators. Stine also wrote and published his first adult novel, *Superstitious,* in 1995. It was a critical and commercial flop, but the author found solace in the fact that he remained the best-selling author: "I might sell 30 million books this year, and no one else comes close. Of course...no one else writes 24 a year."[27]

Series books, especially young reader series, proved popular in general during the decade, particularly *The Baby-Sitters Club* and *American Girls* series, geared towards a female audience. The *American Girls* series was, in fact, several series, each following a particular young girl protagonist, living in a particular time period and region of America, subject to day-to-day routines, as well as to the sweeping historical forces of the day. Another very successful series and the series that would help lift Scholastic up after the *Goosebumps* decline, was K. A. Applegate's *Animorphs. Animorphs* told the story of a group of youths granted the power to morph into various animals. The power was given to them by an alien who hoped to recruit them to stave off the invasion of Earth by another hostile alien race. The series appealed to a number of interests: thriller, science fiction, and animals. Introduced in June 1996, *Animorphs,* assisted by a considerable promotional push, received an even greater initial interest than did either The *Baby-sitters Club* or *Goosebumps* series.[28]

Of course, no discussion of children's books in the 1990s would be complete without mention of J. K. Rowling's Harry Potter books, about a child, raised in ignorance by his aunt and uncle, who discovers that he is heir to a family of sorcerers and to some very powerful magic. The first volume, *Harry Potter and the Sorcerer's Stone,* was released in the U.S. (it was originally published in Rowling's native England as *Harry Potter and the Philosopher's Stone*) in September 1998. It became a quick success and enchanted many readers with its richly drawn fantasy, reminiscent of that of C. S. Lewis. That it became a children's best-seller is perhaps no surprise. But it became much more than that in time. Book two in the projected seven-book series, *Harry Potter and the Chamber of Secrets,* was published in the U.S. in June 1999, and the third volume, *Harry Potter and the Prisoner of Azkaban,* later that same year. At decades end, three *Harry Potter* books occupied three spots on the best-seller lists simultaneously. Such was the success of the first three books that in 2000, prior to the publication of the next novel, the *New York Times* began a separate best-seller list for children's books, thereby freeing four slots in the straight fiction list for adult works.

MAGAZINES

The magazine market grew greatly in the nineties, despite fears that on-line magazines might stifle the demand for the print variety. In a few cases this was true. Certainly, newspapers continued a decline that had started decades earlier, as Americans turned increasingly to television for news. Likewise, in the nineties online news cut further into newspaper profits. The difficulty of the newspaper business forced many independent publishers to close their doors, or to sell out to media conglomerates. By 1995, eight companies, Gannett, Knight-Ridder, Advance Publications, Times Mirror, Tribune Company, Cox Newspapers, Hearst, and the Washington Post Company owned over 185 daily newspapers. The challenge posed by online news content also led many papers to themselves explore online publishing, and in 1995, these eight conglomerates formed a national network of on-line newspapers.[29]

Some men's magazines suffered as a result of the Internet's growth. *Penthouse* and other adult periodicals found that the easy accessibility of pornography on-line undercut their sales considerably. *Playboy,* which did not rely strictly on nudity for its content, fared considerably better, and so too did a new breed of men's magazine. *Maxim,* originally published in Britain, made its U.S. debut in 1997 to immediate success. The magazine bridged the gap between *Playboy* and magazines like *GQ* and *Esquire* with its mix of fashion, news, sports, entertainment, and, especially, women. Less naughty than *Playboy, Maxim* featured plenty of pictures of scantily clad women. That the women were not nude (or, at least, provocatively obscured) made *Maxim* less risqué than other men's magazines, so it could be carried in a wider number of locations, even in supermarkets. Moreover, famous actresses and models who were not willing to pose nude were happy to pose for *Maxim,* which gave the magazine a further boost in sales. The magazine also sought a more populist tone than other magazines, or as publisher Lance Ford claimed, "The tone of the old guard, the *GQ*s, the *Playboy*s, is snooty."[30] The formula was repeated by numerous other magazines, including *Stuff, Bikini,* and the most successful this side of *Maxim, FHM (For Him Magazine).*

It has been estimated that by 1990 there were more than 10,000 magazine titles being published in the U.S. The number is difficult to confirm given the continued popularity of small-press low-circulation 'zines. Although a growing number of these moved their operations to cyberspace, the advances in desktop publishing also made it easier than ever for individuals to create hard-copy publications. Widely distributed magazines seemed to cover every possible category, geared towards niche audiences: parents, Christians, hip-hop listeners, rock collectors, and so on. Like newspapers, many magazines coupled their paper content with on-line publications. The sheer number of magazines makes a comprehensive consideration unreasonable, but a few new titles deserve mention. In 1992, Time Warner began publishing *Entertainment Weekly*, but one of a surfeit of popular entertainment/celebrity magazines. A new major beauty and fashion magazine, *Allure*, first published in 1991, attempted to set itself apart from the crowded field by emphasizing a non-traditional approach to beauty. One of the most important periodicals to begin publication during the decade was *Martha Stewart's Living.* Launched in 1991, the magazine's focus on house and home, cooking and entertaining, and crafts, propelled Martha Stewart, already widely known for her books, to even greater fame.

CONCLUSION

Children's books, self-help, religion, history, memoir, fiction, both popular and high literature: the best-seller lists of the 1990s saw them all. The literary market in the last decade of the twentieth century certainly proved diverse, suggesting a wider breadth of book buyers than ever before, despite what fear might continue about the decline of literacy. Titles that appeared on the lists represented a mixture of the predictable and the surprising, but the true excitement of the decade was not merely contained between covers, but in the very nature of the literary world. With the changes in the way literature was disseminated, the book industry entered a brave new world, one in which books might soon become available on demand, or perhaps eliminated altogether in favor of electronic displays of texts. In any case, the direction of the book market changed, and publishers, distributors, and retailers scurried to anticipate the latest developments. Yet for all of this, readers remained largely the same, subject to trends as they might be, voraciously seeking wisdom, enlightenment, and entertainment in the pages of a growing multitude of books.

The 1990s

9

Music

NIRVANA

In the May 13, 1999 issue, *Rolling Stone* magazine proclaimed singer/songwriter Kurt Cobain their "Artist of the Decade,"[1] and perhaps there is no better place to begin a treatment of music in the 1990s than with consideration of Cobain, not only for his popularity as the front man for the band Nirvana, but also as a representative of changes happening in the 1990s music industry. In the 1990s, a great deal of music that had previously been directed to a niche audience—not only alternative rock and pop, but also soul, country, rap, and more—became mainstream. And although it would be a grand generalization to suggest that Nirvana alone was the reason for this, the band's influence on the opening up of the mainstream media to new kinds of music should not be underestimated.

Alternative rock, which had its roots in the punk rock and new wave of the 1970s and early 1980s, had, by the start of the 1990s, established a strong outlet, mostly through college radio and a few commercial stations. In fact, commercial radio in many cities found that there was indeed a sizeable market for rock and pop that existed outside of the established top forty programming formats. It is primarily through these alternative commercial and college stations that bands like Nirvana were first heard by many listeners, but it is a single song, with an aggressive guitar riff, bleak lyrics, and Cobain's screaming voice that made much of America sit up and take notice. The single, "Smells Like Teen Spirit," from the 1991 album *Nevermind*, seemed overnight to become an anthem for the nation's malaise, and particularly for America's youth culture. In writing about Nirvana, one critic stated "The teen spirit that is always in the ether can hover for years

Nirvana posed after receiving an award for best alternative video for "In Bloom" at the 10th annual MTV Video Music Awards, September 2, 1993, in Universal City, California. Members from left are, Chris Novoselic, Dave Grohl, and Kurt Cobain. Man at right is not a member of the band and is unidentified. © AP/Wide World Photos.

without coalescing into anything more than a haze—that vague, uneasy, something-in-the-air feeling rising like swamp gas as a byproduct of living young and unsteady in a hostile world that hasn't yet made its intentions clear. But it can also go off with a spectacular atmospheric bang."[2] There certainly seems to be some truth to the claim that "Smells Like Teen Spirit" was such a catalyst. Moreover, this song also signaled that supposed niche music could indeed find a wider audience, and even, as was the case with *Nevermind*, merit enormous commercial success.

Nirvana had its birth in the late 1980s, as part of Seattle, Washington's Sub Pop scene. The Sub Pop record label had made a name for itself as the label of numerous bands whose inspirations came in part from punk, but also infused other musical styles, especially the melodicism of 1970s hard rock, into the mix. The most notable of these bands was Soundgarden, who predated Nirvana (even though, ironically, Nirvana's success would open commercial avenues for Soundgarden). Nirvana released their first album, *Bleach*, in 1989 and was, along with much of Sub Pop's catalogue, immediately well-received by alternative radio. But although it demonstrated the aggression and melodicism that would become Nirvana's hallmark, *Bleach* lacked the spirit and the popular accessibility, the catchy song writing that would bring the band its great acclaim. Two years and two EPs later, Nirvana released *Nevermind*, which would eventually sell over seven million copies. On this record, original members Cobain and Chris (later Krist) Novoselic were joined by drummer Dave Grohl, and the music coalesced into a melodic wall of sound that was impossible to ignore. "Smells Like Teen Spirit," the opening track, demonstrated a hallmark of Cobain's writing style, alternating between cleanly played guitar chords, with lyrics sung in a lazy, almost mumbled style, and then an explosion of distortion and shrieking. But formula aside, the key to the song and the band's success was Cobain's sense of melody. Behind the aggression and the noise was a remarkably well constructed pop song, one that took listeners to another place, one to which listeners could hum along. Although no song could hope to capture the success (and status) of "Smells Like Teen Spirit," the Cobain formula resulted in numerous hits from *Nevermind* and its follow-up album, *In Utero*.

Part of Nirvana's appeal was undoubtedly the implied lack of control suggested by Cobain's lyrics. The songs of Nirvana were haunted by self-deprecation, paranoia, disassociation, and even a sense of contempt for the world of pop music and its fans, as in the song "In Bloom," which lambasted the fans who had no appreciation or understanding of lyrics. Unfortunately, the lack of control that seemed very carefully constructed on *Nevermind* began to manifest itself in more troubling ways, both in Nirvana's music and Cobain's life. While an exciting record, *In Utero* seemed more fragile and lacked the self-control of *Nevermind*. The result was a less commercial album whose every twist and turn was a surprise, but which also very likely reflected the instability of Cobain's mental and emotional state. Although the band managed a performance on the TV show *MTV Unplugged* that would later be released as a CD, *In Utero* would be their final studio record, as Cobain fell further under the thrall of drug, health, and emotional problems. In April 1994, a short five years after Nirvana's debut, Cobain died in his Seattle home of a self-inflicted shotgun wound.[3]

Although many noted an increasingly self-destructive impulse on Cobain's part, his death sent shockwaves throughout the country. His suicide at the age of 27, followed by a funeral vigil by fans and an around-the-clock tribute on MTV, led many to proclaim Cobain the latest rock 'n' roll martyr, in line with Keith Moon, John Lennon, Janice Joplin, and others. True or not, Cobain and Nirvana were far from forgotten, as the subject of numerous books and movies. Moreover, those associated with Nirvana went on to other projects, keeping the memory of the band alive. Novoselic formed a band called Sweet 75, while Grohl found enormous success with his new band, The Foo Fighters. Meanwhile, Cobain's widow, Courtney Love, found continued fame as the front woman for the band Hole and as a minor film actress, in movies like *Feeling Minnesota* (1996) and *The People vs. Larry Flynt* (1996).

GRUNGE AND ALTERNATIVE HARD ROCK

Ultimately, Nirvana's influence was far more wide-reaching. Even as Nirvana emerged from the world of punk and alternative rock, that world was dragged into the limelight with them. The term *grunge* came to be applied to numerous bands that came to light during the early 1990s, and especially to those on the Sub Pop label and coming out of Seattle. Several grunge bands, including Soundgarden, Alice in Chains, and Stone Temple Pilots, would find considerable commercial success, in part due to the trailblazing of Nirvana. Second only to Nirvana in fame was Pearl Jam, led by singer Eddie Vedder. Pearl Jam's melodies drew more from heavy metal and seventies rock than did Nirvana's, and also left out much of the self-deprecating humor of Cobain's lyrics, instead opting for pseudo-cerebral existential sensitivity. The real appeal of Pearl Jam was Vedder's almost hyper-emotive vocals. Pearl Jam's 1991 debut *Ten*, which sold over six million copies, offered up a sense of seriousness and profundity (more attributable to Vedder's voice than his lyrics). It was clear from *Ten* and the records that followed, including *Vs.* (1993), *Vitalogy* (1994), which both entered the charts at number one, that Pearl Jam was a band that took itself very seriously, and one that warmed up to its commercial success far more easily than did Cobain, and as a result, their music provided a higher comfort level for fans of the grunge sound than did other bands.[4]

The success of grunge also opened doors for bands with an equally aggressive sound that might not be strictly considered grunge. Smashing Pumpkins, for instance, developed a rather unique sound of its own, melding not only grunge, but also seventies rock and the gothic rock sound of the 1980s. Smashing Pumpkin's songs on their debut *Gish* (1991), their breakthrough recording *Siamese Dream,* and their sprawling two-disc concept album *Mellon Collie and the Infinite Sadness,* were marked by deep (and often bleak) introspection and full-out rage, but what particularly stood out was front man Billy Corgan's distinctively thin and reedy voice.

Also stirring up the flames of alternative rock was Rage Against The Machine, a multi-ethnic band marked by a mixture of hardcore punk, hip hop, and heavy metal, with a dash of reggae, and fiery political lyrics. That political polemics (particularly of the radical left) were not widespread in the pop music of the 1990s makes Rage Against The Machine that much more remarkable. The band's self-titled debut in 1992 introduced themes to which the band would return frequently: social injustice, power politics, and especially racism. Punk rock had long explored such themes, but Rage Against The Machine were a commercial success well beyond other such groups. Moreover, they masterfully made sure that they were seen, often playing benefit concerts and openly protesting what they saw as unjust, such as the imprisonment of Native American Leonard Peltier.[5]

Similar in sound, if not in politics, to Rage Against the Machine were a number of new hard rock bands that blended crunching guitars with hip hop beats and vocals. From Bakersfield, California, Korn gained a large following, constituted mostly of men in their late teens and early twenties, with unrelentingly aggressive music and lyrics. Though not especially melodic, Korn's hostility, along with occasional interesting instrumentation—singer Jonathan Davis played bagpipes—made them a mainstay of hard rock radio. Their 1998 release, *Follow the Leader,* their third after *Korn* (1994) and *Life is Peachy* (1996), debuted at the top spot of *Billboard* magazine's list of top 200 albums and spawned the hit singles "Got the Life" and "Freak on a Leash." The album also included "All in the Family," which featured guest vocals by Fred Durst, the front man for a like-minded band, Limp Bizkit. Leaning more heavily on rap, were rap-rock performers like Insane Clown Posse, known as much for their costuming and makeup as for their music, and Kid Rock, who also threw country stylings in the mix. These bands inspired no shortage of other bands into mixing rock and rap, a trend which continued at full strength into the new millennium.

Also of note is the success of Marilyn Manson, which had its roots in the noise-laden industrial pop of the late 1980s, as pioneered by bands like Ministry and Nine Inch Nails. The music of Marilyn Manson incorporated the same power guitar riffs, amusical noise, and distorted vocals often found in the music of its progenitors. However, it is less likely that the band will be remembered for its music than it will be for its shtick. Marilyn Manson, the man whose stage name leant itself to the band, became as well known for his costuming, which combined drag queen with horror movie walking undead, and onstage antics. The sex-and-death motif of their music, shows, appearance, and stage names combining those of sex starlets and serial killers (à la Madonna Wayne Gacy), earned Marilyn Manson immediate and widespread publicity, but also raised the ire of more than a few parents and community leaders. Performances by the band were barred in several areas, and the music of the band was linked to several acts of high school violence, used as a scapegoat to explain why teenage boys would be moved to act out so violently. The criticisms of Marilyn Manson spread to include all *gothic* music, and while many were quick to point out that Marilyn Manson had little to do with the gloomy gothic rock that was born in the 1980s, the term *gothic* nonetheless became identified with bands like Marilyn Manson.[6]

THE MAINSTREAMING OF ALTERNATIVE ROCK

With the popularization of this kind of alternative music, came the rise of alternative commercial radio. Previously, alternative rock had largely been the domain of the college radio stations, which were not subject to the same kind of rating and advertising pressures as commercial radio. There

People throw debris into one of the many bonfires set at Woodstock '99 near the end of the three-day event on the former Griffiss Air Force Base in Rome, N.Y., July 25, 1999. © AP/Wide World Photos.

had been commercial alternative stations since at least the early 1980s, and that number did increase somewhat throughout that decade, but these were mostly confined to coastal urban areas, such as Los Angeles and New York. But the 1990s saw the spread of alternative radio to much wider markets. Particularly, large corporations came to control local stations, and they would play alternative rock, but the same alternative rock from region to region. In addition, alternative rock festivals, like Lollapalooza and several festivals starting in 1994 under the name "Woodstock," became some of the most successful live music events in the nation. Woodstock '99, however, demonstrated how different these were from the original Woodstock of the 1960s. The crass commercialism of the festival as well as widespread violence, fully distanced this disastrous concert event from its namesake. Combined with the continued popularity of MTV music television, corporate radio and the rock festival tours contributed to a growing homogeneity, even in the traditionally eclectic and localized world of alternative rock. Among other things, this encouraged the popularity of bands that were only mildly alternative, veering closer to a kind of adult-contemporary sound, like Hootie and the Blowfish and Barenaked Ladies. These bands found a generally older audience than did the Nirvanas and Pearl Jams, ultimately providing an alternative for listeners who didn't require a particularly hard edge to their music.

One of the particular bright spots among these bands was The Dave Matthews Band. This group, led by Matthews, a South African relocated to Charlottesville, Virginia, garnered much attention for the multicultural, multiethnic lineup of musicians, including a saxophonist and a violinist, which was echoed in their music, a melding of many styles. The band's base was acoustic rock, but the audible influences were much wider, including folk, jazz, and world music. With their early independent releases (on the Bama Rags label), including their debut, *Remember Two Things* (1993), the Dave Matthews Band developed a solid following, even though they had yet to gain much radio airplay. With 1994's *Under the Table and Dreaming* and 1996's *Crash,* however, the band established itself as a major act, both on radio and live. Indeed, by the end of the decade, The Dave Matthews Band would become one of the most sought-after live act, their musical virtuosity, catchy songs, and front man's affable nature routinely packing venues.

WOMEN IN ROCK

There was also a strong female presence in alternative music during the 1990s, which is perhaps best represented by the establishment of an annual festival primarily devoted to women's music: the Lilith Fair. The festival was primarily the brainchild of Sarah McLachlan, who was a part of a swell of popular women artists that began in the late 1980s. McLachlan's first album, *Touch* (1988), made her a pop star in her native Canada, but it's with her follow-ups *Solace* (1991) and *Fumbling Towards Ecstasy* (1994) that she truly established herself in the United States. Influenced by the music of Kate Bush, these layered, guitar- and piano-driven records most prominently featured McLachlan's rich, airy voice and introspective, and frequently melancholy lyrics. McLachlan, very aware that her music had found a large audience of female listeners, became a strong proponent of women's music and argued that the music industry, particularly in terms of live performance, was not terribly kind to female artists other than those whose prime asset was their sex appeal, like the Spice Girls and Britney Spears. The Lilith Fair was her largely successful attempt to rectify this, at least in part.

The popularity of Lilith Fair, as well as that of McLachlan and other women working in the same vein, like Tori Amos, whose quirkiness perhaps worked against her achieving McLachlan's level of success, served as an inspiration to other women as well as creating a more welcoming environment in the music industry. While there was no shortage of McLachlan imitators, there were many women developing their own distinct sound. Ani DiFranco, whose professional career began nearly as early as

McLachlan's, gained a considerable boost in popularity from that singer's success. Graced with skills both as a vocalist and guitar player, DiFranco was also notable for her do-it-yourself attitude, which inspired her to handle most of her own production work and to self-release her albums on her own label, Righteous Babe. Alanis Morissette, another Canadian, had made several innocuous pop albums in the early 1990s before the 1995 release of *Jagged Little Pill,* a multi-platinum album of often cynical, frequently angry, yet catchy pop songs. Jewel (surname Kilcher) released her first record, *Pieces of You,* in 1995. A highly skilled if sometimes self-indulgent vocalist, Jewel drew as much from traditional folk music as from the pop world. Sheryl Crowe, initially as popular for her statuesque good looks as for her music, proved herself with folk- and blues-based rock 'n' roll, and an appealing mixture of tough and vulnerable vocals. Fiona Apple, a teenaged singer with a voice sounding much, much older, released her debut *Tidal* in 1996 to critical and commercial applause, and occasional accusations that her sexually charged material (and videos) were inappropriate for someone of her age. Apple also gained a reputation for her tirades, including one at the MTV music awards, wherein she announced that "this world is bullshit." But this didn't stop her popularity; she sold several million copies of *Tidal* and, in 1998, was voted Female Performer of the Year by readers of *Rolling Stone.*[7]

HEAVY METAL

Alongside the popularization of alternative rock, there were inroads made by other genres of music as well. Heavy metal, while still limited in its radio appeal, continued to accumulate a significant following, particularly among young men in their teens and twenties. In the late 1980s, heavy metal seemed to be acquiring some of the respect that had previously evaded it. Although this was the age of *hair* bands, like Poison and Cinderella, there was also a ground swell of harder metal bands that eschewed the glam of the mainstream. A Grammy Award for best hard rock/heavy metal act was introduced in 1989, and while its first recipient, the classic rock group Jethro Tull, raised the eyebrows and the ire of many heavy metal fans, the award marked a change in the general conception of the genre. Both the 1980s and 1990s saw the genre spread into a number of sub-genres, such as thrash metal, speed metal, and death metal. Death metal, particularly received considerable criticism for its frequent use of violent imagery and its almost obsessive attention to the theme of death and decay. An offshoot of death metal in the 1990s was black metal, which took the themes and sounds of death metal to further extremes, frequently mingling sacrilegious imagery with that of death, and filtered them through heavily distorted and artificially deepened vocals. These bands, perhaps best exemplified by Morbid Angel, were frequently lumped together with bands like Marilyn Manson, and cited as corrupting influences on America's youth.

Unsurprisingly, despite its growing sales, most heavy metal failed to garner much radio play, as stations instead latched on to grunge-derived sounds for their aggression. But there were exceptions, such as Metallica. From its beginnings with the 1983 speed metal record *Kill 'Em All*, Metallica built the strongest following of any band of its kind, kicking off the 1990s with a bang as it grabbed the 1990 heavy metal Grammy. Throughout the 1990s, the band continued to prosper as it became more melodic, while never losing its bleak and aggressive outlook. While heavy metal may have influenced the grunge bands that were so popular in the 1990s, Metallica remained unarguably the most successful true metal band of the decade, meriting high sales for its albums *Metallica* (1991), *Load* (1996), *Re-Load* (1997), *Garage Inc.* (1998), and *S&M* (1999).

RAP AND HIP-HOP

Like heavy metal, rap and hip-hop largely went ignored by most commercial radio, even as the sales figures for the genre shot sky high, and controversy plagued it. Many Americans first became aware of rap through the relatively accessible and non-controversial rapping of MC Hammer, Run-D.M.C., and the like in the 1980s. But in the early 1990s, a different side of rap came to light. In 1990, the group 2 Live Crew drew attention from around the world when a federal judge in Florida ruled its album *As Nasty as They Wanna Be* (1989) to be obscene, due to its explicitly sexual lyrics. The ruling gave 2 Live Crew the dubious distinction of being the first musical group of any kind to have a record legally declared obscene in the United States, but it also pushed their sales way up. Despite (or perhaps because of) the group's popularity, authorities, especially those in Florida, continued to target the group and their music, raiding live shows and arresting and prosecuting record store owners and clerks for selling the record to minors and adults alike. After the arrest of several members of 2 Live Crew at an adults only show at a Florida night club, the group went to trial. At the trial, Duke University English professor Henry Louis Gates argued that the group was "engaged in sexual carnivalesque," a "part of a venerable Western tradition."[8] Even some less in tune with cultural history questioned the merits of the trial, noting that equally explicit material could be found in other musical forms, as well as in recently published literary works. This led some to suspect that 2 Live Crew were singled out in part because they were black, and therefore more threatening, say, than a white comedian with equally lascivious material, like the popular Andrew Dice Clay. Ultimately, 2 Live Crew was acquitted and the obscenity ruling on their album reversed, but the controversy surrounding rap was far from over.

Particularly targeted for attack, on counts of misogyny and encouraging violence, was so-called Gangsta Rap. This genre of rap can arguably be said to have its source in the music of Public Enemy, whose records, including *It Takes a Nation of Millions to Hold Us Back* (1988), *Fear of a Black Planet* (1990), and *Apocalypse 91 . . . The Enemy Strikes Black* (1991), brought a new political consciousness to rap. But while Public Enemy reported on the conditions of African American communities, it was groups like N.W.A. (for Niggas With Attitude) that dragged their listeners deep into that world. N.W.A. painted a brutal picture of their home, Compton in South Central Los Angeles. Their lyrics detailed drug deals and gang wars in explicit and violent terms, and while these helped drive all of their albums up the charts, they also opened the group up to attack. While some critics lambasted them for the violence and disrespect towards women in their lyrics, others applauded the group for their honest portrayal of life in the lower-class African American 'hood. Several individual members of the group would go on to their own solo success during the course of the decade. Ice Cube had perhaps the greatest success, with a string of critically praised albums, starting with *AmeriKKKa's Most Wanted* in 1990, that continued with the themes established in N.W.A., though arguably with greater sophistication. He also started a modest career acting in film. Eazy E also began a successful solo stint, but was cut short by his death of AIDS in 1995. Meanwhile, Dr. Dre cofounded his own label, Death Row Records.[9]

The name Death Row was chosen in part because of the criminal background of many of the executives and recording artists on the label, so it is perhaps not surprising that the label was plagued with violence and run-ins with the law. Cofounder Marion "Sugar Beat" Knight was surrounded by rumors of violent behavior, and, while he denied such rumors, he openly admitted to ruling by intimidation as much as by business acumen, an attitude that may well have contributed to a major rivalry with Sean "P. Diddy" Combs and his Bad Boy label. Meanwhile, Death Row's top artist Snoop Doggy Dogg was being tried on murder charges. Though treating the usual themes of gangsta violence, womanizing, and drug use, Snoop Doggy Dogg was unusual in his oddly sing-song, playful raps. Employing the more traditional swagger and aggression of gangsta rap, Tupac "2Pac" Shakur was actually recruited from his jail cell by Knight, even as his record *Me Against the World* (1995) was selling phenomenally, topping the charts. This all lent credence to the accusations of rap's violent nature, as did the growing rivalry between Death Row and Bad Boy. Although it was never proven that the conflict resulted directly in violence, the period saw the murders of several involved with the labels, including Tupac Shakur in 1996 and Bad Boy's most popular artist, the Notorious B.I.G., in early 1997. Death Row eventually dissolved as it was abandoned by Snoop Doggy Dogg and by Dr. Dre who formed his own label, Aftermath Entertainment. Knight was ultimately incarcerated for violating parole.[10]

Another important figure in gangsta rap was Ice-T who, like Ice Cube, would eventually take up acting as well, even as he continued to explore various musical genres. Ice-T had spent his early years engaged in gang and criminal activity in Los Angeles. In the early 1980s, Ice-T became interested in rapping, eventually releasing his first album in 1987. He quickly developed a considerable following and stirred up considerable controversy, both of which would hit their peak in 1992 with the formation of his heavy metal band, Body Count, and the release of the band's self-titled album. The band was rather simplistic both musically and lyrically, but Ice-T's intentions seemed less aesthetic than political. For starters, the band itself was an anomaly: heavy metal, the traditional domain of young middle-class white men, was now being performed by an angry black man from the 'hood. Were that not enough, Body Count's songs certainly made it clear that Ice-T was not one to steer away from controversy. A song called "Cop Killer" sparked more than a little hostility towards the rapper-cum-rocker from the law enforcement community, and even vice-president Dan Quayle blamed the song for encouraging violence against police officers. Amidst the controversy, the Body Count album would eventually be re-released without "Cop Killer," a move which garnered less praise from authorities than criticism from other artists who derided Ice-T for caving in to external pressure.[11]

Ice-T, N.W.A., Death Row Records and the ilk opened the floodgates to a barrage of other rappers engaging in like gangsta rhymes, including The Geto Boys, Compton's Most Wanted, and others. The *Gangsta* label had long been questioned by many of the rappers whose work was being labeled as such, but there was no question that calling something gangsta was a wise commercial move. Former N.W.A. member M.C. Ren, for instance complained about how "Everyday a new rapper comes out. They label him a gangsta rapper. And they be in the videos with a million guns. In the pictures and the magazines everybody's got a gun, everybody's wearing the same clothes. They've commercialized it."[12] Indeed, many rappers viewed gangsta as having become more concerned with fashion than with personal and political expression.

Because of this, as well as the violence and misogyny in so much of the music, it's unsurprising that there should be a backlash against gangsta and hardcore rap from within the hip hop community. The Native Tongues family, a loose-knit conglomeration of rap artists coming originally out of New York in the mid-eighties, eschewed themes of violence and criminality. Native Tongue bands like De La Soul, the Jungle Brothers, and A Tribe Called Quest explored political issues, but in a generally less bombastic way than did Public Enemy, less interested in attacking the dominant culture as in celebrating their own *Afrohumanist* culture. More importantly, these rappers explored the bounds of rap musically, frequently drawing from soul, blues, and jazz for their melodic and rhythmic structures. This style of rap also tended to be friendlier to women, whose Native Tongue

voices provided a welcome counter to the sexism of much rap. Queen Latifah stands as one of the most important female rap artists. Her first record,
released in 1989, received immediate critical and commercial success,
which she used as a springboard in the 1990s to further musical success, as
well as an acting career and significant activism in support of AIDS research
and ecology. On the other hand, the duo Black Sheep was an anomaly
among the Native Tongue Posse, with their decidedly lascivious and sexist lyrics. But even here, the sexism was playful, with the duo frequently
making self-deprecating fun of their own sexist attitudes.[13]

This kinder, gentler rap sound quickly spread throughout the nation,
reaching its commercial peak in the form of a Georgia group called Arrested
Development. This group not only celebrated their African roots, but also
their Southern upbringing, both in their clothing and their sung and rapped
vocals, which drew heavily from Southern Black music. Their first record,
released in 1992, was called *3 Years, 5 Months and 2 Days in the Life of...*, mark-
ing the time it took for the band to be signed to a record label. The album
went platinum within the year. Arrested Development showed many hip-
hop artists and the general American populace that rap need not be simply
about Black anger (nor had it always been prior to Arrested Development).[14]

Other bands followed in experimentation with musical styles and lyrics.
Cypress Hill made a name for themselves, particularly with their self-
titled debut in 1991 and 1993 follow-up *Black Sunday*, which went platinum
and spawned the hit single "Insane in the Brain." The two-thirds Latino
group gained notoriety for their frequent mingling of English and Span-
ish, and for their advocacy of marijuana use.[15]

Of course, with the success of rap, it was only natural that whites would
also make ventures into the world of hip hop. There had been white rappers before the 1990s, but Marky Mark and Vanilla Ice never did gain the
respect of the hip-hop community in the 1980s that white rappers did in
the 1990s. This may be because many of the newer white rappers were not
content merely copying the styles of a black music, but of expanding it to
capture their own experiences. The Beastie Boys, for instance, went well
beyond the silliness of their 1986 debut, developing a sound on *Check Your
Head* (1992), *Ill Communication* (1994), and *Hello Nasty* (1998) that borrowed
significantly from rap—rhythmically spoken lyrics and heavily layered
samples, for instance—but was almost a genre unto itself. The Beastie Boys
also started their own label, Grand Royal, which allowed them full creative
freedom and provided an avenue for others mining similar aural territory,
like the all-female group Luscious Jackson.

Following a similar pattern, was Beck, a singer-songwriter, who sprang
to nationwide popularity with the single "Loser," which despite its lo-fi
sound and sloppy vocals (by design) became a surprise hit. The single was
rereleased on Beck's debut, *Mellow Gold*, in 1994. *Mellow Gold* was an entertaining but uneven record which in no way prepared listeners for what

was to come on Beck's 1996 release, *Odelay,* on which, like the Beastie Boys before him, Beck delved into altogether new territory, leaving behind the amusing childishness of "Loser" in favor of surprisingly intelligent songs that only bore the slightest resemblance to traditional rap.

At the end of the decade, the most popular white rapper was Eminem. By his arrival on the scene, much of the controversy about rap had died down, as rappers expanded into new musical territories and the gangstas had largely dissipated (or were at least getting less attention than they had been). But with 1998's *The Slim Shady LP,* Eminem brought the controversy back to the front page. Eminem—Marshall Bruce Mathers III in his civilian guise— became a target almost immediately, even as *The Slim Shady LP* sold 480,000 in its first two weeks. Eminem's lyrics were accused of encouraging violent behavior, particularly against women and homosexuals. Indeed, the lyrics presented some of the most brutally graphic images to appear not only in rap, but in all of pop music. Eminem was defended as having created a persona. The Slim Shady of the title, it was argued, was not the same person as Eminem, nor was Eminem the same person as Mathers. Indeed, the defense was quite the opposite of that frequently used for gangsta rap, that it represented the violence of life in the 'hood. Instead, Eminem's raps were a twisted fiction—if laced with considerable truth—that ought to be taken as such. Eminem also received early flack for being a white artist performing black music, but such criticism was shortly diffused and Eminem was soon largely accepted, if not always approved of, by the hip-hop community. His debut album, after all, had been released on a real hip-hop label, Dr. Dre's Aftermath records. Dre admitted the awkwardness of the act, all the while standing by his choice to sign Eminem, saying "It's like seeing a black guy doing country and western, know what I'm saying?...You know, 'He's got blue eyes, he's a white kid.' But...If you can kick it, I'm working with you."[16]

The success of African-American performers was not limited to the world of rap, but also that of rhythm and blues (R&B). Yet interestingly, many artists, in looking to forge new ground, drew heavily from traditional soul. R&B performers like Janet Jackson and Mariah Carey successfully stuck to the familiar dance-pop sound that had carried their careers thus far. Yet on *The Miseducation of Lauren Hill* (1998), for instance, the former member of bohemian hip hop group the Fugees, found a new sound in mingling soul and doo-wop of earlier eras with a very modern hip-hop feel. Moreover, by the end of the 1990s, Macy Gray had become one of the top selling R&B performers, with a brassy soul sound that could well have come from decades earlier.

LATINO POP

Latinos also experienced numerous successes in the 1990s. There was, of course, a continued presence in various musical genres, from punk to heavy metal to hip hop, but the greatest successes were those working firmly in the world of mainstream pop, with Latin American stylings. Although performers like Gloria Estefan had garnered a certain amount of attention for Latin pop, no such performer had ever come even close to the visibility of one man: Ricky Martin. Martin, originally a member of mid-eighties teen pop vocal group Menudo, had already established himself in Latin America, especially his birthplace of Puerto Rico, when, in May of 1999, he released his first English language album, entitled simply *Ricky Martin*. Propelled largely by the energetic dance single "Livin' La Vida Loca," the album shot to the top of the pop charts. The song itself became virtually inescapable. As much a key to Martin's success, however, was his personality and performance style. A charming figure, it was hard not to like Martin, and whatever one thought of his music, none could deny that his onstage charisma and energy was something to be admired.[17]

Ricky Martin ultimately came to be seen as the spearhead of a new wave of Latin music, opening doors for other performers, including Mark Anthony, Enrique Iglesias, and singer/actress Jennifer Lopez. There is, however, a valid argument that Martin was at least as much of a product of the changes occurring in Latin music as their architect. In fact, Martin's attempts at crossover success are very much in the footsteps of singer Selena, who had made significant moves to expand her fan base to include non-Latinos, before her 1995 murder put a premature end to her promising career. Ultimately, the growth in Latin music's popularity was phenomenal, with annual sales reaching more than $570 million in 1998.[18] The success of Latin music in America was not especially surprising, given the rapid growth of the Latino population in the U.S. What is perhaps more surprising is that performers like Ricky Martin found such a warm welcome with a white, English-speaking audience. As Joe Trevino, the vice president of Hollywood Records Latin division explained, "We're the fastest-growing genre of music, and you're seeing more and more non-Latinos purchasing Latin music." The situation consequently put record companies in an interesting position, wherein they were required to market their wares both to Latino and Anglo audiences. Niche marketing was no longer sufficient given the breadth of the potential audience for Latin music.[19]

COUNTRY MUSIC

Country music also continued the move into the mainstream which was started in earnest in the 1980s, with the groundswell of younger performers and a move towards a much stronger adult-contemporary pop sound. Yet, as for so many other musical genres, the turn of the decade from the '80s to the '90s, signaled a major change in country's mainstream acceptance. 1989 saw the rise of country superstars like Travis Tritt, Clint Black, Vince Gill, and Mary Chapin Carpenter. And, more importantly, 1989 saw the chart debut of Garth Brooks. This Oklahoma singer-songwriter openly admitted to having rock as well as country influences, and both were clearly audible in his music, which, if stripped of Brook's country twang vocal and the occasional country instrumentation (i.e., slide guitar and fiddle), could easily be mistaken for mainstream soft rock. The combination of styles, in any case, proved phenomenally successful for Brooks, who would become the best-selling recording artist of the 1990s, selling over 100 million records. Interestingly, Brooks capped off his 1990s career by assuming the guise of a noncountry, rock 'n' roll artist, Chris Gaines.[20]

Brooks and his sort, however, were not accepted on all fronts. Some country purists complained that as these artists moved toward a stronger pop sound, they stripped country of its soul, taking away from it what made it unique. Ultimately, there was still an audience for old style country, and, fortunately, there were still old stalwarts, such as Johnny Cash and Waylon Jennings, making that kind of music. And there were fresh faces as well. Although possessing definite pop sensibilities (as evidenced by a later duet with Elton John and her subsequent recordings), singer LeAnne Rimes shot to stardom in 1996 with "Blue," a song which clearly nodded to the likes of Patsy Cline and which helped Rimes grab a Best New Artist Grammy. This is all the more remarkable for Rimes having been only 13-years-old at the time of the release of "Blue." Others that followed also gleefully stuck to the traditions of the country genre, in a movement alternately referred to as Americana, roots revival, and (ironically, given its closer adherence to traditional sounds) alternative-country. One of the most notable groups in this vein was the Dixie Chicks, a trio of women who had no compunction about flaunting their looks and fashion sense, but who also had a keen interest in preserving country's heritage. As lead singer Natalie Maines explained, "We take pride that we're bringing back older, traditional sounding things and making it sound more modern."[21]

MAINSTREAM POP

Even as the musical world seemed to expand in the 1990s, even as record companies became more adventurous with their releases, hoping to find the next Nirvana that would tap into a new (and profitable) sound, there was no shortage of traditional pop. Bubblegum pop had an enormous resurgence during the decade, with the music of young, mostly blonde girl singers and *boy bands* becoming virtually inescapable by the end of the decade. In truth, it could well be argued that the music of these youths was secondary, as they were largely being sold on their image. The boy bands, for instance, provided fans with non-threatening heartthrobs and playful, and never sexual, love songs. The girl singers, on the other hand, were frequently overly sexualized, raising no small bit of controversy, easily dwarfed by record sales.

Singer Britney Spears smiles as she holds one of her four MTV awards at a photocall in Dublin, Ireland, Nov. 11, 1999. The singer from Louisiana won the Best Female, Best Breakthrough, Best Pop Act, and Best Single for "Hit Me Baby One More Time," reflecting the 17-year-old's popularity with some two million telephone-voting MTV viewers across Europe. © AP/Wide World Photos.

Certainly skin and sex appeal were a very real part of the Spice Girls' success. This British group of five singers, bearing monikers like Sporty Spice and Ginger Spice, were almost immediately showered with criticisms: that they were style over substance, that they were more marketing than musical, that they catered to feminine stereotypes, even that they were racially inequitable (the one black member being called Scary Spice). Whatever the criticisms, however, the group's debut album, *Spice,* and the first single, "Wannabe," quickly reached the number one spot on the charts. In defense against the criticism, Posh Spice (Victoria Adams) suggested, "Everyone's entitled to an opinion. I don't think everyone's great. But, I mean, who's having the last laugh, eh? Come on."[22]

The Spice Girls found a considerable audience among young teen and pre-teen girls, and given this audience, some felt troubled by their sexed up image, especially that of Baby Spice, who was in her early twenties and capitalized on being the youngest member of the group. By the end of the decade, there would be a new breed of sexed-up teen singer that would make Baby Spice's sexuality seem tame by comparison. In 1999, singer Britney Spears released her debut album, ... *Baby One More Time,* which became one of the biggest selling records of the decade, selling over ten million copies before the end of the year. The music, buoyant dance pop, was derided as vapid by some critics, yet tapped into the same kind of audience to whom the Spice Girls music appealed, young teens and pre-teens. Also like the Spice Girls, Britney Spears's image was equally important to her appeal. But at the time of her debut, Spears was a mere 17-years-old, and some thought she provided a bad example for young girls, while also appealing to prurient interests among adults. Spears staunchly denied that her scanty outfits were worn in the interest of sex appeal, claiming that the clothing simply reflected the fashion of the day: "Sure I wear thigh high's, but kids wear those—it's the style."[23] Given the hyper-sexualized presentation of Spears in the video for "Baby One More Time," in her April 1999 *Rolling Stone* pictorial, and elsewhere, her defense largely fell on deaf ears. In the years to come, even Spears herself would reflect on how her image was being received, stating "I don't want to be part of someone's *Lolita* thing. It kind of freaks me out."[24] Spears took to slightly downplaying her sexuality, albeit still with considerable bare skin, but her popularity continued unabated into the 2000s, along with that of similar performers, such as Christina Aguilera and Jessica Simpson.

The boy bands of the late 1990s were almost diametrically opposed to the image created for most of the young female pop singers. Instead of being highly sexualized, these groups were largely presented as nonthreatening. Thus, a group like The Backstreet Boys might come across as fun-loving and mischievous, but never dangerous. The image was one that paid off, as The Backstreet Boys would be named Artists of the Year in *Rolling Stone*'s 1999 readers poll, followed closely by similar groups, especially 'N Sync. Although compared to the New Kids On The Block of a decade earlier, The Backstreet Boys, nonetheless, were the boy band pioneers of the 1990s. The Backstreet Boys downplayed their similarities to the earlier group, eldest member Kevin Richardson suggesting that "New Kids never claimed to be a vocal groups—they were entertainers. We're a vocal group. We'd like people to look at us like Boyz II Men or New Edition, only we're white."[25] The Backstreet Boys were formed in 1993, the product of an open audition in Orlando, Florida, held by businessman Lou Pearlmen, but it wouldn't be until 1997, after considerable touring and moderate success in Europe that the group would finally break through in the U.S., with "pretty love songs for guys and girls to slow dance to, up-tempos to make you dance and midtempos for in your car, to make you forget about the traffic," as described by Richardson.[26] They had repeated success with songs like "Quit Playing Games (with My Heart)," "As Long As You Love Me," and "I'll Never Break Your Heart." The Backstreet Boys would eventually break from Pearlman (resulting, in part, in a lengthy legal battle over revenues), and successfully venture forward on their own, but not before Pearlman had put together a similar group, 'N Sync.[27] As another five boys in their late teens and twenties, singing similar love songs, 'N Sync could be seen as simply a carbon copy of the Pearlman era Backstreet Boys, but 'N Sync, who would also break from Pearlman in time, proved to be no slouch in the sales arena themselves, selling more than nine million copies of their self-titled debut album by the end of the 1990s.[28]

Of course, the veteran pop divas continued to prosper. Madonna enjoyed a particularly active decade, complete with continued film exposure, especially in *Evita* (1996), and childbirth. Musically she continued to experiment with electronica and other musical forms on her albums *I'm Breathless* (from and inspired by her role in the 1990 film *Dick Tracy*), *Erotica* (1992), *Bedtime Stories* (1994), and *Ray of Light* (1998). Another diva, Celine Dion, had one of the most popular singles of the decade with "My Heart Will Go On," recorded for the soundtrack of *Titanic* (1995). The song won an Oscar and enjoyed virtually inescapable radio airplay.

The tried and true, then, remained tried and true in the 1990s. But the cracks that appeared in the veneer of popular music in the 1980s, which showed that there was an audience for a great multitude of musical styles, exploded into massive fissures, and truly changed the music industry. While the 1990s may have seen more criticism hurled at popular music than perhaps ever before, they also proved to be an extremely exciting decade for pop music. Indeed, one could argue that pop music had not felt so dangerous since the dawn of rock 'n' roll. And a great deal of this danger (and consequent vitality) was born of the cacophony of new voices, from so many different social fronts, that hurled from speakers across the country, not merely in isolated regions. The multivoiced nature of popular music at the end of the twentieth century, ultimately, is one of the 1990s greatest claims, and has revitalized musical production for years to come.

10
Performing Arts

TELEVISION DRAMA

Perhaps the most significant television development in the 1990s was the birth of two new networks. Spurred by the continued success of the Fox network, two major studios, Warner Brothers and Paramount, decided to start their own networks. The WB and Paramount networks both started rather slowly in 1995. Each network spent considerable time fishing around until they finally found their niche. The WB was particularly successful in finding large markets for its teen-oriented dramas and its African American sitcoms. The Paramount network, spearheaded by its successful *Star Trek* properties, also found success with these genres, and also became a major outlet for TV science fiction.

One could pose a sound argument that the 1990s was something of a golden age for television drama. The decade saw more critically acclaimed dramas than had ever been seen before, and, moreover, a greater variety of dramas. Many dramas, especially police and medical dramas, cultivated a gritty realism, in contrast to the generally held concept that television gussied up reality. But there were also dramas that were decidedly unrealistic, like filmmaker David Lynch's bizarre *Twin Peaks*, which intrigued and often baffled audiences for two seasons (1990–1991). Science Fiction television also enjoyed unprecedented success, driven largely by *The X-Files*, and the last years of the decade saw the phenomenal rise of the teen drama. Of course, among all this, there was still room for a show like David Hasselhoff's lifeguard drama, *Baywatch*, generally regarded as one of the silliest shows on television, which sold largely on the basis of pretty people in bathing suits. Although *Baywatch* had a slow start in the U.S., it proved an international phenomenon, highlighting the importance of the overseas market for American television programming during its decade-spanning run, from 1989 to 2001.

The 1990s are also notable for the number of filmmakers—producers, directors, and actors, including Lynch, Oliver Stone, Steven Spielberg, Barry Levinson, and George Lucas—who foraged into network television, lending it a bit more cachet than it had before. Yet despite these successes, TV dramas, especially non-domestic and therefore more expensive dramas, had to struggle in the 1990s. Given that drama generally costs more than comedy, these shows were forced to bring in higher revenues in order to make their continued existence justifiable to network executives. Moreover, the 1990s saw the continued growth of the news magazine show and the rise of reality TV, both of which directly threatened to cut into drama's audience. On the side of the dramas was the fact that they retained their position as the prestige broadcasts of any network.

SCIENCE FICTION TV

Science Fiction television experienced something of a renaissance in the 1990s. The continued strength of the *Star Trek* franchise ensured that there was always at least one *Star Trek* series on the air. *Star Trek: The Next Generation* completed its television voyages in 1994, to continue it journeys on the big screen, starting with the lackluster *Star Trek: Generations* (1994) which sought to bridge the original series with *The Next Generation,* with Captains Kirk (William Shatner) and Picard (Patrick Stewart) fighting back-to-back. From 1993 to 1999 aired *Star Trek: Deep Space Nine,* a series set not on a starship but on a space station. The series, headed by an African American, Avery Brooks, who played Benjamin Sisko, involved considerably more political intrigue than prior *Star Trek* series. It never did garner as large a viewership as *The Next Generation,* which perhaps allowed the creators a bit more creative freedom. By the series last season, a number of critics were suggesting that this might well be remembered as the best and most ambitious of the *Star Trek* series. In 1995, yet another *Star Trek* series was aired, *Star Trek: Voyager.* In this series, a starship was flung by a spatial anomaly to a galaxy far from its own. The following seven seasons entailed the crews attempt to return to their home galaxy, impeded by technical crises and hostile alien races. Like all *Star Trek* shows, *Voyager* presented a multicultural crew, featuring an Asian, a Latina, and a Native American, as well as a black Vulcan. The show also starred the first female lead in the *Star Trek* franchise, Captain Kathryn Janeway, played by Kate Mulgrew. There were also numerous star-faring imitations of *Star Trek,* particularly *Babylon 5* (1994–1995), which quickly garnered a cult following not unlike that which developed around the 1960s *Star Trek* series, *SeaQuest DSV* (1993–1995), and *Earth: Final Conflict* (1997–2002), created by Star Trek creator Gene Roddenberry.

The X-Files, produced by Chris Carter, made its debut in 1993 and quickly became one of the Fox network's cornerstone shows. The show focused on two FBI agents, Fox Mulder (David Duchovny) and Dana Scully (Gillian Anderson), who were charged with investigations into the supernatural. Scully, a generally skeptical medical examiner, served as a foil to Mulder's quick intuitive leaps to the most outlandish of conclusions, which nonetheless proved true more often than not. Yet despite the degree of inherent antagonism between the pair, the series also showcased a growing friendship, which ultimately proved as central to the series as the investigations into reports of vampires, werewolves, and killer insects. While the moody cinematography, clever writing, and skillful performances by central and secondary actors garnered the show praise, many attributed its success in part to how it tapped into a general state of paranoid malaise infecting the American psyche. A running storyline suggested that elements within the government not only knew about the existence of extraterrestrials, but were also running experiments on human subjects, involving alien genetic material. Mulder and Scully's investigations into extraterrestrial activities would consequently bring them into frequent conflict with the authorities who they served. Thus, while the pair were clearly the good guys of the series, the agency for which they worked was shadowy and menacing, reflecting an attitude towards the government held by a sizable segment of the American population, who saw themselves as cogs in a machine over which they had little or no control. The catchphrase "Trust no one" which often appeared in the opening credits—the other was "The truth is out there"—thereby found a warm reception from viewers. *The X-Files* also tapped into millennial fears, as it frequently suggested that epochal changes were on the immediate horizon, changes that would forever affect humanity. The 1998 theatrical, *The X-Files* movie, therefore, was appropriately subtitled *Fight the Future.* Chris Carter in fact attempted to appeal to the same fears in a second, less successful series, *Millennium* (1996–1999). The success of *The X-Files* inspired considerable imitation, like *Dark Skies,* (1996–1997) and even another Carter show, *Harsh Realm* (1999–2000). Even *Baywatch* got into the act when its spin-off *Baywatch Nights* (1995–1997) switched from detective drama to supernatural thriller. *The X-Files* even had its own spin-off, starring the show's conspiracy-mongering misfits, *The Lone Gunmen* (2001).

The success of the science fiction and horror genres also encouraged the development of new fantasy, a genre that, though not new to television, had long been retired from the small screen. The earliest of these was *Hercules: The Legendary Journeys,* which aired from 1995 to 1999. This series starred Kevin Sorbo in the title role and featured elaborate fight sequences and special-effect laden action reminiscent of the Hercules and Sinbad movies of old. The series swung easily from melodrama to slapstick, capturing some of the spirit of the B-horror movies of the series' producer Sam

Raimi. Early in the series *Xena* was introduced, a character that in no time at all would be given her own series, *Xena, Warrior Princess*, which would become the most successful series ever produced in the genre. Xena, played by Lucy Lawless, was a character torn between her violent, mercenary upbringing and her desire to do good, cultivated by her young companion, Gabriel, played by Renée O'Connor. Like *Hercules, Xena* demonstrated a skillful blend of melodrama, action, humor, and revealing costumes, as well as a playful twisting of world history and mythology. The closeness of the relationship between these two women, initially intended as simply a cherished friendship, soon lent itself to lesbian readings of the series, which was embraced by a gay, as well as straight, viewership. Rather than take umbrage at this reading, the producers of *Xena* took to playing up the angle, alluding to, but never confirming nor denying, something greater than friendship between Xena and Gabriel. With various degrees of success, other producers sought to emulate *Hercules* and *Xena.* These shows were followed by *Conan* (1998), *The Adventures of Sinbad* (1996), *The Epic Adventures of Tarzan* (1996), *Beastmaster* (1999–2002), and *The New Adventures of Robin Hood* (1997–1999) among others. The flood of such shows, or perhaps the wearing off of the schmaltzy novelty, eventually led to a very sudden decline in the popularity of television fantasy, and by the time *Xena* bowed out in 2001, few other examples of the genre still aired.

RELIGION IN TV DRAMA

That a number of these shows flirted with the occult did not sit well with all television viewers, and on some minor fronts, *The X-Files* and its offspring were soundly condemned. In contrast to this, the 1990s saw the birth of a number of shows with a religious bent. Foremost among these was *Touched by an Angel* (1994–2003), starring Roma Downey and Della Reese as angels. In a pattern similar to that of *Highway to Heaven* (1984–1989), each week Downey's character Monica would come down to Earth to help people through their trials, inspiring faith all the while. Although the show received some criticism from secular fronts on account of its pat solutions to social troubles, from alcoholism to racism, and from religious fronts for its sentimental portrayal of angels, the show nevertheless garnered a sizable viewership by virtue of its wholesome, uplifting storylines.

On a more earthly front, *7th Heaven* (1996–) detailed the day-to-day life of the family of Eric Camden (Stephen Collins), a reverend raising his family in the heart of the Bible Belt. While the show and its conservative values were highly praised on some fronts, others criticized its lack of realism and general didacticism. Nonetheless, the show's success suggests that there was a very definite audience for family oriented shows with uncomplicated morals. Shows like *Touched by an Angel, 7th Heaven,* and the similarly designed *Second Noah* (1996–1997) tended to downplay the gray areas of life that were so significant to other dramas in the 1990s. But one short-lived series with a religious bent, *Nothing Sacred* (1997), did in fact deal with the more troubling questions of modern life and religion. The show focused on the tribulations of an urban Catholic priest, who found himself confronted with typically controversial issues, like abortion and pre-marital sex. Although the show, written by a priest, was well-received critically, the Catholic church attacked the show for its ambivalence towards issues that were clear-cut in Catholic ideology. This, combined with the skittish network's constant shifting of the show's timeslot, prevented the show from finding a strong audience.

POLICE AND MEDICAL DRAMA

The police drama had long been a staple of television production, and the 1990s were no exception to this. In fact, dramas involving law enforcement came and went with a particular frenzy, and this may be in part attributed to the loosening of content restrictions in the later decades of the twentieth century. Television producers were allowed to show police work in a new and visceral light. The bulk of the police dramas of the 1990s owed much to their greatest predecessor, *Hill Street Blues* (1981–1987), but there was also a great deal of innovation. Of the many such dramas to air during the 1990s, including such titles as *Third Watch* (1999–), *Brooklyn South* (1997–1998), and *New York Undercover* (1994–1998), three particularly stood above the rest, both critically and commercially.

Produced by Steven Bochco, David Milch, and David Mills, among others, *NYPD Blue,* which first aired on ABC in 1993, garnered much early attention, mostly because it pushed the boundaries of what was permissible on television. Profanity was common on the show, as was brief partial nudity. In fact, actors' contracts commonly included a nudity clause stating that they would disrobe for the camera if necessary. Responding to the violence, language, and nudity, nearly one-quarter of the network's 225 affiliates refused to carry the first episode, and ABC instituted a "viewer discretion advised" warning before each episode aired. Although it was these potentially salacious details that started the initial buzz regarding the series, *NYPD Blue* soon proved to have much more in its arsenal than skin and swearing. The show enjoyed a long run as it cast harsh light on the lives of detectives in the New York city police department. It depicted men and women who, while following a noble vocation of police work, were themselves flawed human beings. Over the course of its run, the show saw numerous cast changes, including a rotation of leading men—David Caruso, Jimmy Smits, and Rick Schroder—but one of the shows stalwarts, Dennis Franz, a *Hill Street Blues* alumnus, contributed to the creation of one of the most fascinating characters to ever appear on the small screen. Franz's Andy Sipowicz began the show as what could almost be characterized as a bad cop. Sipowicz was violent, brutish, and mean. He was also intolerant, frequently peppering his profanity-laden speech with racism, homophobia, and sexism. But over the course of the show's run, and as the character's life and relationships with his fellow detectives developed, he made an effort to change, controlling his temper and his intolerance, and even becoming a loving family man. Such transformations had been seen on television before, but never had they unfolded so gradually and so realistically. At the end of the decade, Sipowicz was far evolved from the show's first season, but the darker aspects of his personality had never totally vanished, and the character continued in his evolution. For his portrayal, Franz won four Emmys throughout the decade. The show received numerous awards and recognitions, including Emmys for actors Gordon Clapp and Kim Delaney, and for Outstanding Dramatic Series.

Named "the best show you're not watching" by *TV* Guide in 1996, NBC's *Homicide: Life on the Streets* (1993–1999) was another important contributor to the police drama genre. In fact, Joseph Wambaugh, the author of the *TV Guide* article, went so far as to call it "the best police series ever produced by American television."[1] The show was created by Paul Attanasio, and was based on a book by David Simon detailing a year in the life of the Baltimore police department. It was produced by Tom Fontana and noted filmmaker Barry Levinson, who had grown up in Baltimore and frequently situated his films in the locale. In addition, the show assembled a top-notch cast, including many actors best known for their work in cinema, such as Yaphet Kotto, Ned Beatty, Daniel Baldwin, and Andre Braugher, who would quickly become one of the shows' greatest assets. *Homicide* quickly became a critical success, though for the full length of its run it found itself struggling with the network and trying to grab a larger share of the audience. Despite continued critical success after the departure of Braugher from the series in 1998, shortly after winning the Emmy for Outstanding Actor in a Dramatic Series, the show finally lost its battle with network executives in 1999. Still the show continues to be hailed for how it realistically depicted the lives of homicide detectives and concentrated on the cerebral and emotional pressures of the job far more than on gunfire and sensationalism (though cases did tend to become a bit more sensational late in the series, as the threats to its existence increased). The show also paid close attention to the victims of violent crime, such that in a number of episodes, the survivors of murder victims took center stage as much as the regular cast. Praised for its stylish verité cinematography and sharp writing (especially by James Yoshimura), *Homicide* also earned acclaim for its portrait of minorities. At certain junctures of the series, nearly half the cast was African American, presenting a rare demographic for a television drama, though quite representative of urban Baltimore.

Notably, *Homicide: Life on the Streets* enjoyed several crossover episodes with *Law & Order*, the third of the major police dramas of the 1990s. *Law &*

Order, however, was somewhat different. As the title suggests, the show functioned in two parts, the first half hour dealing with the investigation of a crime by New York city police detectives, and the latter half treating the prosecution of the crime by the district attorney's office. Thus, by having what amounted to two shows in one, *Law & Order* allowed the viewer to see the ultimate results (or lack thereof) of the police work in a way less often seen in other police dramas. Jerry Orbach, who played detective Lennie Briscoe, even suggested that the show was the TV drama equivalent of comfort food in that viewers could tune in and have some idea of the general direction and format of the show. This is not to say that the show was devoid of surprises. The show regularly resorted to twist endings, and frequently advertised its storylines as ripped from the headlines, and, although *Law & Order* focused less on the private lives of its characters, they nonetheless suffered as flesh and blood beings, subject to emotional turmoil, personal problems, injury, and death. These tribulations were perhaps all the more striking given the fact that viewers never could be sure how long a character would stay on the show. While other 1990s dramas saw characters come and go, nowhere was this more true than on *Law & Order,* which saw constant cast changes, such that no actor could claim to have been on the show for the whole of its existence. Surprisingly then, while the show starred many highly acclaimed actors, including Sam Waterston, Jill Hennessy, and Paul Sorvino, its success was not star-bound. Instead, it stood its ground with whomever might be in the cast in any one season by virtue of its consistently solid storytelling. Such was its success that it would spawn several spin-off series, *Law & Order: Special Victims Unit* and *Law & Order: Criminal Intent. Law & Order* kept the legal thriller alive and well in the 1990s, though for most of the decade none came close to matching its success until 1997 when *The Practice* appeared. This David Kelly law firm drama started slow with audiences, but shot to prominence when, in its first year, it won a number of major Emmys, including Outstanding Drama Series.

The medical drama also proved popular, with two shows, both debuting in 1994, rising to considerable heights: *ER* and *Chicago Hope. ER* (1994–) focused specifically on the emergency room operations of a hospital. Produced in part by novelist Michael Crichton, the show was unflinching in its camera work, making it one of the bloodiest shows on television. As the series progressed, however the emphasis turned away from the emergency room procedures and more towards the interpersonal relationships. Some early fans criticized the show as turning into a melodramatic prime-time soap opera, while others were troubled by the move away from the realism of the early episodes to a more sensationalistic tone. Whatever the attitude might be towards the later years of the series, the early episodes were unquestionably some of the most groundbreaking broadcasts in realistic television drama. In addition, the persistently well-rated series helped propel a number of actors to stardom, including Eric LaSalle, Julianna Margulies, Anthony Edwards, and especially George Clooney, who became a top film star after his departure from *ER*. *Chicago Hope* (1994–2000) starring, among others, Mandy Patinkin and Hector Elonzo, was a somewhat darker show, and less strictly realistic in its portrayal of hospital life. The show seemed to bask in the unusual, and employed a much greater degree of gallows humor.

YOUTH DRAMA

Of course, not all 1990s television drama sought hard-hitting realism. Indeed, this was also the decade of *Beverly Hills 90210* (1990–2000) and *Melrose Place* (1992–1999), both produced by Aaron Spelling. Both shows debuted to tremendous popularity. *Beverly Hills 90210* began as a high school–based soap opera, and had immediate appeal to young viewers, while *Melrose Place* was aimed at a older audience with stories of betrayal, seduction, and infidelity, in a kind of 1990s variation of the sixties prime-time soap opera *Peyton Place*. Although critics generally considered the shows juvenile at best and puerile at worst, *Beverly Hills 90210* and *Melrose Place* nevertheless became a guilty pleasure for many viewers, and even as their popularity began to wane in the late 1990s, their core audience propelled them to respectable runs. Moreover, both shows helped to launch the careers of numerous young actors. Although many of the actors in *Beverly Hills 90210* were decidedly overaged, even at the show's start, for high school students, they nonetheless became teen idols of a sort, and so Jason Priestley, Shannen Doherty, Luke Perry, and others gained renown as the most famous "teenagers" of their time.

The late 1990s also saw the rise of a new kind of teen drama. While taking a cue from earlier such series as *Beverly Hills 90210*, these new teen dramas—perhaps best exemplified by *Dawson's Creek* (1998–2003), *Party of Five* (1994–2000), and *Felicity* (1998–2002), three staples of the WB Network's lineup—seemed to connect even more strongly to young viewers. The principal reason for this was that the teenaged characters in these shows simply seemed more realistic, coming from middle-class backgrounds, and played by a talented pool of teen actors, rather than by adults. While these shows were attacked on some fronts for their alleged depiction of teen promiscuity, and on others for the whiny self-importance of the characters, in fact the troubles faced by the young protagonists often echoed the issues facing the young audience, tapping into teen malaise and finding a common bond with them.

A new spin on the teen drama was introduced with *Buffy the Vampire Slayer* (1997–2003), in which Sarah Michelle Geller played the title character, who defended her town of Sunnydale from vampires and other forces of darkness. The series, created by Joss Whedon, was based on a minor movie of the same name, but far exceeded the expectations set by the film.

Whedon explained the series as a twist on the traditional horror film, in which the young blonde girl was always menaced by some horror. In this series, the young blonde was in fact more than able to take care of herself. The show skillfully mingled teen drama with horror movie thrills, and considerable humor, as well as clever writing and often stunning cinematography. And while the show was largely ignored for major awards, most likely because of its genre, it regularly landed on critics' lists of best TV shows, and became the WB's top series. Similar genre-mixing experiments were undertaken, including *Roswell* (1999–2002), featuring teen extraterrestrials, *Charmed* (1998–), about young witches, and the *Buffy* spin-off, *Angel* (1999–), about a moral vampire who fights evil.

It should not be construed, however, that all of the TV dramas of the 1990s were derivatives of traditional genres. In fact, the 1990s saw some truly innovative dramatic programming that confounded any attempts at easy categorization. Certainly *Twin Peaks* set a precedent for bizarre television in its blending of small-town strangeness with murder-mystery and supernatural occurrences. And while *Twin Peaks* may never have been an enormous commercial success, the critical praise and cult following certainly inspired some producers to push the bounds, as in the eerie *American Gothic* (1995–1996) and *Picket Fences* (1992–1996), a show centered on the sheriff of a decidedly off-kilter small town, which, while not strictly supernatural, was certainly unusual, going so far as to have one major secondary character die of spontaneous combustion. Another important show was *Northern Exposure* (1990–1995), which told the story of a physician, played by Rob Morrow, sent to an Alaskan town filled with endearingly odd characters. The series walked a fine line between drama and comedy, ultimately confounding the artificial generic distinctions between the two.

The end of the decade also saw important developments in cable broadcasting. Besides a growing number of made-for-cable movies, the waning years of the nineties successfully explored the possibilities of cable series TV. The most notable of these were *Sex and the City,* which debuted in 1998 and detailed the daily lives of a number of young urban professional women, and *The Sopranos,* a critical and commercial coup for cable network HBO. First aired in 1999, *The Sopranos* focused principally on the family and professional life of a mobster, Tony Soprano, played by James Gandolfini. Unrestricted by network censors, the show happily employed violence and coarse language, which offended some, but which most took as appropriate to the show's subject matter. *The Sopranos* also became the first cable broadcast to win an Emmy for best drama series.

TELEVISION COMEDY

The situation comedy also thrived in the 1990s. While most of this comedy was fairly standard fare, with domestic and workplace sitcoms dominating, there were important steps forward in the genre, as well. Two shows in particular dominated the world of TV comedy in the 1990s. The first of these, *The Simpsons,* introduced in 1989 by the Fox network, was in fact the first successful prime-time animated series since the *Flintstones* (1960–1966), and like that show, *The Simpsons* was modeled on the traditional family sitcom. The series, developed by cartoonist Matt Groening, featured Homer Simpson, the dull-witted father, Marge, the straightlaced mother with frightful blue hair, Lisa, the super-intelligent daughter, Bart, the mischievous son, and the perennially silent baby, Maggie. The show was, at first, principally a parody of the family sitcom genre, but as the show's run gradually outran the ages of its child characters, *The Simpsons* turned into one of the wittiest satires on television, taking swipes at conservative and liberal values alike. Whereas the show began by focusing mostly on Bart, it increasingly highlighted Homer, who became the prime vehicle through which the show mocked ignorance and mob mentality. The world of the series, the middle-American town of Springfield, was also populated with hundreds of other characters, including the fat police chief, the apathetic reverend, and the town drunk, all of whom added considerably to the variety of issues available for satire. Moreover, in exposing the foibles of these various characters, the show ultimately made the dysfunctional title family the moral center of the series. Remarkably then, while the series displayed a scathing wit, viewers nonetheless sympathized with the characters, even as those same viewers might be the target of the show's satire. The show spawned an enormous marketing franchise, and made television primetime seemingly friendly to animation again. But it is a testament to *The Simpsons* long-lived success that none of the many animated series to follow in its footsteps, including *The Critic* (1994–1995), *The Family Guy* (1999–2002), *Capitol Critters* (1992), *Fish Police* (1992), and Groening's own *Futurama* (1999–2003), came close to approximating its consistently high ratings.

Two other animated series, which aired not on network television, but on cable, also created quite a stir in the 1990s. The first of these was Mike Judge's *Beavis and Butt-head* (1993–1997), which aired on MTV. Much of this series was dedicated to showing the two adolescent stars as they watched and mocked music videos. On the occasions that they left the sofa, they typically did very stupid things, usually inflicting some kind of self-injury with the use of fire or chainsaw. There was considerable outrage about the series, particularly after a five-year-old set fire to his house, killing his sister, apparently imitating the doltish characters. Nevertheless, the pair were popular enough to have a hit movie based on their adventures, *Beavis and Butt-head Do America* (1996). Following in their footsteps was the Comedy Central series *South Park,* first aired in 1997. The foul-mouthed third-graders of this series, Stan, Kyle, Kenny, and Cartman, were the creations of Matt Stone and Trey Parker. Although lovingly laced with toilet humor, the series still managed to offer frequently smart social satire, particularly

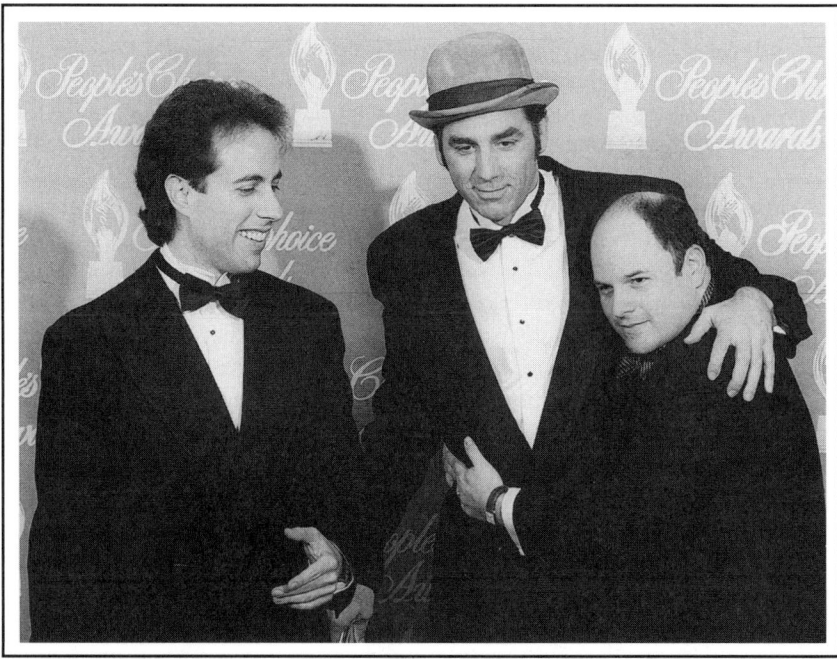

Jerry Seinfeld, left, poses with Michael Richards, center, and Jason Alexander after their show *Seinfeld* won a People's Choice award for Favorite Television Comedy Series at the 1997 People's Choice Awards in Santa Monica, Calif., Jan. 12, 1997. © AP/Wide World Photos.

in its indictment of moral hypocrisy in America. Propelled by animation nearly as crude as that of *Beavis and Butt-head,* as well as by running jokes, like a talking piece of excrement named Mr. Hankey and the killing off of Kenny each episode, *South Park* also reached the big screen in *South Park: Bigger, Longer & Uncut* (1999).

Along with *The Simpsons,* the other cornerstone sitcom of the 1990s was NBC's *Seinfeld,* which debuted in 1990 and aired until 1998. Created by stand-up comedian Jerry Seinfeld and Larry David, this show focused on four friends, Jerry, George, Elaine, and Kramer, living in New York City. Ostensibly the show was about "nothing." The characters simply went about their day's business, talking about the minutia of their day-to-day lives while lunching in the neighborhood coffee shop. Viewers applauded the reality of the show, as similar conversations were indeed a significant part of their own lives, but the characters of *Seinfeld* were, in fact, anything but typical Americans, or even typical New Yorkers. Instead, the show offered an acute satire of modern life's banality by pushing this banality to such extremes that it became quite surreal. The most inconsequential things—a tuna on rye sandwich, the board game Risk, Pez candy dispensers—ended up having extraordinary ramifications. Moreover, the show, much like *The Simpsons*, frequently made fun of its own conventions and those of the sitcom in general. This practice reached its height with a series of episodes involving the creation of a TV pilot called *Jerry* by George and Jerry. This show within a show closely approximated *Seinfeld*, with fictional actors cast to play the part of the *real* characters, themselves fiction constructs of *Seinfeld*. The ultimate bizarrity of *Seinfeld* would not be imitated, which is a credit to the skill of the shows' writers and producers, and also to the chemistry between the show's principal cast, Jason Alexander, Julia Louis-Dreyfus, Michael Richards, and Seinfeld. The show, with its reputation as a *water cooler show*—that is, a show that viewers would, theoretically, discuss at work while taking breaks at the company water cooler—made its final bow in 1998, its final episode garnering 76 million spectators, the largest viewership ever for a sitcom.

There were other significant entries into the sitcom genre, including *Friends*, created for NBC by Marta Kauffman and David Crane. Launched in 1994, this series detailed the relationship between a group of six friends in their twenties and early thirties. The show garnered consistently good ratings due to the chemistry between the characters, with whom viewers could easily relate. Moreover, it helped propel the careers of its young cast, Jennifer Aniston, Courtney Cox (Arquette), Lisa Kudrow, Matt LeBlanc, Matthew Perry, and David Schwimmer. The show received numerous awards and nominations, including Kudrow's 1998 Emmy win for outstanding supporting actress. Another noteworthy sitcom was *Frasier* (1993–), a spin-off of *Cheers* (1982–1993). In this show, Kelsey Grammer's *Cheers* character, the barfly psychologist Frasier Crane, relocated from Boston to Seattle where he began a call-in radio psychology show. The real focus of the show, however, was Crane's relationship with his injured father, Martin (John Mahoney), a retired police officer, who moves in with him, as well as with his father's caretaker, Daphne (Jane Leeves), and his brother Niles (David Hyde Pierce). *Frasier* simultaneously offered unusually cerebral writing for a sitcom, and made light-hearted fun of the intelligencia, and this combination leant to its success among an educated, but middle-class audience. Moreover, the show proved very popular with critics and won numerous awards, including Emmys for outstanding comedy series every year from 1994 to 1998. *Mad About You*, starring Paul Reiser and Helen Hunt, was another major 1990s sitcom. This series ran from 1992 to 1999 and traced the romance of the protagonist couple, through their quick courtship, their marriage, and the birth of their daughter. Another important series to be introduced in the 1990s was *Will and Grace*, significant for its positive portrait of homosexuals. The title characters of the series, introduced in 1998, were a gay man and a straight woman who live in an apartment together. The show used this situation to not only explore new comic ground (as most prior portraits of gays were derisive), but also to make a political point about the very real place of gays in American culture and society. *Sports Night* (1998–2000) was yet another sitcom of note. Created by Aaron Sorkin, the show used more dynamic cinematography than most sitcoms and was written with a sharp, almost theatrical patter. Set at the studio of a sports-news program, the show's stylization and blend of drama and comedy found mixed reception among viewers, but it was critically praised and stands as one of the more adventurous sitcoms ever produced.

The 1990s also saw major activity in the production of African American sitcoms, with the WB and UPN networks leading the way. These included *The Fresh Prince of Bel Air,* starring Will Smith, *Martin,* starring comedian Martin Lawrence, *Moesha*, starring singer Brandy, *Hangin' with Mr. Cooper,* and *The Jamie Fox Show.* Although these shows garnered considerable ratings and revenues, critical opinion was split. The shows did find large audiences among African-Americans, and many claimed that the shows offered funny variations on the true lives of the African American communities. Others claimed that the cachet of such shows was that they played on long-lived racial stereotypes of buffoonish blacks. Among these critics was filmmaker Spike Lee, who offered his ultimate critique of them in his movie *Bamboozled* (2000).

COMPUTERS AND CINEMA

The 1990s proved to be quite a lively decade for the cinema, with the growth of many new studios and with the introduction of numerous young, exciting directors. But perhaps the most significant developments in cinema were not so much aesthetic as technological. The 1990s saw the dramatic influence of digital technology, with, most notably, the bulk of movie theaters turning to digital sound. In 1990, *Dick Tracy* became the first major release with a digital soundtrack. While digital picture had not yet been instituted by the end of the decade, though the technology had been developed, it seemed that it would only be a matter of time before virtually the whole movie-going experience was turned digital. Moreover, advances in technology allowed for special effects imagery the likes of which had never been seen before. In 1993, the technologically groundbreaking *Jurassic Park* hit theatres. This Spielberg-directed thriller about a zoo filled with prehistoric creatures was not so notable for its story, which was similar to many monster movies of the past, but for the fact that the dinosaurs seemed to truly come alive. More remarkably, these realistically rendered beasts in fact lived largely in the memories of computers, were digitally modeled and animated, and were placed seamlessly onscreen with live-action performers and settings. These kind of special effects reached their peak with the long-awaited new movie in the *Star Wars* series, *Episode One:*

The Phantom Menace (1999), which was virtually bursting at the seams with computer-generated effects, including one character, Jar Jar Binks, who was entirely computer created. Highly anticipated as this film was, it proved to be a disappointment to many fans, but dissatisfaction stemmed from the script and performances, not from the absolutely eye-popping complexity and sophistication of its effects.

Nor would this be the only way that computer technology would lead to startlingly new methods of filmmaking. The 1995 film, *Toy Story*, was the first full-length computer-animated feature. In this case, it was not only select objects, but the entire film that was computer animated, from the backgrounds to all the characters, primarily a bunch of living children's playthings. *Toy Story* opened new vistas in animation, and with each fully computer-animated film that came out in *Toy Story*'s wake (including the 1999 sequel, *Toy Story 2*), computer animation was slicker and more convincing.

The 1994 Robert Zemeckis film, *Forrest Gump*, also demonstrated new uses of computer technology in film. This movie, about how the simple-minded title character, played by Tom Hanks, managed to become a significant player in a number of historic events of the latter half of the twentieth century, didn't play itself up as a technological breakthrough. But the movie used computer technology to have Gump meet such historical figures as John F. Kennedy and Lyndon B. Johnson. Hanks was not on screen next to actors playing the part of these figures, but was, in fact, digitally placed onto existing footage of them, which was itself computer manipulated to make the figures appear to be interacting with Forrest Gump. This technique which was so astounding in *Forrest Gump* stirred up considerable controversy about the appropriate use of such technology. The debate was propounded by the advent of commercials featuring dead stars, such that James Cagney, Louis Armstrong, and others appearing resurrected in Diet Coke ads, and John Wayne seemingly risen from the grave to hawk Coors Light beer (see Chapter 3.)

Another important use of computers in special effects could be seen in the 1999 film, *The Matrix*, directed by the Wachowski brothers. The filmmakers used a new kind of digital effect which they called "bullet time." Using multiple still cameras, special effects teams could effectively photograph scenes in rapid sequence from multiple angles, and then, assisted by computers, animate these still photos seamlessly. A kind of stop-action animation using live actors, bullet time allowed the makers of *The Matrix* to create stunning action scenes in this science-fiction thriller, in which time seemed to bend at the will of the directors, without any of the artificiality of earlier experiments with sped-up or slowed-down film.

Mention must also be made of the most commercially successful movie of the 1990s, *Titanic*, directed by James Cameron. This 1997 release which retold the story of the sinking of the famed luxury ocean liner, was indeed a triumph of computer and other special effects. But more than the special effects, the production of *Titanic* seemed to hearken back to the classic era of cinematic spectacle. Indeed, considerable buzz about the film preceded its release, the result of Cameron's rather flamboyant filmmaking. The director went so far as to hire a submersible craft from which he could view, and film, the actual wreckage of Titanic, and he also spent considerable time and effort to erect elaborate sets, duplicating sections of the ship. In short, Cameron reconstructed much of Titanic not only on screen, but in the real world. The costs of such a project were understandably excessive, reaching some $200 million, which evoked some concern on the part of 20th Century Fox. Such was the studios concern that Cameron forfeited his salary and percentage of the gross. But in the end, *Titanic* more than earned Cameron his keep. The film, which entailed a rather traditional star-crossed love affair amidst the ocean liner's voyage and destruction, not only made back its money, but broke all box-office records and won several major awards, including Best Director and Best Picture Academy Awards.

INDEPENDENT FILM

While it is certainly true that the film industry turned out much of the kind of blockbuster material that had been its bread and butter for years, the 1990s offered new opportunities for independent film and filmmakers. Independent producers proved that there was a market for independent film, and the big studios took notice, with many of them starting their own "independent" division, as in the case of 20th Century Fox's Fox Searchlight line. The independent film market was further bolstered by the growth of the *indy* film festival circuit, spearheaded by the Sundance Film Festival. By the end of the decade, however, many were raising red flags about how the major film corporations, with their co-opting of independent talent, their purchases of major independent studios, like Columbia TriStar's purchase of Miramax, and their domination of distribution channels, threatened to truly stifle independent film. On the bright side, many suggested that in the years to come, computer technology might make it far more easy for independent films to be made and to be seen. Whatever predictions might be made, however, it is clear that the 1990s truly pushed the boundaries of cinema.

One of the most significant, as well as most debated, independent films of the 1990s was *The Blair Witch Project* (1999), a faux documentary about three film students who go into the woods to make a film about a local legend, and then are assaulted by forces beyond their comprehension. The film was produced on a shoe-string budget of $35,000, and looked it. The camera work was handled by the principal actors, the film students, so it appropriately appeared amateurish. The ultimate quality of the film was debatable, but its success was not. *The Blair Witch Project* became one of the top-grossing films of the year. After its release, as much, if not more, attention was cast on the publicity campaign as on the film itself. Directors Daniel Myrick and Eduardo Sanchez marketed the film on the Internet and elsewhere as a true story, producing a sizable amount of extra documentation, so that seeing the film was only a part, if a major part, of the Blair Witch experience.

The very beginning of the decade saw the release of *Henry and June* (1990), detailing the affair between writers Henry Miller and Anais Nin, a landmark film by virtue of its being the first movie to be released with the NC-17 rating, which had been instituted as a replacement for the X rating, which had come to be associated strictly with pornography. NC-17 was meant to designate a film with strong adult, but not pornographic, content. The new designation had little effect, however. Although *Henry and June*, directed by Phil Kaufman, was rated NC-17, distributors, theaters, and video outlets nonetheless resisted the film just as if it wore the X rating. Consequently, the film, though critically praised, remained largely unseen by the bulk of the American moviegoers. Indeed, while *Henry and June* proved that there was no real restriction on the content of movies, it also proved that there was also no way of forcing the industry to actually show such a film.

NEW TALENT

Arguably the most significant film of the 1990s, however, was seen by a great many people, becoming a cinematic icon of the decade. The film was *Pulp Fiction* (1994), written and directed by Quentin Tarantino. In 1992, Tarantino directed his first feature, *Reservoir Dogs*, a low budget picture that told of the aftermath of a bank robbery gone bad. The film gained immediate attention for its ultra-violent portrayal of the criminals. The bloodshed of the movie merited comparison with the films of Sam Pekinpah, but Tarantino also brought something new to the film. The script snapped with an almost theatrical patter, very stylized and hiply retro in tone. Moreover, as in *True Romance* (1993), written by Tarantino, the dialogue was filled with references to popular culture, from film to TV to comic books to pop music. All of these features would be revisited in *Pulp Fiction*, a much more complex film than its predecessor. With the success of *Reservoir Dogs* behind him, Tarantino was now able to cut loose with a non-linear movie which traced the interweaving threads of numerous narratives. Critical applause, Tarantino's reputation, and considerable star power (including Bruce Willis, Uma Thurman, and John Travolta, whose career was reinvigorated by *Pulp Fiction*), brought viewers to the movie in droves, and perhaps surprisingly, the film's complicated structure was very well-received commercially, as well. Despite such popularity, however, the ultimate value of *Pulp Fiction* would be the subject of considerable debate. Some complained that Tarantino's overwhelming references to pop culture suggested a lack of truly original ideas on Tarantino's part, and the arguably gratuitous violence of his films was also the subject of attack. Certainly *Pulp Fiction* was much imitated by other filmmakers, and more often than not, in their shallow celebration of violence and "hipness," these imitations demonstrated the excellence of *Pulp Fiction*, which won Tarantino and Roger Avary an Academy Award for their screenplay. Perhaps in reaction to the number of imitators, Tarantino would follow *Pulp Fiction* with *Jackie Brown* (1997), starring Pam Grier in the title role. Though still preoccupied with the criminal element, still filled with violence and snappy dialogue, *Jackie Brown* was nonetheless a decidedly less flashy film than *Pulp Fiction*, focusing in on a single linear storyline and a single character's plight.

There were other important young filmmakers, as well. Among these was Paul Thomas Anderson, whose first feature *Hard Eight* (aka *Sydney*) was released in 1997. Although that film was well-received critically, Anderson's next film *Boogie Nights* (1997) really made people sit up. The movie, which took place in the late 1970s and early 1980s, explored the rise and fall of a male performer in X-rated films. The film's content was startling for a mainstream film, but beyond this preoccupation, *Boogie Nights* was the work of a startlingly talented filmmaker, who weaved a many layered story about love and fidelity, and who employed remarkable cinematographic techniques to capture the mindsets of his characters. Anderson followed *Boogie Nights* with *Magnolia* (1999), an elaborate tapestry of many interrelated narrative threads. The film, which starred Tom Cruise, Jason Robards, Julianne Moore, and many others, was nominated for a number of Oscars, including Best Actor for Cruise and Best Original Screenplay.

Another major new directing talent in the 1990s was Steven Soderbergh, who first gained widespread attention in 1989 with *sex, lies and videotape*. While much of Soderbergh's output in the early 1990s was only moderately well-received, late in the decade he would cause many to take notice, with the films *Out of Sight* (1998) and *The Limey* (1999), both of which offered strikingly original visual experiences. In these films, Soderbergh displayed a sense of visual timing that seemed almost musical. *The Limey* particularly played with chronology in such a way as to demonstrate the unique properties of the cinema. In short, Soderbergh told stories that could not be effectively told in any other medium. Though a frequently experimental director, Soderbergh also proved himself an effective commercial director, particularly at the dawn of the new century, with such films as *Erin Brokovich* and *Traffic* (both 2000).

ESTABLISHED FILMMAKERS

The 1990s were also a vital decade for many of the old hands, as major directors, who had already made their reputations, came back to the cinema with restored vitality. Certainly the 1990s proved fruitful for Steven

Spielberg. Although established as a highly successful and popular director, the 1990s would see Spielberg finally recognized as a serious director,
something he had striven for since, at least, making *The Color Purple* (1985).
Two Spielberg films deserve particular attention. The first is *Schindler's List*
(1993), an unflinching recounting of the Holocaust and of the title character who attempted to lessen its devastating effect. The film, shot mostly in
black and white, was Spielberg's masterpiece, and this was recognized with
multiple Academy Awards, including those for Best Picture and Best Director. The second film is *Saving Private Ryan,* released in 1998. This film,
though a fairly standard war movie in certain respects, was notable for its
first twenty minutes, which depicted the invasion of Normandy on D-Day,
June 6, 1944. Never before had World War II been depicted so viscerally,
with jerky cinema verité camera work, and considerable gore. The film was
applauded for its realistic depiction of an invasion whose survivors were
dwindling and whose violence ran the risk of fading from American popular memory. *Saving Private Ryan* was nominated for a best picture Oscar
and Spielberg won the award for best director. Given the seriousness of
these films, it is important to remember that Spielberg also stuck close to
his roots, with plenty of films designed for pure escapist entertainment,
two *Jurassic Park* films foremost among them.

Other major directors also made their mark in the 1990s, including Martin Scorsese, who directed numerous films, including *GoodFellas* (1990) and
Casino (1997), which are regarded by many as his masterpieces. Scorsese
also proved himself quite an adventurous director, making films like an
adaptation of the Edith Wharton novel, *The Age of Innocence* (1993), and
Kundun (1997), about the Dali Lama. The pictures showed that Scorsese
was more than capable of extending himself beyond the usual urban mi-
lieu of his movies, even as *Bringing Out the Dead* (1999) showed that he had
not abandoned it. Robert Altman added to his already illustrious career
with *The Player* (1992), about the surreal life of a Hollywood film producer,
Short Cuts (1993), an interweaving of numerous storylines based on the
short stories of Raymond Carver, and others, like *Pret-á-Porter* (1994), and
Cookie's Fortune (1999). Oliver Stone explored several real-life figures in such
films as *The Doors* (1991), *JFK* (1991), and *Nixon* (1995). He also contributed
to his oeuvre with *Heaven and Earth* (1993), *Any Given Sunday* (1999), and
Natural Born Killers (1994), a graphically violent film which owed much to
the spate of ultra-violence in the wake of *Pulp Fiction.* David Lynch, who
continued to startle audiences with weird films like *Wild At Heart* (1990),
Twin Peaks: Fire Walk with Me (1992), and *Lost Highway* (1997), truly as-
tounded the world by directing the G-rated *The Straight Story* (1999), a
quiet, touching story about a man who rides a lawnmower miles to recon-
cile with his dying brother. Clint Eastwood, who had made a name for himself principally as an actor in Westerns and movies about tough, even brutal
police detectives, became a prolific directing force in the 1990s, during

which were released some eight features with Eastwood at the helm. Although many of these films garnered critical acclaim, including *White Hunter, Black Heart* (1990), *A Perfect World* (1993), and *Absolute Power* (1995), Eastwood's greatest triumph in the 1990s was unquestionably *Unforgiven* (1992). With this picture, Eastwood not only returned to the Western, helping temporarily revitalize the genre, but he also managed to offer an acute commentary on the violent nature of the Western. The movie, which won Oscars for Best Picture, Best Director, and Best Supporting Actor (Gene Hackman), solidified Eastwood's status as a director.

The vitality (and material wealth) of American cinema, drew many foreign directors to the United States, much as had happened early in the "golden age" of American film. The Taiwanese director Ang Lee, for instance, brought his subtle eye for family relationships to *The Ice Storm* (1997), and even made a movie of the American Civil War, *Ride with the Devil* (1999). John Woo, known for his ultra-violent Hong Kong action movies, contributed to American film with *Hard Target* (1993), *Broken Arrow* (1996), and *Face/Off* (1997). Meanwhile, Swedish director Lasse Hallstrom brought his off-beat sensibilities to films like *What's Eating Gilbert Grape?* (1994) and *The Cider House Rules* (1999), and Germany's Wolfgang Petersen made such films as *In the Line of Fire* (1993), *Outbreak* (1995), and *Air Force One* (1997), about the hijacking of the president's personal aircraft.

When, late in the decade, The American Film Institute released a list of the 100 greatest movies, a number of movies from the 1990s proved worthy of inclusion, a noteworthy accomplishment given that the Institute had put a cap on the list, allowing only movies made in 1996 or before to be considered. The list included *Schindler's List, Forrest Gump, GoodFellas, Pulp Fiction,* and *Unforgiven.* It also included Jonathan Demme's serial-killer thriller, *Silence of the Lambs* (1991), Kevin Costner's elegiac Western about a Civil War soldier living amongst the Lakota Sioux, *Dances With Wolves* (1990), and Joel and Ethan Coen's updated *film-noir, Fargo* (1996). Since the list came out, opinion on these specific films has shifted somewhat, even as other overlooked films have climbed in estimation. But the list and more recent critical response to nineties cinema has indicated that the decade was among the most vital, and that the very nature of cinema changed because of pioneering efforts in the 1990s.

THEATRE

Throughout the twentieth century, the theatre faced a difficult struggle. With the advent of cinema, and later of television, the theatre saw itself displaced as the most popular form of public entertainment, and as the century came to a close, the theatre came to be seen as something of an elitist form of entertainment. Partly this had to do with the shift from light entertainment (a task largely taken over by film and television) to more thematically serious drama. Another reason was that the cost of tickets, which frequently broke the triple digits dollar amount, particularly on Broadway, proved prohibitive to many. For many, attending the theatre was a far more laborious process than switching on the TV or hopping down to the cinemaplex, entailing not only the expense, but also, given the relative sparsity of live theatre compared to film, frequent travel time. This said, the theatre certainly was not dead in the 1990s, which saw the rise of numerous small theatre companies, and some truly adventurous new playwrights. Ultimately, for most of the small theatre companies which popped up all over the country in the 1990s, putting on plays was a labor of love, since the revenues were limited such that for most the dream of making a living in the theatre remained a dream.

MUSICAL THEATRE

On Broadway, theatre producers made efforts to entice a more general audience, to counter the notion of the theatre as elitist, and met with considerable success. While the number of Americans who could actually travel to Broadway and pay to see a major show remained small, enough interest was mustered to fill theatres. But, interestingly, in seeking a more popular appeal, Broadway seemed to look into its past for inspiration. The most popular theatrical form in the 1990s was the musical, a long staple of Broadway. Concerns developed in the late 1980s with the deaths of many major names in musical theatre, including Michael Bennett and Bob Fosse, but the genre did not fade out. It is perhaps notable, however, that those shows which met with the most success were not new to the 1990s. Englishman Andrew Lloyd Webber, the top producer of Broadway musicals in the decade, enjoyed continued success with shows like *Cats* and *Phantom of the Opera*. Interestingly, these two tremendously successful musicals of the 1990s started their runs in 1981 and 1986, respectively. When Webber attempted to give birth to a new hit musical, *Sunset Boulevard*, based on the Billy Wilder film, he was disappointed. The show opened in 1994 with record-breaking advanced ticket sales of $37.5 million, but failed to sustain the initial excitement, closing as a financial failure. Webber's American counterpart, Stephen Sondheim, fared little better in the 1990s, rarely scoring the success of his earlier ventures. Among his 1990s productions were *Assassins* (1990), a dark musical in which all of the characters merit the title description, and *Passion*, which opened in 1994. It is perhaps telling that *Passion*, like Webber's *Sunset Boulevard*, was based on a film, in this case Ettore Scola's *Passione d'Amour*. Notably, one of the most successful musicals of the 1990s was also based on a movie, the 1994 Disney film, *The Lion King*. The Broadway musical version, launched in 1998, was produced by Disney with music by Elton John and lyrics by Tim Rice. Another of the great musical success stories of Broadway was *Rent*, written by Jonathan Larson and directed by Michael Greif. *Rent*, which opened on Broadway on April

29, 1996, was inspired by Puccini's opera, *La Bohème*, though it brought the story to an urban setting. With lively music and dance, the show involved the trials and tribulations of several young New Yorkers "facing the soaring hopes and painful realities of contemporary life."[2] The show proved to be one of the most successful Broadway musicals ever, earning a place among its longest-running shows, and also winning the Tony Award and Pulitzer Prize.

Several major dance-musical shows also met with resounding success, though, interestingly, many of these were actually European imports. Started in 1991 in England by Luke Cresswell and Steve McNicholas, *Stomp* combined percussion, industrial noise, dance, and visual comedy in a lively, adrenaline-pumping way that caught on across the globe. The *Stomp* performers quickly gained a positive reputation, and by the second year they were making commercials across the globe, including a high-profile Coca-Cola television ad. By the time the troupe came to the states, they were virtually guaranteed sold-out shows across the country. This kind of performance inspired many imitations and variations, drawing from the same sense of urban creativity.

Another vital form of dance in the 1990s, and one that also inspired much imitation, was Celtic dance. *Riverdance* was the trailblazer in this form, combining the traditions of Irish dance with a modern sensibility. The show was started in 1991 and was gradually refined, with Bill Whelan serving as composer, Moya Doherty as producer, and John McColgan as director. With the success of *Riverdance*, a number of other Irish dance troupes came to the fore, most importantly, *Lord of the Dance*, headed by dancer Michael Flatley, with Ronan Hardiman as composer and Marie Duffy as dance director.

THEATRICAL DRAMA

In 1996, Sondheim launched his first non-musical Broadway show, a thriller written with George Furst called *Getting Away With Murder*. This play was met with a lukewarm reception, but it was a significant sign that Broadway had not completely closed its doors to serious drama, as had been proclaimed by playwright Marsha Norman in 1987.[3] Indeed, it had become difficult for non-musical plays to find a reception on Broadway, but certainly not impossible. Tellingly, one of Broadway's most celebrated productions in 1999 was Arthur Miller's *Death of a Salesman*, first produced in 1949, and celebrating its fiftieth anniversary with Brian Dennehy in the lead role. Other classic plays were also exhumed, such as Tennessee Williams's *Not About Nightingales*, which was written in the 1930s, but not produced until the 1990s, after actress Vanessa Redgrave discovered the manuscript and got it produced in London. It opened on Broadway in 1999.

On and off Broadway, many established playwrights continued fruitfully, in some cases creating some of the most acclaimed work of their careers. Such was the case with Neil Simon, long a Broadway favorite for his nostalgic comedies, who continued his successful career with *Lost in Yonkers* (1991), which won the Tony Award and a Pulitzer Prize and was recognized as one of the best works of his career. Simon followed this with *Jake's Women* (1992), *Laughter on the 23rd Floor* (1993), *London Suite* (1995), and *Proposals* (1997). While none of these gained the same acclaim as *Lost in Yonkers,* they nonetheless helped establish Simon as an indelible part of American theatre into the 1990s. Despite the success of the revival of *Death of a Salesman,* Arthur Miller's 1990s output, including *The Last Yankee* (1993), *Broken Glass* (1994), *Mr. Peters' Connection* (1998), and *The Ride Down Mt. Morgan* (1991, 1998), was received tepidly. This was true of other established playwrights, as well. Several new Sam Shepard plays also saw light in the 1990s—*States of Shock* (1991), *Simpatico* (1994), and *Eyes for Consuela* (1998)—but these were considered minor plays and were largely outdone by revivals of older Shepard plays. Other more successful players in the 1990s included David Mamet—with *Oleanna* (1992), *The Cryptogram* (1995), and *The Old Neighborhood* (1997)—and Wendy Wasserstein, who wrote *The Sisters Rosensweig* (1992) and *An American Daughter* (1997).

Ultimately, however, the place for most serious playwrights, and especially new playwrights, was off Broadway, in New York and off off Broadway elsewhere, and it was in these theaters that the vitality of the theatre truly showed itself. The number of new plays and playwrights in the 1990s is large, but some specific figures deserve particular attention. Among these is Tony Kushner, who made his debut in 1991 with *A Bright Room Called Day*, about the rise of fascism in 1932 Berlin. *A Bright Room Called Day* ran for two weeks and met with mixed reviews, but Kushner would achieve considerable fame in a few short years for his *Angels in America*. The first installment of this two part play, *Part I: Millennium Approaches*, first appeared in London and Los Angeles, and then debuted on Broadway in May of 1993. The play, set during the Reagan era, involved three overlapping storylines and numerous characters, from a former drag queen to a conservative Mormon lawyer. The play commented on politics, race, and religion, but was perhaps most notable for its frank treatment of AIDS and homosexuality. The play won not only several Tonys, for both the production and several of its actors, but was also awarded a Pulitzer. *Part II: Perestroika* appeared later that year, in November 1993. Although Kushner was not the first playwright to address the AIDS epidemic (Larry Kramer and others preceded him), his plays nonetheless opened the floodgates and many others followed his lead in addressing the issue, including Joe Pintauro (*Raft of the Medusa*, 1991), Cheryl L. West (*Before It Hits Home*, 1992), Paul Rudnick (*Jeffrey*, 1993), and Chay Yew (*A Language of Their Own*, 1995).

Another important figure in nineties theatre was Paula Vogel, a controversial playwright whose first major play, *The Baltimore Waltz*, was produced in 1992. *And Baby Makes Seven* (1993) and *Desdemona–A Play About a*

Handkerchief (1993) followed, but like *The Baltimore Waltz,* were received with mixed reviews. It was with *How I Learned to Drive* (1997), which revolved around a sexual relationship between an older man and a young girl, that Vogel came into dramatic renown. The play earned strong reviews and a solid run of 400 performances. The play also won the Pulitzer Prize. Vogel's next play, *The Mineola Twins,* while less well-received, nonetheless continued to establish Vogel as an important writer of sexually charged plays with a strong feminist and sociopolitical bent.

The costs of producing a play made the theatre prohibitive for many producers, so an according rise could be seen in the number of one-man or one-woman shows. John Leguizamo, also known for his film acting, created three of the most highly regarded one-man shows, starting with *Mambo Mouth,* which opened in November of 1990. This show was followed by *Spic-O-Rama* in 1992, and *Freak* in 1998. In each of these productions, which became gradually more autobiographical, Leguizamo explored various aspects of Hispanic culture, alternately playing various characters from his family and the American Latino community in general. Spalding Gray, a master of the one-man monologue since the mid 1980s, continued in this vein as well, writing and performing *Monster in a Box* (1990), *Gray's Anatomy* (1993), *It's a Slippery Slope* (1996), and *Morning, Noon and Night* (1999). A third major figure in the one-man play movement was Eric Bogosian, who wrote and performed several caustic monologues satirizing the general mean-spiritedness of modern America. These included *Sex, Drugs, Rock & Roll* (1990) and *Pounding Nails in the Floor with My Forehead* (1994). Ana Deavere Smith was also a major figure in the one-person show, starting with *Fires in the Mirror* in 1992, which dealt with the 1991 Crown Heights riots, during which violence broke out between local African Americans and Jews. Smith, herself African American, offered, as one critic would have it, "the most compelling and sophisticated view of urban racial and class conflict."[4] Another series of riots would provide the source for Smith's next presentation, *Twilight: Los Angeles, 1992* (1994). The success of these performers, and the fact that they were able to put their productions on with such a limited budget, stimulated the one-player show considerably, and many followed in their footsteps, including Wallace Shawn (*The Fever,* 1990), James Prideaux (*Lyndon,* 1990), Dan Butler (*The Only Thing Worse You Could Have Told Me . . .* , 1995), Josh Kornbluth (*Red Diaper Baby,* 1992), David Drake (*The Night Larry Kramer Kissed Me,* 1992), Claudia Shear (*Blown Sideways Through Life,* 1993), and Eve Ensler (*The Vagina Monologues,* 1996).

CONCLUSION

Perhaps no other arts were more telling about the American public than the performing arts, especially television and film. It seemed as if all of the fears and hopes of the American people were manifested in *The X-Files* and *The Simpsons*. However, as more than one cultural critic has pointed out, the media has at least as much power to shape the public's perceptions as the public has to shape the media. We may as yet lack the historical perspective to determine exactly how it did so in the 1990s. We can confidently talk of how the domestic sitcoms of the 1950s reinforced gender roles. But what are we to determine from the success of *Seinfeld*, other than that it was funny? One can make assumptions about how it revealed the banality of urban life, but most would also argue that the show revealed nothing to them that they didn't already know about it. Likewise, it is difficult to determine whether shows like *The X-Files* instilled millennial fears or merely tapped into them. The ultimate significance of American performing arts in the 1990s remains to be seen.

11
Travel

GENERAL TRAVEL TRENDS

Undoubtedly, the 1990s were a boom decade for travel and the tourism industry, with more people moving themselves into, out of, and around the United States than ever before. Yet it was also a very volatile decade, with new challenges brought about by developing technologies, competitive business practices, and new notions on the part of many Americans about the nature of travel. Travel and tourism to this country had continued to grow consistently throughout the twentieth century, particularly in the latter half of it. This trend continued in the 1990s, and, in fact, by 1991 tourism in all its forms—including airlines and hotels—had become the largest employer. The travel industry, heavily reliant on service workers, was also notable in its hiring of non-white female immigrants, who, frequently working for minimum wage, accounted for as much as 80 percent of the new hires of the 1990s. In 1999, the number of international arrivals to the United States reached 663 million. Not surprisingly, then, travel proved itself to be the third largest retail industry, behind the automobile and food industries. A 1999 study of the prior year revealed that travel and tourism accounted for an economic impact of 1.3 trillion dollars and over 16 million jobs.[1] Interestingly, during the decade the United States slipped a spot on the list of top travel destinations, coming in third place behind France and Spain. Still, this created limited concern in the travel industry given the steady increase in sheer numbers of tourists. Additionally, the United States maintained its position as the top tourism income earner. A 1998 study showed that the United States tourism receipts equaled some $74,240 million, more than double that made by Italy, the second place on this list with $30,427 million.[2]

The airline industry particularly enjoyed a prosperous decade. By 1997, the airline industry was launching over 22,350 flights a day and netted record annual profits of over $5.2 billion. By the end of the 1990s, the industry consisted of about 800 different airlines, employing more that three million people, carrying more than one billion passengers a year. These airlines were complemented by some 14,000 airports across the world, including giant new constructions, like the Denver International Airport, which in 1995 became the first major new U.S. airport to be built in twenty years, and Hong Kong's twenty billion dollar airport built in 1998. This is perhaps surprising given that the first few years of the 1990s were, in fact, rough ones for the industry, with losses of approximately $12.8 billion. The turnaround was largely due to an increase in the sheer number of travelers, as well as low fuel costs.[3]

The amount of business travel grew in the nineties, in part because of the changing nature of many companies. With improvements in communication technologies, especially with the abilities to transmit so much information via computers and the Internet, one might well imagine that business travel would be less of a necessity. But in fact, such technology allowed businesses to function smoothly with locations on either coast and numerous other remote locations, or even locations overseas. The greater spread of such businesses led to an increase in business travel in order to facilitate important face-to-face interaction within a company and with clients. In the world of pleasure travel, consumerism was a driving force, with shopping playing a major part in the tourism industry of any city or country. But more than mere physical goods, travel itself became an object of conspicuous consumption, with the ability to tell of one's travels and adventures amounting to a considerable status symbol. The status associated with travel was not new to the 1990s, but with the growing ease of travel and relative decrease in expense, the game of one-upmanship became more fervent, with consumers zealously pursuing the latest ground-breaking trend in travel. It has also been suggested that the length of the average workday increased during this period, as did the number of stressful and sedentary jobs. This, along with the increased pace of life in general, may well have added new imperative to the desire to get away for a vacation.[4]

The travel book industry, no doubt in reaction to the growth of the travel industry itself, expanded considerably in the 1990s, with new publishers leaping into the fray and older publishers printing more books than ever before. While much of the market tapped into actual travelers, the sheer quality of many of the books, in terms of photography and textual content (including not only travel tips, but also cultural and historical information) also garnered a significant share of buyers who were not active travelers. There was also a growth in specialization in the travel book industry, with books geared specifically to families, or the elderly, or ecotourists, or gay male and lesbian travelers.

Naturally, there was sharp rise in tourism at the end of the decade, as many Americans sought to be somewhere special on New Year's Eve when the twentieth century came to an end. There were, of course, some who very specifically chose not to stray too far from home, given fear of millennium-related terrorism and the Y2K bug, a potential disaster for a travel industry which had come to rely so much on computers. And, then, there were many who stayed near home simply in the interest of avoiding unprecedented crowds at New Year's celebrations. Certainly, even with those hesitant to travel, there was no shortage of revelers, and the travel and hospitality industries did well to gird themselves. There were numerous hot spots in the United States, including Washington, D.C., and New York's Times Square, as well as internationally. Major cities worldwide filled up with tourists, and lodging rates reflected this, with hot spot hotel rooms not uncommonly costing more than a thousand dollars for the night of December 31, 1999.

DEMOGRAPHICS

A 1999 study identified five separate generational groupings for the purpose of defining, and marketing to, the American traveling population. The first of these was the *Depression Kids,* born between 1915 and 1930, which constituted about 25 percent of the population, but held some 50 percent of the nation's discretionary income. This group was a significant one in considering the nature of American travelers, contributing to about 30 percent of domestic travel. Additionally, this group amounted to 65 percent of cruise tourism and a full 80 percent of recreational vehicle (RV) travel. The second generational grouping identified by the study was the *Swing Generation,* born 1931 to 1945, which, in the 1990s, found itself moving into similar travel patterns as those of the Depression Kids. Without question, constituting the dominant travel market for the 1990s were the *Baby Boomers,* born 1946 to 1964. Now middle-aged, this group typically sought nonstressful vacations and sport-oriented trips, so these were naturally the kinds of vacations pushed the most by the travel industry. But with the fourth generation, *Generation X,* a new goal of travel could be seen. Generation X, being the youngest independent traveling generation (with the fifth grouping, *Echo Boomers* still too young, by and large, to travel independently), sought a different kind of vacation experience, one which did not merely allow them to get away and relax, but one which also offered challenges. Self-testing sports, including hiking, skiing, rock climbing, and bicycling, became extremely popular with this generation of travelers, offering not only escape, but adventure.[5]

WORLD TRAVEL

Globalization became an increasingly pressing concern in the 1990s. In the United States, major cities began to resemble one another more as the same kind of large chain businesses moved in. Concern arose about how a city could stand out and remain distinct—thereby remaining a worthwhile tourist destination—even as it acquired the same retailers, the same restaurants to be found from city to city. This was also a factor internationally, as much more of the world came under the shadow of a kind of American corporate imperialism. As one tourism expert suggested, "The homogenized global village emerged as the initial specter as the Americanization of the world spread via CNN and by construction of some 23,000 Golden Arches in 110 countries. Why travel when there is a Benneton in every French village?"[6]

In 1990, the Berlin Wall came down, which was shortly followed by the reunification of Germany. Naturally, this opened what had been East Germany to a whole new tourist market that had largely been stifled due to its Communist regime and internationally imposed travel restrictions. But the fall of the Berlin Wall was also symbolic of the general collapse of Communism in the late 1980s and early 1990s. Some formerly Communist countries, as well as former Soviet republics, remained dangerous places to visit as political and social power struggles, even civil war, filled in the gap left by Communism's fall. But many others, including Poland and Russia, found their now open borders access points to numerous travelers, driven largely by curiosity about these nations that had been hidden away from them in the past.

THE INTERNET

The rapid growth in travel, particularly air travel, was aided considerably by the development of the Internet, which allowed prospective travelers to make travel arrangements from home. Those offering accommodations, be they hotel chains or independently run bed and breakfasts, quickly became aware of the Internet's potential, and set up Web sites on which travelers could investigate the accommodations, including rates and room availability. They could even reserve lodging online. The same was also true when it came to airlines, with Alaska Airlines becoming the first carrier to offer online booking. But as more took to the Web to offer their services, the competition among airlines soon became fierce. For lodging, customers tended to think in terms of locations and lodging quality, but to most travelers, the differences between airlines was negligible. Therefore, online airline shopping encouraged a more rigorous kind of price comparison. In a matter of minutes, a customer could find out the cost of a particular destination as serviced by several different airlines. Internet service providers took this a step further, providing patrons with engines that would search out all available flights, ranking them according to the individual's preference, largely dictated by travel schedules and price. Many other companies flourished in this period, including American Express,

Preview Travel, TravelWeb, and Travelocity, a particularly elaborate service announced in 1995 by corporate partners Worldview Systems and Netscape. Some online services, most notably Priceline.com, marketed themselves as services that would find the lowest price for consumers. Online shoppers also had unparalleled opportunities to book at the last minute and claim, at dramatically diminished prices, unsold space on flights. Such ease with which consumers could compare prices led the already competitive airline industry into unprecedented price wars, and with lowering prices came a comparable increase in the number of Americans who could afford travel by air. Equivalent advances were made for lodgings, particularly by the company Promus. The Promus Web site displayed a U.S. map. Customers could use the map to zoom in on their intended destination and find up-to-the-minute details on room types, availability, and cost.[7]

Additionally, much time and money was spent by tourist destinations to promote themselves online. The *1997 Survey on Technology Uses* found that individual state tourism offices spent over $1.7 million that year developing and maintaining Web sites.[8] Many tourist destinations also had sites with virtual tours, which allowed those using the sites to get a sense of what a location had to offer before undertaking the task of planning a trip. Some viewed such virtual tourism as a kind of substitute for actual travel, as individuals could travel the routes of their choice to destinations marked by colorful photographs, animations, or even live Web-cam shots of the locale. The advantages of this kind of travel were obvious, with far reduced expense, no travel time cooped up in an airplane cabin, no environmental impact, and no real risk to personal safety. Of course, no sort of virtual environment could truly duplicate an actual destination. Despite all of the advances, computer technology still fell well short of providing complete immersion in a virtual world, but even if it succeeded, there is much doubt that this kind of activity would truly sate the lust for travel. At least one scholar suggested that, in fact, this kind of virtual tourism would further foster the notion of a dream vacation, and that people's "use of the Internet may further instill an interest for *real* tourism, as did *National Geographic* and the stereopticon in the days of their grandparents."[9]

Of course, the Internet certainly had its limitations. As more reputable companies, including airlines, travel agencies, and Internet service providers, got involved in online travel planning, security likewise strengthened. But early in the decade, Internet fraud posed a major problem, which still existed to a certain degree later, especially for travel to more isolated locations. The general security of booking through a travel agency was less certain online than in person. Travel agents themselves, realizing the limitations of the Internet, but also aware that they were losing many customers to online self-booking, found themselves becoming less travel arrangers than information brokers, who could assist travelers in their arrangements and provide information on avoiding the pitfalls of online booking and travel in general.

THE DANGERS OF TRAVEL

On September 11, 2001, terrorism horrifically thrust itself into the public consciousness, and delivered a mighty blow to the airline industry and tourism as a whole. But it should not be thought that terrorism was a phenomenon new to the twenty-first century. Indeed, terrorism was a concern for travelers well before even the 1990s, but several high-profile incidents increased the awareness of the dangers of flying overseas (though domestic flights were still considered relatively safe). Notably, since the 1991 Gulf War (reiterated in 1998's Desert Fox operations against Iraq), there was a sharp increase in terrorist activity, especially in the Middle East. Strife in some former Soviet republics made these equally dangerous travel destinations, along with regions of Northern Africa, Latin America, and the Baltic states, among others. Indeed, there was no continent not affected by terrorism in the 1990s, and this had a distinct effect on tourism. Furthermore, much of this accelerated terrorism was directed towards American targets. Tourists and tourism hot spots became what have been described as "soft targets," that is, easy targets, difficult to defend yet high-profile enough to garner terrorist groups the attention they desired.

Unlike the terrorist attacks of September 2001, however, the terrorism of the 1990s slowed tourism to particular destinations, but did not bring the American airline industry to a halt. Suffering more from terrorism were the countries that relied on tourism for a significant amount of their national revenue. Egypt, for instance, felt a considerable economic loss in the wake of a November 1997 terrorist attack on tourists visiting a historic temple. The attack killed 58 people. One study, however, suggested that the effects of such terrorism on at least some tourist sites was fleeting, with tourism returning to full visitation within six weeks.[10] This claim notwithstanding, other experts still saw terrorism as a major detriment to travel overseas, as noted repeatedly in textbooks on the subject.[11] Whatever the case may be on this front, there was no question that the 1990s saw a very distinct rise in terrorism, especially that directed at American targets, a troubling precursor of events to come.

Perhaps one of the oddest developments out of the increasingly threatening world was an unusual book series issued by notable travel book publisher Fielding, Robert Young Pelton's *The World's Most Dangerous Places*. Though prefaced with stern warnings that the destinations listed in the book were indeed dangerous, and that typically these should not be considered as tourist destinations, the book was nonetheless marketed as a travel handbook, and it became a *New York Times* best-seller, at that. Ultimately, the annual editions of the books served mostly as interesting reading for people who would never actually see the destinations in question. At most, the book served as a handbook for people who might be forced to visit such destinations for work or other reasons. But even if few of the purchasers of this book actually ever considered visiting the war zones and such listed therein, the book's very existence and success suggests an important aspect of travel and the tourist mentality of the 1990s.

ADVENTURE AND SPORTS TRAVEL

For many Americans, no longer was it acceptable to merely go out and visit the typical tourist sites. The desire now was for adventure, travel off the beaten track. It might be argued that the growth in adventure travel was a response to the increasingly restrictive nature of urban life and work. As many Americans settled into daily routines, working at sedentary jobs within densely populated office buildings, the appeal of an outdoor, out of town challenge likewise increased. Many travelers found what they were looking for via the sports vacation. These travelers pursued vacations involving hiking, camping, bicycling, rock climbing, boating, and numerous other physical activities. Skiing, river rafting, and similar activity oriented industries flourished. The number of American's engaging in outdoor sports increased notably in the 1990s, as did travel of this sort. Travel emphasized not so much being somewhere as doing something. Camping and backpacking trips became increasingly popular as Americans sought temporary solace from the hustle of urban life. One survey found that more than 53 million people went camping in the 1994–1995 season, over 10 million more than a decade before. Even more remarkable was the increase in camping in primitive areas. Rather than simply visiting established camping areas, Americans sought out areas that were isolated, that were as far as possible from civilization. Indeed, the 1994–1995 study found that the number of primitive area campers had almost doubled from the 1982–1983 season.[12] Likewise, skiing vacations increased in popularity, with snowboarding's growing popularity (driven by the rise in popularity of *extreme* sports, as well as by its induction into Olympic competition) adding significantly to ski resorts' revenues. An estimated average of 400,000 people a year visited North Lake Tahoe alone, with other resort areas posting similar numbers. There was a corresponding boom in the number of travelers visiting the country's national parks. Additionally, there was a significant increase in the number of tourists who pursued marine activities like swimming with dolphins, or close-quarters whale watching. These attractions proved problematic for marine biologists, who certainly saw how they could serve to educate the public about ocean life, but also remarked that hoards of tourists also infringed upon the natural environments and behaviors of sea creatures.

Many travelers took a new approach to international travel, as well. The 1990s saw a significant increase in travel to less developed (or third world) nations, which included much of the South American and African continents. Similarly, many took to backpacking across Europe or the Orient, or any other destination they might reach. It should be noted that adventure travel differed from what might be called exploration travel. In earlier times, exploration travel was significant, but with the rapid diminishment of land still to be explored, adventure traveling of the 1990s tended towards less developed, but more or less known lands. The interest of adventure travel was not to accumulate knowledge of the world for the benefit of mankind, per se (nor to find exploitable resources), rather it was generally seen as contributing to personal growth. Interaction with native populaces outside of well-worked tourist destinations, it was reasoned, must be more enlightening than the usual tourist traps. Likewise, first-hand experience with exotic locales certainly must be more personally enlightening and invigorating than simply reading about such places in *National Geographic*. Such travel was not without critics, however, who noted that adventure travelers often lacked contextual understanding of the cultures they visited and upon whom they passed judgment. Additionally, adventure travel was also unquestionably a status builder, offering bragging rights, rather than enlightenment, to whomever visited the most exotic locales.

As mentioned above, adventure travel's appeal was amplified for a fairly young segment of the population, those pegged with the label Generation X. No longer minors restricted by the wishes of parents, the individuals of this generation came into their own as independent consumers, and consequently were for the first time, en masse, planning their own vacations. This was also the generation seemingly most dissatisfied with the growing urbanization of the U.S. and also the growing homogeneity of America's urban spaces, perceived as instituted by earlier generations. Additionally, it has been suggested that Generation X travelers, having been raised by media and in largely suburbanized areas, were seeking a real sense of identity, defined neither by the media nor their parents.

ENVIRONMENT AND SUSTAINABLE TOURISM

One of the major problems of tourism is that tourist destinations simply experience the wear and tear that comes with increased traveler traffic. Such has long been the case with tourism, but the latter decades of the twentieth century seemed to demonstrate an increased awareness of the damage that could be inflicted by tourism. England's Stonehenge, for instance, saw increased levels of protection. The ancient monument which could once be viewed by visitors close up, even touched by them, was cordoned off in 1989. Ultimately, the separation of traveler from artifact diminished the experience of visiting Stonehenge and like destinations, but so, too, would the gradual degradation of the monument.

Naturally, the concern about man-made destinations was echoed in consideration of natural attractions, including natural parks and preserves. Visits to federally owned natural sites increased some 40 percent from 1986 to 1996.[13] The increase in the number of travelers to national parks by and large outpaced the parks service's efforts to provide accommodations and to reduce the detrimental environmental effects of the tourist crowds. As one tourism expert noted, "Vehicular travel to national parks such as the Grand Canyon, Yellowstone, and Yosemite already exceed[ed] comfortable carrying capacity."[14] At issue was how the government and park managers were to deal with the effects of increased tourism. Obviously, the infrastructure of the parks was fast becoming insufficient for the tourist load, but to increase the size of roads, to build more tourist accommodations, posed the very real risk of infringing upon the natural environment, the very attraction drawing visitors.

As concern over the state of the environment increased in the late twentieth century, so, too, did the attention given to the effects of tourism on the environment. The great irony of the situation is that many of those same travelers who contributed to the degradation of a site, visited with the intent of getting back in touch with nature, driven to impede into natural environments by the same impulse that would have them endeavor to protect them. It has been suggested that "*all* forms of tourism function as agents of change for host communities," regardless of how benign traveler intentions might be.[15] Thus arose the concept of environmental tourism, also called "green" tourism and, from the travel industry side, sustainable tourism. The early 1990s saw several pioneering books espousing the ideas of environmental tourism, particularly *Ecotourism: The Potentials and Pitfalls* by E. Boo, which outlined the problems and set a precedent for exploring ways to sustain both the desires of travelers and the environments to which they traveled. On a global level, tourism's environmental impact was indirectly addressed at a 1992 Earth Summit, where government representatives from 179 countries unanimously endorsed an agenda designed to address the problem. This agreement, Local Agenda 21, demonstrated a shift from the paramount concern of tourism development in the mid-twentieth century. Whereas, previously governments were principally concerned with tourism growth, this agenda encouraged the sustaining of destination lands with additional funding, land grants, and tax incentives on the part of host governments. While the initial agenda did not specifically name tourism, a 1999 meeting of the U.N. Committee on Sustainable Development refined Local Agenda 21, calling for further government efforts in this matter, and also calling on the travel industry itself to educate travelers—through in-flight videos and publications, for instance—about how to reduce their environmental impact.

Of course, one important issue was also how tourism, even ecotourism, might affect local populations. Tourism certainly had an effect on native populations, and some experts expressed their concerns about how sustainable tourism was being applied to the environment of destinations without consideration of other factors. At least one writer addressed the issue vehemently: "Unfortunately, well-intentioned travelers and even some officials advise indigenous villagers or remote rural residents, 'you ought to develop ecotourism—it will create jobs and cash income.' Such statements are often irresponsible and a disservice to residents because these well-intentioned advisors fail to fully comprehend sustainability and its complexities."[16]

Ultimately, however, most travelers sought pleasure, and were not looking to become environmental crusaders. Nonetheless, the number of ecotourists increased, as did the number of general travelers with an eye to the environment. This growth was visible in the increased attention on the part of transportation services and hotels to the environment, and, perhaps more importantly, to making their attention to the environment visible to the consumer. The most common example of this was the posting of signs encouraging hotel lodgers to reuse towels for several days in order to reduce water use and the dissemination of laundry detergents into the environment. Additionally, many tourists sought to lessen their impact on the environments visited by camping, rather than staying in hotel lodgings, or relying increasingly on hiking and biking than on less environmentally friendly modes of vehicular travel. Indeed, this kind of travel tapped into impulses other than conservation, as well. In essence, ecotourism went hand in hand with adventure travel.

GAMBLING DESTINATIONS

Traditional gambling destinations—Atlantic City, Las Vegas, and Reno—suffered in the 1990s on several counts. First, legalized gambling grew as an industry throughout the country in the latter part of the century, with many states allowing for limited casino development and the installment of state lotteries. Moreover, in 1988, congress passed the Indian Gaming Regulatory Act, which limited how much states could regulate Native American–run casinos on Indian lands. As a result, hundreds of largely unregulated and untaxed Indian casinos sprouted up across the country. In part spurred by the growth in Indian casinos, many states instituted limited legal gambling. In 1990 alone, Colorado, Illinois, and Mississippi enabled some degree of gambling. These were shortly followed by Louisiana, Missouri, Indiana, and Michigan. Canada also relaxed its gambling restrictions in the early 1990s. While many of these regions limited gambling to waterways or rural locations, the casinos still reduced the need for travelers to go the distance to Nevada or Atlantic City to place their bets.[17] The 1990s also saw the development of Internet gambling. Gamers could now wager without leaving the comforts of home, and while early online casinos were fairly simplistic, later models offered elaborate virtual casino environments.[18]

Still, even with the rise in online gambling, a study revealed that in 2000 some 72.8 million travelers, about 7 percent of domestic travelers, made trips that involved significant gaming.[19] A significant part of this continued success was due to the development of new luxury hotel-casinos, such as the Luxor Hotel, Treasure Island, Mandalay, and others in Las Vegas and the Silver Legacy in Reno. These new casinos marketed themselves differently than the gambling industry had in the past. Instead of emphasizing gaming, these hotels mostly publicized the non-gaming entertainment, particularly spectacular shows with big name entertainers. Moreover, many of these hotels emphasized the family aspect of the casinos, a precedent set by the Circus Circus hotels back in the 1970s, come to full fruition in the 1990s. A casino like the Luxor, opened in 1993 as the world's third largest hotel, for instance, could market itself by its elaborate Egyptian theming, complete with pyramid and sphinx. Treasure Island offered an extravagant pirate spectacle designed to appeal to the entire family. The draw of these new hotels, however, resulted in no small amount of suffering on the part of smaller, older casinos, many of which went out of business during the decade, leaving much of downtown Reno, for instance, filled with vacant buildings by century's end.

AUTOMOTIVE TRAVEL

Not surprisingly, automobiles continued to dominate by far as the most popular mode of transportation. A 1996 study found that auto travel (including rental cars, trucks, and recreational vehicles) accounted for about 80 percent of personal travel in the United States. Air travel accounted for 17 percent, with bus and train travel barely registering with but 1 percent each. The rental car industry itself grew at a pace at least equaling, perhaps even exceeding, that of the airline industry.[20] Clearly, the appeal of auto travel was the same as it had always been, as cars granted a sense of personal control and flexibility that other modes of transport did not. If anything, this sense was amplified in the 1990s, with car models often reflecting the desire for freedom and individuality on the part of drivers. This should not imply that the auto industry produced a great variety of vehicles in the 1990s, but that common models tapped into these desires. Starting in the mid-1990s, for instance, Pontiac and Chevrolet produced the Sunfire and the Cavalier, respectively. These cars were virtually identical in appearance, but both exploited sporty looks to tap into the desire for affordable automotive excitement that many drivers felt.

This is also important to consider in light of the sports utility vehicle (SUV) boom of the 1990s. The SUV bridged the gap between the family car and the truck, and added an extra dash of sportiness to the whole package.

Volkswagen's new Beetle at the Insurance Institute for Highway Safety in Ruckersville, Va. The Beetle received an overall "good" rating meaning it tops the 11 other small cars crash-tested by the Institute in the past few years. © AP/Wide World Photos.

The vehicles were rugged, large, four-wheel drive powerhouse autos, designed to take on all kinds of terrain. Advertisements for SUVs typically showed them climbing mountains, racing through mud, and the like. Moreover, the names given these vehicles frequently tapped into the notion of adventure unfettered by the constraints of urban life: Blazer, Cherokee, Expedition, Tahoe, Yukon, and Bronco. The Bronco, particularly, experienced an odd increase in sales on the heels of O.J. Simpson's fugitive run up Los Angeles freeways in 1994. Interestingly, despite, or more likely as a result of their reputation as untamed, wide-ranging, adventuresome vehicles, SUVs found some of their greatest patrons in urban and suburban areas. SUVs were significantly more expensive than the average pick-up one might find in rural areas, and consequently, the SUV appeal was mostly among young urban professionals. SUVs also found a major market among women, who may well have made up the majority of the SUV market. In fact, the SUV was an ideal vehicle for professional women with families, and with suburban housewives, since it could accommodate many passengers and goods. Moreover, it may well be that such large, powerful vehicles also gave the drivers a sense of empowerment, and a sense of arrogance according to some detractors. Indeed, despite the proliferation of SUVs, many still questioned the mentality that would purchase and drive an SUV, as well as the need for such a vehicle on well-paved city streets. SUVs were also taken to task because of their truly awful gas mileage, and were accurately marked as the greatest gas guzzlers of the road. Whatever their disadvantages, however, the SUV craze continued unabated. There was a not insignificant 7 million SUVs on American roads in 1993, but at the end of the decade this number had risen to a whopping 20 million with sales still on the rise.[21]

Several car manufacturers also tapped into the nostalgia held by many Americans, especially those of the baby-boom generation, for the seemingly simpler days of their youth. The prime example of this is the reintroduction of the Volkswagen Beetle in 1997. U.S. sales on the classic Beetle came to an end in 1978, though Volkswagen continued production in Mexico into the 1990s. The reintroduced Beetle was, in fact, only superficially similar to the earlier models, bearing more resemblance under its shell to the more conventional VW Golf. But that shell, a modernized variation on the classic Beetle, made all the difference. The Beetle became one of the most popular small cars of the late 1990s, and was given even more retail fuel when Bill Clinton bought one for his daughter.[22] The Beetle was followed by other nostalgia vehicles, most notably Chrysler's PT Cruiser, a combination of 1930s style and 1990s minivan engineering, which was introduced in 1999 to immediate widespread popularity.

Of course, more traditional designs continued to flourish in the market, with plenty of racy sport cars and economy cars reaching their traditional consumers. But many of the automotive advances were not so cosmetic. There were considerable advances in automotive safety, especially in terms of body design and increased use of airbags, which was at least one of the reasons for the elimination of a federally-mandated maximum speed law. This change allowed states and cities to determine their own speed limits, or in one area of Montana, to do away with a posted speed limit altogether. Additionally, auto makers began incorporating more elaborate computer systems into vehicles. Some cars had computerized security systems, some had digital dashboard instruments, and some had elaborate computerized entertainment systems, complete with television for those in the back seat. Perhaps most significant was the incorporation of a Global Positioning System (GPS) in some vehicles. When used in conjunction with a computerized map system, the GPS could inform a driver as to his or her exact location, and offer directions to the desired destination. In 1997, one company thought to link the GPS with cellular technology. The company, OnStar, picked up where other services, like Clarion's AutoPC left off. Whereas earlier variations employed fully computerized systems, OnStar connected drivers with live operators using wireless cellular technology. The data conveyed to the human operator included the car's exact location. Consequently, operators could inform customers of not only their location, but of nearby roadways or businesses, and of current traffic conditions. Additionally, the OnStar system had connections to various parts of the car, and was thereby able to relay information about the car's status. Sensors connected to airbags reported when the bags were inflated, so that operators could attempt to contact drivers and authorities in the event of a crash.

Road construction also accelerated in the nineties. Yet by the end of the decade, it was quite clear that road building had utterly failed to keep up with increased traffic, and that roadways were inefficiently funneling far more vehicles than they had ever been meant to. Much of the construction was focused on growing cities, but established urban areas suffered in that the city infrastructure had not initially been designed to accommodate such traffic, and that, in short, they simply lacked space to expand their roadways significantly. The transportation institute of Texas A&M University studied 75 urban areas and found that the average driver spent about 60 hours in traffic in 1999, up from only 16 hours in 1982, when the last similar study was conducted. Another study of traffic in 2000 found that number had gone up still more, to 62 hours. Additionally, the study found that the high traffic period referred to as rush hour had grown from less than five hours long to about seven hours. The study recommended the building of more roads, but also noted that better management of roadways, as well as better promotion of alternative transportation, would also be necessary. Another study conducted in 2001 found that about 6 billion gallons of gas was being wasted annually by cars stuck in traffic.

Moreover, the condition of roads became an important issue of debate in the 1990s. Even as new roads were being built rapidly throughout the 1990s, many of the older roadways were falling into serious disrepair. In California, it is estimated that the number of urban highways in need of serious repair doubled in the 1990s, and that roads in poor condition were costing the average Californian $140 a year in auto repairs. Likewise, the growing dilapidation of California bridges became a major concern. Although a standout state given the sheer number of roadways, California's example was representative of a growing problem facing highways across the nation.

TRAINS, BOATS, AND BUSES

It seems that there were no means of vehicular travel that failed in the 1990s. Even the traditionally antiquated locomotive seemed to hold its own after decades of decline. Railways continued to flourish as a domestic means of travel in other countries, but the U.S. had seen a long downward slide in train travel since its peak in the 1920s. Most rail companies turned away from passenger transport, concentrating on cargo shipping, which left Amtrak essentially unopposed. Despite the decline in rail travel, then, Amtrak still saw significant revenues. In 1997 alone, Amtrak carried over 48 million travelers, including many business commuters, and garnered a record-breaking $1.67 billion. Amtrak was, however, still subsidized by the

The Carnival Destiny, a $400-plus million cruise ship being built for Miami-based Carnival Cruise Lines, cruises past Trieste, Italy, as it returns to its Italian shipyard following four days of sea trial testing. The company says the 892-foot vessel, with a maximum passenger capacity of 3,360 and a crew of 1,040, will be the largest cruise ship ever constructed. © AP/Wide World Photos.

United States government, as an economic and relatively environmentally friendly means of transportation. Amtrak nevertheless strived in the 1990s to reach a level of self-sufficiency, particularly with the production of high-speed Acela Express, which was finally unveiled in 2000 as the American answer to Japan's and France's high speed trains.[23]

In 1993, The White House Conference on Global Climate Change reported that intercity bus service was the most energy-efficient commuter transportation mode, more efficient than air, automobile, and even train service (including subways.) Estimates at the end of the 1990s placed the number of buses in service at between 26,000 and 28,000. While many of these were confined within city limits, bus service flourished not only within cities, but over longer distances as well, with companies like Greyhound Lines, Inc. and the Trailways National Bus System offering charter and tour "motorcoach" service. These companies expanded overseas as well as in the states. The continued stability of the charter bus industry was certainly aided by attempts in the latter part of the century to offer travel comfort comparable to other means of transport, with older rickety vehicles being replaced by luxury buses, complete with reclining seats and climate control.[24]

The cruise liner industry was one of the most rapidly growing travel industries at the end of the century. In 1980, an estimated 1.43 million people took cruise ship vacations, but by 1990 that number had more than doubled to 3.64 million. The number continued to rise throughout the decade, up to 5.05 million in 1997. The greatest number of these were to the Caribbean, accounting for about 48 percent according to 1998 figures, but other destinations, especially the Mediterranean, Alaska, Northern Europe, and the Bahamas, were also popular. While most of the large cruise line companies had established themselves well before, the most successful new company of the decade was Disney Cruise Line. The gigantic entertainment company made a great stir in the industry by offering cruises geared towards the whole family, providing at least as much for children to do as for adults (relieving considerable pressure on parents to keep their children entertained). Additionally, Disney offered a package vacation including not only the cruise, but also time at Florida's Walt Disney World or Disney's Animal Kingdom, a new 500-acre, $800 million park that opened in April 1998.[25]

Pleasure boating also grew as a popular leisure-time activity. By the midnineties, nearly 10 million Americans utilized sailboats, and some 46.9 million participated in motorboating.[26] Although the expense of boating kept it as an activity for the wealthy and upper-middle class, an increase in disposable income for many Americans led to an equivalent increase in boat sales. Technological advancements changed boating significantly. In 1985, a sailboat could travel some 20 miles in 2 hours. But by 1998, high-speed catamarans could travel 75 miles in the same amount of time, and with development of boats progressing unabated, there was no question that this speed would only increase. Consequently, boat tourism increased significantly. A given tropical island which once took a full day to reach just 15 years earlier could now be visited in a matter of hours.

CONCLUSION

With the threat of terrorism in the early years of the new millennium, many thought that there would be a corresponding slide in travel. Indeed, the airline industry certainly felt the pinch after the September 2001 attacks on the United States. Many experts, however, noted that the airlines were also suffering due to poor management in the 1990s. For while more people were traveling by air than ever before, the airlines were also spending steadily and slashing prices. The attacks, then, simply struck at the insta-bility that was already plaguing the industry.

Despite the decline in air travel, one would be unwise to claim an end to, or even a significant decline in American travel. The impulses that drove Americans to travel so much in the nineties remained, and while terrorism gave some pause, the need to escape through tourism was as great as ever. In fact, many continued to fly, but an even greater number took to the roads. Many stuck to closer ground in their vacations, packing into cars, not air-planes. This, along with strong dealer incentives, made the auto industry one of the strongest during the economic woes of the early twenty-first century. Injury to the travel industry, then, was perhaps only minor, and the future looks likely to hold even greater travel activity than the record-breaking years of the 1990s.

The 1990s

12
Visual Arts

ART AND CONTROVERSY IN THE EARLY NINETIES

The 1980s ended with considerable controversy about art, and more specifically, the appropriate subject matter for art. This controversy came to a head with the debate over the federal National Endowment for the Arts (NEA) funding of artists considered by some as obscene. Specifically, work of such artists as Robert Mapplethorpe and Andres Serrano had become the battleground over which the NEA, the artists, and their supporters fought against such groups as evangelist Donald Wildmon's American Family Association. Controversy of this sort would certainly spill into the 1990s, and in fact, color the whole debate about high art in the decade. In July 1989, Senator Jesse Helms managed to sneak an amendment through the sparsely attended senate, that proclaimed that public funds (including, but not limited to, NEA funds) could not be used to support art that featured "depictions of sadomasochism, homoeroticism, the sexual exploitation of children, or individuals engaged in sex acts and which, when taken as a whole, do not have serious literary, artistic, political, or scientific value." Consequently, in the year that followed, the NEA's president vetoed grants to several performance artists, Karen Finley, John Fleck, Holly Hughes, and Tim Miller, claiming their work was too political. That the performers were gay males, lesbians, and feminists—and politically on the left—was not lost on many observers. A lawsuit filed by the artists reinstated the grants three years after the vetoes, and also undercut the potency of the anti-obscenity pledge that NEA grant recipients were required to sign in the wake of the Helms amendment.

Ultimately, this battle resulted in considerable damage to the National Endowment for the Arts. Now it found itself embattled not only by the political right, but also by the left, who felt that the organization's recent attempts to restrict artistic content amounted to an assault on the first amendment's guarantee of free speech. Even many of political middle ground had something to say on the issue. Indeed, works like Mapplethorpe's homoerotic photography and Serrano's "Piss Christ," which featured a crucifix submerged in urine, came to wide public attention as a result of the controversy. As writer Lisa Phillips would have it, many "wondered whether avant-garde art—which has traditionally assaulted mainstream value—should be funded by a government agency at all."[1]

POLITICAL ART

Of course, in the world of high art there were attempts to create works of a more general appeal and that had clear meaning behind them. Far less opaque than much of the avant-garde were works that sought to advance political ideas. AIDS had had a terrible impact on the art world in the 1980s and 1990s, taking the lives of Mapplethorpe (in 1989), Scott Burton, Keith Haring (both in 1990), David Wojinarowicz (in 1992), Felix Gonzalez-Torres (in 1996), and many others. Not surprisingly, then, many of these and other artists created works that directly engaged the AIDS epidemic. And frequently this work was amongst the most direct of the artists' work, backed as it was by a desire to educate. Ultimately, the most famous work of art addressing the AIDS epidemic, however, was more properly qualified as folk art. The NAMES Project Quilt, with each of its many panels representing a different AIDS victim, was started in 1987, and in the 1990s, it continued to grow and to tour the country. The quilt included 1,920 panels when first displayed, but in 1996, the last time it was displayed in its entirety, it included about 38,000 panels and covered the entirety of Washington, D.C.'s National Mall. Since then, the quilt continued to grow—as did the number of NAMES Project chapters and affiliates—reaching in excess of 44,000 panels and 84,000 names, which shockingly only represented 19 percent of American AIDS deaths. The 1996 display was likely the last such presentation of the whole quilt, now weighing some fifty tons, which had simply grown too large for more than partial exhibition.[2]

Additionally, art that advanced feminist and homosexual politics continued to thrive within the world of high art. But even more notable was the growth in exhibitions featuring work by ethnic minorities. In 1990, the New Museum of Contemporary Art in New York launched "The Decade Show: Frameworks of Identity in the 1980s," a groundbreaking exhibition devoted to ethnic diversity and multiculturalism. Many of the artists of color featured in the exhibit had been largely ignored, but "The Decade Show" successfully brought these artists out of obscurity. In the years that followed, major art museums added a great deal of work by ethnic minorities to their permanent collections, and held numerous shows high-

Christie Hughes, 23, a Temple University student and volunteer with the NAMES Project, sits and contemplates panels from the Project AIDS Memorial Quilt, April 16, 1996, at Temple's Mitten Hall in Philadelphia. The quilt is a memorial to the hundreds of thousands of people who have died of AIDS. © AP Photo/Nanine Hartzenbusch.

lighting their work. One of the most notable of these shows was the 1994 Whitney Museum exhibition titled the "Black Male," which took to task representations of black men in popular culture.

PUBLIC ART

Interestingly, even as so much contemporary art seemed to ostracize, there were efforts to connect the popular public with the art world. Many cities held arts and crafts festivals and funded public works. Certainly, public art had existed well before the 1990s—well before the twentieth-century, even—but in the United States, public art projects seemed the be erected at an accelerated pace late in the century. A central force in the creation of public art—mostly sculptures and murals, but also including architecture and museum exhibits—was the attempt on the part of many cities to revitalize urban areas (see Chapter 4). Even when employing abstract design, public art, it was claimed, would help add a sense of life to an area, bringing businesses and patrons back to the abandoned urban areas of a city. Critic Mel Gooding suggested that "Public art serves many purposes, but none can have more point and dignity than that of investing a public space with a renewed vitality, extending its availability as a place to be, in which a sense of identity, and of the possibilities of the civil life, are enhanced."[3] It is notable that in the late 1980s and 1990s, there was a concerted effort to make public art public not only in exposure, but also in process. Whereas prior public art, more accurately thought of as civic art, had been frequently placed without regard to area residents, this period saw public officials seeking to include members of the community and to allow the local populace some say in the kind of art that would decorate their town. Moreover, several cities instituted art education programs in conjunction with the development of public art projects. Such was the case in Dade County, Florida, where the "Dade Art in Public Places" program brought community education and public works development together. As a result, much public art of the 1990s seemed to better reflect the concerns and culture of the community in which it was constructed. An example of this is a statue of the Aztec winged-serpent god Quetzalcoatl erected in San Jose, California. While the statue had its detractors (some objected to its religious implications, others to its design), the statue nonetheless served as a significant work for a city with such a large and active Latino populace.

ART AND TELEVISION

One of the most important figures in bringing high art to a popular audience was also one of the most unlikely. Sister Wendy Beckett, a tiny nun with an animated and passionate way of talking about art, found a wide audience through her BBC/PBS television shows which traced the history of art. Sister Wendy, born in South Africa and later relocated to England, made her first television appearance in 1991 on the BBC, and was shortly re-aired in the United States to critical and popular acclaim. She hosted numerous art documentaries, including 1997's *Sister Wendy's Story of Painting*. She not only explored ancient arts, but also delved into the world of modern art, in such a way that the lay audience could begin to understand the value of the avant-garde which had previously remained largely obscure. Sister Wendy's appeal was that she simply didn't come across as an art critic. There was no jargon and no pretense to her commentary, simply a knowledge of art history, a keen eye for detail, and an obvious passion for art. Television success was supplemented by some fifteen books on art authored by Sister Wendy, along with numerous articles in art magazines.

Though none quite matched Sister Wendy in sheer charm, other art series appeared on PBS to much applause. Among these were the series *American Photography: A Century in Images* (1999) and *American Visions* (1997) hosted by renowned critic Robert Hughes. The art critic for *Time* magazine, Hughes wrote and narrated the eight-part series, which brought him, and the viewer, to over one hundred locations in the United States. More than merely critiquing the art, Hughes sought to explore how art reflected the point of view of various people in various parts of the country at different times in history. Thus, *American Visions* offered not only the history of art, but of the nation and its developments.

PHOTOGRAPHY

Natalie Nodecker, a writer for *American Photo* magazine, wrote at the start of the new millennium that the predominant style of photography, and indeed all popular culture, in the 1990s was "a kind of amalgam of eroticism, technology, and humor, plus a snarky celebration of the mundane and trashy."[4] She cited as prime examples of this the photography of David LaChapelle and France's Jean-Baptiste Mondino, two major forces shaping the look of 1990s fashion and celebrity photography. Their work was emblematic of a move away from realism in photography, instead frequently relying on high stylization, unusual and deliberate posing of the subjects, and garish colors. David LaChapelle produced particularly conspicuous celebrity photography, as one of the most commonly employed cover photographers for *Rolling Stone* and other major magazines like *The Face* and *Interview*. Meanwhile, Mondino found work in many areas of photography, from fashion shoots, to album and magazine covers. Both photographers also directed music videos, informed by and likewise informing their photographic work. Other major photographers working in the field of fashion and celebrity photography included Steven Klein, a frequent contributor to international editions of *Vogue*, and Greg Gorman, who went beyond celebrity photography to produce movie posters, as well. The German-born former model, Ellen von Unwerth, also made a name for herself in the 1990s with her own brand of fashion and celebrity photography, which appeared in major magazines like *The Face* and *Vogue*, as well as in several books, including *Couples* (1998) and *Ellen von Unwerth Wicked No. 1* (1998).

Working in a decidedly different vein, Anne Geddes was perhaps the most popular photographer of the decade. Her best-known work involved babies dressed as various natural objects, including animals, insects, vegetables, and especially flowers. Detractors claimed that her work was schmaltzy, more interested in being cute than being substantive. But a large segment of the American public nonetheless embraced Geddes. Her many books, (particularly the 1996 collection *Down in the Garden*), which were photography bestsellers, spawned a whole cottage industry. Her distinctive baby photos could be seen on note cards, journals, calendars, photo albums, advertisements, and more. In addition, numerous children's books were produced using her photographs, including a popular series of instructional board books like *ABC* and *123*.

Similarly criticized for their lack of substance, were a series of photos by William Wegman. Wegman became enormously popular in the 1990s on the basis of his dog photos. He commonly dressed weimaraners in various costumes and photographed them, as in his picture-storybook adaptation of Little Red Riding Hood, complete with weimaraner wolf and weimaraner Red Riding Hood. This 1993 publication was followed by the like-minded *Cinderella* in 1999. Wegman's highly successful photography albums included *William Wegman's Farm Days* (1997), *My Town* (1998), *What Do You Do?* (1999), and *William Wegman's Pups* (1999). Interestingly, even as critics lambasted Geddes and Wegman, it was also apparent that these were two accomplished photographers. Whatever might be said of the content of their photos, the technique was quite strong. Wegman, particularly, was less known for his edgier non-dog photography, wherein his sense of composition served a more pointed, less commercial purpose.

As in seemingly all areas of visual art, photography, too, was the subject of considerable controversy, particularly in the rise to prominence of several photographers whose focus was the youthful human body. Chief among these was San Francisco Bay area photographer Jock Sturges, who had several books, particularly *The Last Days of Summer* (1993) and *Radiant Identities* (1994), featuring his photographs. These books contained nude photos of young people, particularly girls, just coming into sexual maturity. Defenders of Sturges work argued that his photos were artfully composed depictions of a natural part of adolescence. Detractors claimed they were no better than child pornography. Indeed, Sturges photos, largely taken on nude beaches in France and California, resulted in the photographer being charged, and later cleared, as a pornographer. Other photography books with similar content received similar condemnation. Among these were those of Lexington, Virginia, photographer Sally Mann, whose photos were collected in *Immediate Family* (1992) and *Still Time* (1994). A well-regarded photographer, Mann produced photos that were decidedly moodier than those of Sturges, playing with shapes and shadow almost in abstraction. Thus, while criticisms of her work still abounded, many considered Mann's work decidedly less sexualized than that of Sturges, or that of Australian David Hamilton, whose collection, *The Age of Innocence*, caused considerable outrage upon its 1995 release. Whereas the photography of Sturges and Mann largely stood on its own, Hamilton's photographs were accompanied by captions, quotes and snippets of poetry, which many saw as emphasizing the sexual (even prurient) nature of the photographs. Even many of Hamilton's defenders admitted that the text was banal, but still argued that the photos themselves merely depicted a natural part of human development. These books stirred up considerable resistance in some quarters, not only against the photographers and publishers, but also against retail outlets which carried them, with protests being staged out front of numerous bookstores across the country. Barnes & Noble and other outlets took to keeping the books behind the counter, and eventually making the books available only through special order. The controversy about the books and their photographers eventually diminished to a simmer, having affected little more than a considerable increase in the sales of the books.

An altogether different kind of controversy developed around the digital manipulation of photographs. "Faked photographs," wrote Vicki Goldberg and Robert Silberman in the companion book to the PBS documentary *American Photography: A Century of Images,* "unless made as art of entertainment, seem especially duplicitous, even treacherous."[5] Likewise, contributing editor Russell Hart suggested in a special issue of *American Photo* dedicated to the digital revolution, "the objective 'truth' of photographs has become something of a quaint concept. So has the idea of copyright protection."[6] Although the practice of altering photographic evidence was nothing new, computer technology made the practice much easier, and much more resistant to detection. While this practice did have some worthwhile practical effects—such as the use of computer-generated age progressions in the search for missing persons—it also caused no small anxiety on the part of many, for now even a photograph could not be taken as irrefutable proof. Yet, as Goldberg and Silberman pointed out, this technological advancement also opened up new vistas for those using photography not for reportage, but for art's sake, and that there could even be a "natural delight in tricks and illusion."[7] One cited example of this was George E. Mahlberg's "Oswald/Ruby as Rock Band" (1996), in which Mahlberg doctored the famous photograph of Lee Harvey Oswald's murder by Jack Ruby. In this photo, Oswald is given a microphone, Ruby an electric guitar, and one of the police officers escorting Oswald a keyboard. The alteration of an otherwise grim scene naturally relied on a knowledge of the actual photo, and was in no way designed to be duplicitous. In other cases, the alteration of photographs was not so apparent to the uninitiated. Such was certainly the case with much of Jill Greenberg's work. A frequent contributor to entertainment magazines, Greenberg developed a signature style of, in the words of Russell Hart, "supersaturated colors, quirky perspective, and a visual wit that pokes gentle fun at the trendy world of new media."[8] Greenberg's deft blending of both digital and traditionally filmic effects created a look that was in many ways definitive of 1990s commercial photography.

But not all instances of digital photo alteration were this flamboyant. In fact, this technology became commonplace. Photo technique magazines by the end of the 1990s regularly featured articles on how to manipulate photographs, to center an image, to sharpen (or even alter) a background, and to brighten or mute colors. Moreover, these powers were not granted only to the professional photographer, but came within the reach of the average amateur. The 1990s saw the development of affordable digital cameras, with the later years of the decade giving birth to simple point-and-shoot models. These cameras captured images in a computer memory, allowing them to either be printed or downloaded onto a home computer. In addition, many models allowed for instant review of a photograph, so the picture-takers could immediately discard those photos that turned out badly. While many professional photographers lamented the loss of these "accidental" photos, for most casual photographers, such technology was ideal. Only successful photos needed to be kept, and these could be digitally manipulated for various purposes, or could be easily e-mailed or posted on Web sites.

COMPUTER ART

Digital manipulation of photography was one thing, but the 1990s also saw the development of several new avenues of artistic production wherein the computer itself was used for the creation of art, alternately called cyberart, digital art, or simply computer-generated art. Indeed, works frequently might exist strictly within the memory of a computer, without any true source material for manipulation. In addition, the computer allowed for the creation of art of such a character that it could not be approximated with any other medium.

One prime example of this was the creation of digital stereograms, also know as Magic Eye pictures. Stereograms existed in some form long before the 1990s, with early postcards using duo images. The idea was that by bringing these images into the same visual space, by relaxing the eyes, sometimes with the assistance of vision distorting lenses, the pair of two-dimensional images would appear as a single three-dimensional image. In the 1960s, the application of computers to this concept took place. Dr. Bella Julesz created 3-D images composed of seemingly random patterns of dots in order to study depth perception in humans. By the 1990s, the stereogram techniques had advanced amazingly, such that individuals like Dan Dyckman and Mike Bielinski saw the aesthetic potential of the stereogram. Advanced computer technology simplified the mathematical processes used in stereogram creation, resulting in images of increasing complexity. Most stereograms appeared, at first glance, as chaotic abstract patterns, but with the relaxing of the eye, now without the need for special lenses, previously unseen 3-D images came to light. Other stereograms used non-abstract repeated images—of coins, insects, flowers, and so on—which could create a similar illusion of depth. The stereogram phenomenon first exploded in Japan, and its popularity overseas quickly lead to the popular introduction of stereogram art in the U.S. In 1993, the book *Magic Eye: A New Way of Looking at the World,* which featured images created by N.E. Thing Enterprises, hit bookstores and quickly became a best-seller. The book's success led to the release of many other books of stereograms, both by the N.E. Thing crew and others. Additionally, such images began appearing more frequently in advertising, on posters, and greeting cards, and even in a few art gallery showcases. Although the stereogram's popularity had diminished somewhat by the end of the decade, the "Magic Eye" had become an indelible part of American culture and cultural literacy.[9]

Fractal art, although conceived some years before the dawn of the decade, also found a firm foothold in 1990s popular culture. These designs, the visual representations of complex mathematical formulas, began to appear with greater frequency, like stereograms, on posters, cards, and more. Several books of fractal art were published. Fractal art was, however, a topic of some controversy, as some critics contended that it could not be true art, since the images were the simple playing out of mathematical algorithms. Defenders suggested that art and science were not mutually exclusive, and that, indeed, the artist made certain selections in launching a fractal which, while unable to dictate the ultimate pattern, could nonetheless influence it.[10] In this respect, fractal art could be compared to the seemingly random splatters of paint in a Jackson Pollock painting. Whatever the arguments between the technological and aesthetic elements of fractals, the works themselves, with their complex mingling of both natural patterns and high tech computations, found a ready popular audience, with successful videocassettes and books, such as *Fractal Cosmos: The Art of Mathematical Design* (1994), which sought through vivid fractal displays "to uncover for the viewer the beauty that is inherent in pure mathematics."[11]

Fractals and stereograms were among the most high-profile works of computer art, but by no means were these the only modes of digital creativity. Even the average home computer included illustration software, and those in the business of art utilized such software to create representational art that in some cases was difficult to distinguish from straight photography. The perfection of textural modeling allowed computer artists to closely approximate the look of different materials, from metal to human skin. Also significant was the rise to prominence of computer collages and mosaics. Collage, like its analog predecessor, simply used the computer to juxtapose illustrations, photos, and other images (including backgrounds and color schemes) to create a unified whole. Mosaics took this process further, using perhaps thousands of photos and placing them in such a way that, with some digital manipulation of color and shadow, these small photos formed a larger picture. Indeed, the world of computer art seemed endless in the 1990s. But even as new innovations shaped the way people thought aesthetically, age-old debates arose about what, exactly, constituted art. Could a Web page be art, with its mingling of images and texts? Could computer games be considered art? Indeed, some games created such vivid, even surreal environments, that one could well imagine still images from them on a gallery wall. Ultimately, when it came to theories of art, the rise of digital media certainly created more questions than answers.

COMICS

The 1990s were a volatile decade for the comic book world. As a whole, the comic book market began the 1990s in a boom, riding a wave that started in the 1980s. The first years of the decade saw the rise of several new, and unprecedented successful independent comics publishers, as well as some of the greatest sales that the top two publishers, Marvel and DC, had ever seen in their long existences. In addition, comic books made inroads in terms of respectability, with perhaps the high point being the 1992 awarding of a Pulitzer Prize for Art Spiegelman's comics documentary of the Holocaust, *Maus: A Survivor's Tale* (serialized and published in two volumes from 1980 to 1991.) The late 1980s and early 1990s also saw a continued rise in the number of comic book specialty stores in the nation, and a voracious new class of speculative comics buyers. But the boom did not last and in the mid-1990s, partly due to the glut of product (Marvel at one point was releasing over 150 titles a month), partly due to the dissatisfaction of speculators new to comics who wondered why their purchases weren't making them profits, the comic book market dried up considerably, with many new publishers folding production and comic shops closing their doors. It has been estimated that from 1993 to 1998, comic book profits dropped some 60 percent, from $800 million to $325 million. Additionally, of the approximately 8,500 specialty shops that existed in 1994, less than 5,000 survived to see the new millennium.[12] Even the major publishers were not immune to the bust, with Marvel filing for bankruptcy in 1996. Moreover, most comic book distributors ceased business, leaving Diamond Comics Distributors as the only one left by 1997, and comics no longer found their way into non-specialty stores—supermarkets, convenience stores, and mom-and-pop shops—like they did once. Grim though this period might have been for the comics industry, it ultimately may have left it on sounder footing, having cut away much of the fat of an artificially bloated industry.

In the early 1990s, Marvel Comics was on top of the industry like never before. In 1990, Marvel went public and the company's stock, as detailed in their first annual report, itself cleverly disguised as a comic book, quickly skyrocketed. But a part of this rapid inflation of stock value was the result of an artificially inflated market. 1991 also saw a controlling share of the

Marvel stock being bought by financier Ron Perelman, which would eventually lead to complex financial and corporate wrangling about ownership and control of the company. Meanwhile, those first years of the decade saw the launch of numerous new comic series by Marvel, several of which would merit record-breaking sales and contribute to a significant change in the very look of superhero comics. In 1990, Marvel released a new *Spider-Man* title, written and drawn by fan favorite Todd McFarlane. This was followed in 1991 by Rob Liefeld's *X-Force* and a new *X-Men* title illustrated by Jim Lee, the first issue of which was released in five editions with variant cover art and sold 8 million copies, making it the best-selling comic book of the twentieth century.[13]

These three artists, though of somewhat variant style and quality, helped to usher in a new look in comics. Their dynamic art tended towards high detail, or in some cases the impression of high detail. Detractors called this over-rendering, wherein, as one critic would have it, "It seems nothing that can be drawn with one line is ever rendered without six."[14] Others were kinder to this approach to line, like artist/critic Scott McCloud, who suggested that "when Marvel's reader base grew into the anxieties of adolescence, the hostile, jagged lines of a Rob Liefeld struck a more responsive chord."[15] Even more significantly, these artists also tended to use much larger panels, thereby giving the average comic book fewer (though frequently more complex) individual pictures per page and per comics magazine than found in comics from a decade earlier. Although larger panels had been used on occasion by artists before, the enormous popularity of Lee, Liefeld, McFarlane, and others made such a technique, along with the over-rendered line, almost a standard in mainstream comics.

Moreover, the popularity of these artists led not only to aesthetic, but also to industry shake-ups when, dissatisfied with the work-for-hire system of the major publishers, which denied creators ownership rights to their creations, Lee, Liefeld, and McFarlane, along with other favorite artists, Eric Larsen, Marc Silvestri, and Jim Valentino, left Marvel en masse. In 1992, they began publishing their own creator-owned books under the banner of Image Comics. The venture proved an unqualified commercial success and also proved the draw not only of famous characters but also of individual artists. Image quickly became a more than worthy competitor to the two major publishers, DC and Marvel, with huge sales on books like Liefeld's *Youngblood,* McFarlane's *Spawn,* Lee's *WildC.A.T.s,* Valentino's *Shadowhawk,* Larsen's *Savage Dragon,* and Silvestri's *CyberForce.* While some argued that these books were essentially derivative of Marvel superhero comics, there's no denying that, for many fans, this was exactly what was desired. After all, these artists had made their reputations with these kinds of books and knew that this was what fans expected of them. Ultimately, such an approach paid off, with *Youngblood* #1 selling about a million copies and *Spawn* #1 selling almost two million, well beyond the sales of most comics, even those published by the majors.[16] The early successes of Image, however, were somewhat offset by early difficulties. Frequently late shipment of comics and generally poor management strategies chafed with many fans, retailers, and distributors. In addition, internal conflicts would eventually lead to the departure of many key members of the Image team. Several artists set up their own production companies, and Liefeld went so far as to establish a separate company, Maximum Press, to publish his own work. Liefeld was later voted out of the company. Additionally, Silvestri's production company, Top Cow, left Image, as did Lee's WildStorm Productions. (Top Cow would eventually return to the fold; WildStorm would not.) In time, Image settled into a pattern of consistent sales, taking its place as a major independent publisher, if, by the end of the decade, no longer posing a threat to DC and Marvel.

As important as Image itself was, equally significant is how the company opened the market up to independent comics publishing. Independents had long been around, but Image broke the DC-Marvel stranglehold on the industry. The 1990s saw the birth of many new publishing imprints, a number of which were formed by former Marvel and DC creators encouraged by the early Image success story. The most popular of these was Valiant, which, in addition to developing new superhero characters, resurrected heroes from the Gold Key comics line published from the 1950s to the 1980s. Despite considerable early critical and commercial praise, however, Valiant would not survive the decade. It has been argued that this was in part due to a drop off in the quality of Valiant titles, as well as the loss of solid artists like Barry Windsor-Smith and Bob Layton, but Valiant's demise must also be credited to the drying up of the comics market in the latter half of the 1990s. Other companies that started strong, including Broadway, Continuity, Defiant, Tekno, and Topps, likewise failed to last. Even longer-lasted independents faded away in the 1990s. First and Eclipse comics, which both came out of the 1980s quite strong, closed their doors. So, too, did pioneering underground publisher Kitchen Sink.

But despite these closures, there were independent successes in the 1990s. Whereas most of the aforementioned companies sought to break into the mainstream, other companies—among them Drawn & Quarterly, Slave Labor Graphics, Fantagraphics, and Dark Horse Comics—catered to a generally smaller niche market, with experimental and alternative titles. Even Dark Horse, which found considerable mainstream success with its movie-licensed titles featuring the likes of the Terminator, Aliens, and Predator, maintained their commitment to alternative comics. Alternative publishers also managed to make considerable inroads in terms of comics' respectability, with their books gaining notable attention in the popular and book trade press and finding their ways into chain bookstores like Barnes & Noble and Borders. Thus, even as some bemoaned the death of the comics market, creators on the edge of the industry created some of the most groundbreaking comics seen in some time. Dan Clowes grabbed attention with stories like *Ghost World* (1993–1997), about two recently graduated high schoolers trying to find their place in the world, and the surreal *Like a Velvet Glove Cast in Iron*. Chris Ware's *Acme Novelty Library*, a series started in 1993, also broke considerable new ground, particularly with its rejection of a standardized comic book size or format. In addition, Ware's deft line and masterful page layouts, perhaps reaching their peak in his very personal Jimmy Corrigan stories, not only influenced comics production, but also commercial graphic art in general. Also significant was the autobiographical work of Joe Sacco, particularly his *Palestine* (1993–1995), a comics examination of the contemporary Middle East which drew the attention not only of comics readers, but also of those with general interest in history and current affairs. Equally significant was Scott McCloud's *Understanding Comics: The Invisible Art*, originally published by Kitchen Sink in 1993. In this book, McCloud offered an analytical examination of the comics form. While there had been numerous books on the history of comics and on specific artists, there had been few attempts of this sort. Moreover, rather than presenting a dry consideration of the form, McCloud chose to present his analysis in the form with which he was most comfortable: the comic book. *Understanding Comics*, then, was an easily accessible introduction to a narrative form in that very form, and while some accused McCloud's analysis of shallowness, others saw its value as an introduction. The book even found its way into some college classrooms.[17]

These books along with works by Peter Bagge, Kyle Baker, Howard Cruse, Julie Doucet, Ben Katchor, David Mazzucchelli, Seth, Jim Woodring, and others far too numerous to detail here, proved that the American comics industry was far from being on its creative death bed. The major publishers could not help but notice the inroads being made by the alternative press. The continued stability of many alternative titles led DC to create its Vertigo imprint, which specialized in comics geared towards an older, more sophisticated audience. Central to this line was *The Sandman* and related books, in which writer Neil Gaiman created a metaphysically complex universe with the assistance of popular artists like Dave McKean, Kent Williams, and Sam Keith. Additionally, a number of DC's older properties, like *Swamp Thing* and *Doom Patrol* were reborn into the Vertigo line as new spins on traditional horror or superhero comics. The Vertigo line was a success, though sales were somewhat limited since the core comic book market still consisted of younger adolescents. Other imprints started by DC fell completely flat, like Helix, their science fiction line, and Milestone, a well-intentioned attempt to cater to African-American youths with a line of black superheroes. Of course, in addition to exploring these new avenues, DC stuck with the properties that had put the company into the top tier of comic book publishers, with several comics events garnering the company nationwide publicity. In 1992, Superman died at the hands of the aptly named villain Doomsday (Superman later came back to life), and in 1993, Batman was crippled, his back broken by the bad guy Bane (Batman soon healed.) Superman's death, particularly, was a media coup. The issue featuring the hero's death was published in two editions, a collectors' edition, specially bagged with a black armband, and a standard newsstand edition. The event brought people into comic shops who had never set foot in one before, people who hadn't read a comic book since their childhood, and the sales figures reflected that. Some six million issues were sold of these first editions, and they were followed by a second printing, then a third and a fourth.

ART AND CONTROVERSY IN THE LATE NINETIES

Just as the decade opened with controversy about what was appropriate in art, so, too, did it end. Of particular note was the Brooklyn Museum of Art show, "Sensation: Young British Artists From the Saatchi Collection." This show, which began in October 1999, was combated not only by the usual decency groups, especially the Catholic League, but also came under fire by New York Mayor Rudolph Giuliani. The exhibit, first opened at London's Royal Academy in 1997, offered such viewing as Marc Quinn's self-portrait carved out of eight pints of the artist's own frozen blood, and Damien Hirst's macabre work featuring such things as a bisected pig and a 14-foot tiger shark floated in formaldehyde. But the center of the controversy was Chris Ofili's stylized painting of the Virgin Mary, notable for a lump of elephant dung affixed to the portrait and for the clippings from pornographic magazines surrounding it. Proclaiming the exhibit "sick," Giuliani announced that he would withhold the $7.2 million in city funding to the museum unless the show was cancelled. He also threatened to disband the museum's board of directors and filed a lawsuit on behalf of the city which claimed that the museum had violated its lease.[18] The Brooklyn Museum counter-sued claiming that the denial of funding (which had never before been in question) was an infringement on free speech. And not only did artists across the world jump to the museum's defense, but so, too, did much of the mainstream press. Even respected news commentator Hugh Downes came forward, claiming that, although he, too, found the show disgusting, it was neither his nor Giuliani's place to decide for others what was appropriate viewing. These legal wranglings (settled some months after the exhibit had closed in early 2000), however, had little effect other than to raise awareness of the show. Indeed, those putting on the Sensation show were well aware of what artists had long known: controversy sells. Even the advertising seemed to bear this out. One poster, for instance, presented itself as a Health Warning, reading "The contents of this exhibition may cause shock, vomiting, confusion, panic, euphoria, and anxiety. If you suffer from high blood pressure, a nervous disorder, or pal-

Chris Ofili's *The Holy Virgin Mary*, a controversial painting of the Virgin Mary embellished with a clump of elephant dung and two dozen cutouts of buttocks from pornographic magazines, is shown at the Brooklyn Museum of Art Sept. 27, 1999, in New York, as part of the "Sensation: Young British Artists From the Saatchi Collection," exhibit scheduled to open Oct. 2. The Brooklyn Museum of Art sued the city on Sept. 28, seeking to stop Mayor Rudolph Giuliani from making good on his threat to freeze millions of dollars in funding because of artwork contained in the exhibit. © AP/Wide World Photos.

pitations, you should consult your doctor before viewing this exhibition." Such copy served a dual purpose, laying ground for the claim that no one who had viewed the exhibit had done so without full knowledge of the nature of its content, and enticing attendees with a lurid promise of forbidden sights.

Ultimately, however, art of this nature garnered more in the way of publicity than in the way of applause, at least from the average middle-American. Avant-garde art had always placed itself outside of the mainstream, and this was certainly true in the 1990s. For most Americans, the work in Sensations and like installations, was perhaps a topic of conversation, about the socio-political issues surrounding it, but was not something that was particularly liked. Consequently, then, there were virtually two art worlds: high art and popular art, which encompassed commercial photography, advertising art, computer art, comics art, and the like, and which Americans, even those who did not regard themselves as artistically inclined, consumed in plenty.

Cost of Products in the 1990s[1]

ENTERTAINMENT AND TRAVEL

TV Set (36"): $200–$750

Video Cassette Recorder: $150–$550

Camcorder: $500–$1200

Stereo Receiver: $250–$600

CD Player: $150–$600

DVD Player: $300–$500

Desktop Computer (with Monitor): $600–$3000

Laptop Computer: $1600–$2000

Economy Car: $10,000–$20,000

Luxury Car: $25,000–$35,000

Pick-Up Truck: $15,000–$25,000

Minivan: $20,000–$30,000

Sports Utility Vehicle (SUV): $25,000–$35,000

Tires: $40–$200

Gasoline: $1.25–$2.00/gallon

Round Trip Cross-Country Flight (San Francisco to New York City): $250–$500

America Online Monthly Fee: $20

Hardcover Novel: $20–$30

---

1. Due to item make, inflation, regional differences, and other factors—options on vehicles, for instance—listed costs are roughly estimated. In some cases, great variances existed.

Mass Market (Pocket) Book: $3.50–$7.00
Daily Newspaper: $.25–$1.00
Movie Tickets: $4.00–$7.00
Pre-Recorded VHS Video Cassette: $10–$25
Music Compact Disc: $15–$20

CLOTHING

Running Shoes: $45–$150
Khaki Pants: $20–$60
Print T-Shirt: $10–$20
Dress Shirt: $30–$50
Blue Jeans: $20–$100
Men's Suit: $180–$1000
Panty Hose: $2.00–$9.00

MISCELLANEOUS LIVING EXPENSES

Refrigerator: $450–$2000
Gas Range: $500–$1400
Microwave Oven: $100–$250
Dish Washer: $300–$1500
Blender: $20–$100
Juicer: $10–$40
Washing Machine: $350–$1000
Clothes Dryer: $300–$800
Blow Dryer: $15–$40

Milk: $2.00/gallon
Eggs: $1.00/dozen
White Bread: $1.00–$2.00/loaf
Frozen TV Dinner: $1.50–$4.00
Chocolate Bar: $.50–$2.00
Macaroni and Cheese, Dry: $.35–$1.50/box
Canned Tuna: $1.00
Paper Towels: $1.00/roll
Toothpaste: $2.00/tube
Breakfast Cereal: $1.00–$3.00

Notes

INTRODUCTION

1. There has been no shortage of books dealing with the media's influence by Marshall McLuhan, Neil Postman, Ron Powers, Jerry Mander, Bill McKibben, and others.

2. Ray B. Browne, and Pat Browne, *The Guide to United States Popular Culture* (Bowling Green, OH: Bowling Green State University Popular Press, 2001), 1–4.

CHAPTER 1

1. See http://www.census.gov.

2. Ibid.

3. Ibid.

4. Sarah Anderson, John Cavanagh, Chuck Collins, Chris Hartman, and Felice Yeskel, "Executive Excess 2000: Seventh Annual CEO Compensation Survey," Aug. 30, 2000, http://www.ufenet.org/press/2000/Executive_Excess_2000.pdf.

5. For more information, see Michael A Bernstein and David E. Adler, eds, *Understanding American Economic Decline* (New York: Cambridge University Press, 1994).

6. For more information, see William Julius Wilson, *When Work Disappears: The World of the New Urban Poor* (New York: Knopf, 1996).

7. Harlow A. Hyde, "Slow Death in the Great Plains," *The Atlantic Monthly* 279.6 (June 1997): 42, 44–45.

8. Haynes Johnson, *Divided We Fall: Gambling with History in the Nineties* (New York: W. W. Norton, 1994), 90–97.

9. National Center for Policy Analysis, "Crime and Punishment in America: 1998," http://www.ncpa.org/~ncpa/studies/s219/s219a.html.

10. Eric Scholsser, "The Prison-Industrial Complex," *The Atlantic Monthly* 282.6 (December 1998): 51–52, 54–58, 62–66, 68–70, 72–77.

11. National Center for Policy Analysis, "Crime and Punishment in America: 1998."

12. Alston Chase, "Harvard and the Making of the Unabomber," *The Atlantic Monthly* 285.6 (June 2000): 41–44, 46–50, 51–56, 58–59, 62–65.

13. Roy F. Fox, *MediaSpeak: Three American Voices* (Westport: Praeger, 2001), 132–133.

14. Chandler Burr, "The AIDS Exception: Privacy Vs. Public Health," *The Atlantic Monthly* 279.6 (June 1997): 57–63, 64–67.

CHAPTER 2

1. Federal Interagency Forum on Child and Family Statistics, *America's Children: Key National Indicators of Well-Being, 2000.* http://www.childstats.gov/.

2. Barbara Schneider and David Stevenson, *The Ambitious Generation: American Teenagers, Motivated but Directionless* (New Haven: Yale University Press, 1999), 31.

3. Federal Interagency Forum on Child and Family Statistics, *America's Children.*

4. "The Rolling Stone Poll: Young America Talks Back," *Rolling Stone* 799 (November 12, 1998): 79–80.

5. Schneider and Stevenson, *The Ambitious Generation,* 3–4.

6. David Brooks, "The Organization Kid," *The Atlantic Monthly* 287.4 (April 2001): 40–46, 48–54.

7. Schneider and Stevenson, *The Ambitious Generation,* 190–191.

8. Ibid., 191–194.

9. Federal Interagency Forum on Child and Family Statistics, *America's Children.*

10. Ibid.

11. Quoted in Jon Steel, *Truth, Lies, and Advertising* (New York: John Wiley & Sons, 1998), 87.

12. Schneider and Stevenson, *The Ambitious Generation,* 75.

13. Ibid., 5.

14. Peter Schrag, "The Near-Myth of Our Failing Schools," *The Atlantic Monthly* 280.4 (October 1997): 72–74, 76, 78, 80.

15. Brooks, "The Organization Kid."

16. Schrag, "The Near-Myth of Our Failing Schools."

17. Lucy Rollin, *Twentieth-Century Teen Culture by the Decades: A Reference Guide* (Westport: Greenwood Press, 1999), 323–324.

18. Schneider and Stevenson, *The Ambitious Generation,* 170–172.

19. Ibid., 11.

20. Jane D. Brown, Jeanne R. Steele, and Kim Walsh-Childers, eds, *Sexual Teens, Sexual Media* (Mahwah, New Jersey: Lawrence Erlbaum Associates, 2002), 5–6.

21. Rollin, *Twentieth Century Teen Culture by the Decades,* 313–314.

22. Federal Interagency Forum on Child and Family Statistics, *America's Children.*

23. Peter A. Witt and John L. Crompton, "Trends in the Development of Recreation Services for Youth at Risk," in *Trends in Outdoor Recreation, Leisure and Tourism* (Wallinford, U.K.: CABI Publishing, 2000), Ed. W. C. Gartner and D. W. Lime, 393–402.

24. Brooks, "The Organization Kid."

25. Ted Halstead, "A Politics for Generation X," *The Atlantic Monthly* 284.2 (August 1999): 33–34, 36–42.

26. "The Rolling Stone Poll: Young America Talks Back."

27. Halstead, "A Politics for Generation X."

28. Ibid.

29. Federal Interagency Forum on Child and Family Statistics, *America's Children*.

30. Allison S. Wellner, *Americans at Play: Demographics of Outdoor Recreation and Travel* (Ithaca: New Strategist Publications, 1997), 277–297.

31. Brooks, "The Organization Kid."

32. Wellner, *Americans at Play,* 277–297.

CHAPTER 3

1. Jean Kilbourne, *Deadly Persuasion: Why Women and Girls Must Fight the Addictive Power of Advertising* (New York: The Free Press, 1999), 34–35.

2. Roy F. Fox, *MediaSpeak: Three American Voices* (Westport, Connecticut: Praeger, 2001), 108–110.

3. Kilbourne, *Deadly Persuasion,* 33–34.

4. Ibid.

5. Fox, *MediaSpeak,* 115–116.

6. Ibid., 55–60.

7. Ibid., 110.

8. James B. Twitchell, *Twenty Ads That Shook the World: The Century's Most Groundbreaking Advertising and How it Changed Us All* (New York: Crown Publishers, 2000), 194–203.

9. Ibid., 215.

10. Linda K. Fuller, "We Can't Duck the Issue: Imbedded Advertising in the Motion Pictures," in *Undressing the Ad: Reading Culture in Advertising* (New York: Peter Lang, 1998), Ed. Katherine Toland Frith, 109–129.

11. Fox, *MediaSpeak,* 133.

12. Eric Schlosser, *Fast Food Nation: The Dark Side of the All-American Meal* (New York: Houghton Mifflin, 2001), 43.

13. Fox, *MediaSpeak,* 108–109.

14. Schlosser, *Fast Food Nation,* 51–53.

15. Fox, *MediaSpeak,* 93–95.

16. Schlosser, *Fast Food Nation,* 55.

17. Fox, *MediaSpeak,* 95–96.

18. Ibid., 101–104.

19. "This is Your Government on Drugs," editorial, *Rolling Stone* 794 (September 3, 1998): 43–44.

20. Paul Taylor, "Stumped Speech," *Mother Jones* (May/June 2000).

21. Kilbourne, *Deadly Persuasion,* 37–38.

22. Ibid., 39.

23. Robbin Zeff and Brad Aronson, *Advertising on the Internet* 2nd ed. (New York: John Wiley & Sons, 1999), 7–10.

24. Ibid., 14–15.

25. Ibid., 17–18.

26. Zeff and Aronson, *Advertising on the Internet*, 4.

CHAPTER 4

1. James S. Russell, "Profound Forces are Reshaping American Cities: Is There a Place for Architecture?" *Architectural Record* 188.3 (March 2000): 76–82, 206–208.

2. Andres Duany and Elizabeth Plater-Zyberk, *Suburban Nation: The Rise of Sprawl and the Decline of the American Dream* (New York: North Point Press, 2000), 4.

3. James Parsons, "A New World (Made To) Order," *Architecture* 88.5 (May 1999).

4. Duany and Plater-Zyberk, 43–45.

5. Edward Blakely and Mary Gail Snyder, *Fortress America: Gated Communities in the United States* (Washington D.C.: Brookings Institute Press, 1997.)

6. Thomas Angotti, "New York: Challenges Facing Neighborhoods in Distress," in *Rebuilding Urban Neighborhoods*, (Thousand Oaks: Sage Publications, 1999), Eds. W. Dennis Keating and Norman Krumholz, 177–190.

7. Roberta Brandes Gratz and Norman Mintz, *Cities Back from the Edge: New Life for Downtown* (New York: Preservation Press, 1998), 152–156.

8. Russell, "Profound Forces are Reshaping American Cities."

9. Ibid.

10. Andrea Oppenheimer Dean, "Our Critic Goes Behind the Scenes at This Year's AIA Honor Awards," *Architectural Record* 187.5 (May 1999).

11. Michael Cannell, "Brain Drain," *Architecture* 88.12 (December 1999): 125–127.

12. Ibid.

13. Jerry Laiserin, "Form Follows Information," *Architectural Record* 187.10 (October 1999): 124–127.

14. Robert Ivy, "Major Museums and Medals: Frank Gehry's Big Year," *Architectural Record* 188.1 (January 1999): 45.

15. Robert Ivy, "Frank Gehry: Plain Talk with a Master," *Architectural Record* 187.5 (May 1999): 185–192, 356, 359–360.

16. Hugh Pearman, *Contemporary World Architecture*, (London: Phaidon, 1998), 78.

17. Ibid., 61–62.

18. C. E. Kidder Smith, *Source Book of American Architecture* (New York: Princeton Architectural Press, 1996), 633.

19. Jeffrey Hogrefe, "The Ascent of Glass," *Smithsonian* 32.4 (July 2001): 80–88.

20. Ibid., 82. See also http://www.amnh.org/org/rose.

21. James Wines, *Green Architecture* (New York: Taschen, 2000), 172–176.

22. Ibid., 180–188.

23. Ibid., 233–234.

24. Kidder Smith, *Source Book of American Architecture*, 629.

25. Pearman, *Contemporary World Architecture*, 25.

26. Dennis McCafferty, "Breaking New Ground," *USA Weekend* (Aug. 30–Sept. 1, 2002): 6–7.

CHAPTER 5

1. See http://www.mcfarlane.com/.

2. Cynthia True, "Master of the Game," *Rolling Stone* 800 (November 26, 1998): 94, 99–101.

3. Haynes Johnson, *The Best of Times: America in the Clinton Years* (New York: James H. Silberman, 2001), 11–16.

4. Alison S. Wellner, *Americans at Play* (Ithaca: New Strategist Publications, 1997), 114–116.

5. Ibid., 265–268.

6. Lynette Lamb, "Can Women Save Sports?" *Utne Reader* 97 (Jan.–Feb. 2000): 56–57.

7. David Deardorff II, *Sports: A Reference Guide and Critical Commentary, 1980–1999* (Westport: Greenwood Press, 2000), 31.

8. Ibid., 31.

9. Ibid., 31.

10. BBC News Online, "Business: The Economy: Woods Holes $90m," http://news.bbc.co.uk/1/hi/business/the_economy/429698.stm (August 25, 1999).

CHAPTER 6

1. Dennis Hall, "Delight in Disorder: A Reading of Diaphany and Liquefaction in Contemporary Women's Clothing," *Journal of Popular Culture* 34.4 (Spring 2001): 65–74.

2. Elsa Klensch, CNN Online, http://www.cnn.com/STYLE/9812/23/trend.yearender/, (December 23, 1998).

3. William Hamilton, "Suitably Attired," *The Atlantic Monthly* 288.2 (September 2001): 122–125.

4. Quoted in Joan Nunn, *Fashion in Costume 1200–2000,* 2nd ed. (Chicago: New Amsterdam, 2000), 252.

5. Amy Merrick, "Tired of Trendiness, Former Shoppers Leave Gap, Defect to Competitors," *The Wall Street Journal* (December 6, 2001).

6. Jancee Dunn and Patti O'Brien, "How Hip-hop Style Bun-Rushed the Mall," *Rolling Stone* 808 (March 18, 1999): 54–57, 59.

7. "School Uniforms," http://www.pbs.org/newshour/infocus/fashion/school.html (July 25, 2002).

8. Ruth P. Rubinstein, *Society's Child: Identity, Clothing, and Style* (Boulder: Westview Press, 2000), 259–260.

9. Nancy Rutter and Owen Edwards, "Ready to Ware," *Forbes ASAP,* April 5, 1999, 30–32.

10. "The Name Game," http://www.pbs.org/newshour/infocus/fashion/namegame.html (July 25, 2002).

11. Urban Decay Web site, http://www.urbandecay.com/aboutudframe.html (July 25, 2002).

12. "Sephora—Liberating Beauty Products," Corporate Design Foundation Web site, http://www.cdf.org/7_2_index/sephora.html (July 25, 2002).

13. "Aging Baby Boomers Drive Surge in Sales of Personal Care Products," Merchandisegroup.com, http://www.merchandisegroup.com/password/archive/102102.html (January 21, 2002).

14. Mim Udovitch, "Breasts, Reassessed," *Esquire* 131.2 (February 1999): 86–89.

15. Debra L. Gimlin, *Body Work: Beauty and Self-Image in American Culture* (Berkeley: University of California Press, 2002), 75.

16. Deborah Caslav Covino, "Outside-In: Body, Mind, and Self in the Advertisement of Aesthetic Surgery," *Journal of Popular Culture* 35.3 (Winter 2001): 91–102.

17. Gimlin, *Body Work*, 75.

18. Ibid., 5.

19. Rubinstein, *Society's Child*, 249.

CHAPTER 7

1. Charles R. Goeldner, J. R. Brent Ritchie, and Robert W. McIntosh, *Tourism: Principles, Practices, Philosophies*, 8th ed. (New York: John Wiley & Sons, 2000), 178.

2. *Los Angeles Times*, http://www.com/la-000030033apr28.story (April 4, 2002).

3. For a number of articles on this subject, see the Economic Research Service Web site at http://www.ers.usda.gov.

4. Food Marketing Institute Web site, http://www.fmi.org.

5. Eric Schlosser, *Fast Food Nation: The Dark Side of the All-American Meal* (New York: Houghton Mifflin, 2001), 120.

6. Red Bull Web site, http://www.redbull.com.

7. Schlosser, *Fast Food Nation*, 3.

8. Ibid., 47–48.

9. Ibid.

10. Ibid., 9.

11. T.G.I. Friday's Web site, http://www.tgifridays.com.

12. Jim Adamson, *The Denny's Story: How a Company in Crisis Resurrected Its Good Name* (New York: John Wiley & Sons, 2000).

13. Emeril Lagasse Web site, http://www.emerils.com.

14. Starbucks Web site, http://www.starbucks.com.

15. Andy Murray, "Microbreweries Focus on Close-to-Home Connoisseurs," *Eagle-Tribune* online, http://www.eagletribune.com/news/stories/20020303/BV_001.htm (March 3, 2002).

16. "Craft-Brewing Industry Keeps Growing," http:/www.beertown.org/PR/industry_growth.htm (July 13, 2002).

17. Schlosser, *Fast Food Nation*, 53–54.

18. Michael F. Jacobson, "Liquid Candy: How Soft Drinks are Harming Americans' Health," http://www.cspinet.org/sodapop/liquid_candy.htm.

19. Ibid.

20. Schlosser, *Fast Food Nation*, 140.

21. Haynes Johnson, *The Best of Times: America in the Clinton Years* (New York: James A. Silberman, 2001), 91–102.

22. Elizabeth Larsen, "Bossy's Lament," *Utne Reader* 100 (July–August 2000), 18–19.

CHAPTER 8

1. A report published at the end of the 1980s attested some 45 million Americans were functionally illiterate. Mortimer B. Zuckerman, "The Illiteracy Epidemic." *U.S. News & World Report* June 12, 1989. 72.

2. See http://www.amazon.com/exec/obidos/subst/misc/company-info.html.

3. See http://www.aol.barnesandnoble.com/help/a_bn_com.asp?.

4. *Publishers Weekly,* November 15, 1999.

5. *Publishers Weekly,* January 20, 1997.

6. Daisy Maryles, "Connecting the Numbers," *Publishers Weekly,* January 10, 2000, 25–27.

7. *Publishers Weekly,* January 20, 2000.

8. Isabella Reitzel quoted in Barbara Kinsella, "Is Oprah Bringing in New Readers?" *Publishers Weekly,* January 20, 1997, 276.

9. *Publishers Weekly,* January 3, 1994.

10. Robert K. J. Killheffer, "Inter-Galactic Licensing," *Publishers Weekly,* September 25, 1995, 27–31.

11. Robert K. J. Killheffer, "Creative Experimentation Reigns," *Publishers Weekly,* June 17, 1996, 34–41.

12. Ibid.

13. Robert Dahlin, "Expanding the Scene of the Crime," *Publishers Weekly,* April 22, 1996, 38–47.

14. "John Grisham," *Current Biography,* September 1993, 21–24.

15. Jonathan Bing, "Sue Grafton: Death and the Maiden," *Publishers Weekly,* April 20, 1998, 40–41.

16. John Blades, "David Guterson: Stoic of the Pacific Southwest," *Publishers Weekly,* April 5, 1999, 215–216.

17. Lucinda Dyer, "Love, Thy Magic Spell is Everywhere," *Publishers Weekly,* May 13, 1996, 41–47.

18. Daisy Maryles, "The Medium Makes the Sale," *Publishers Weekly* January 3, 1994, 55.

19. John Spaulding, "Poetry and the Media: The Decline of Popular Poetry," *Journal of Popular Culture* 33.2 (Fall 1999): 147–153.

20. Mallay Charters, "The Different Faces of Poetry," *Publishers Weekly,* March 3, 1997, 38–41.

21. Harriet Lerner, "When Bad Books Happen to Good People," *Ms.,* November/December 1993, 62–64.

22. Dennis Mclellan, "Deepak Chopra: The Guru Turns to Fiction," *Publishers Weekly,* July 24, 1995, 43–44.

23. Kenneth Woodward, "Angles," *Newsweek,* December, 27 1993, 57.

24. Robert Dahlin, "Turning the Page on the 20th Century," *Publishers Weekly,* May 17, 1999, 35–36.

25. Jim Milliot, "Slow Growth Ahead in Consumer Spending on Children's Books," *Publishers Weekly,* August 15, 1994, 24.

26. Jim Milliot and Diane Roback, "1996 a Difficult Year for Children's Publishers," *Publishers Weekly,* November 3, 1997, 35–38.

27. "Weaving a Web of Horror, the Author Lures Millions into His Spooky Parlor," *People Weekly* v. 44 (December 25, 1995): 102–103.

28. Sally Lodge, "Scholastic's Animorphs Series Has Legs," *Publishers Weekly*, November 3, 1997, 36–37.

29. Fredric A Emmert, "U.S. Media in the 1990s," http://usinfo.state.gove/usa/infousa/media1rd.htm, (November 7, 2002).

30. *Maxim* Web site, http://www.Maximonline.com.

CHAPTER 9

1. Greil Marcus, "Kurt Cobain: Artist of the Decade," *Rolling Stone* 812 (May 13, 1999): 46–48.

2. Ira Robbins, *The Trouser Press Guide to '90s Rock* (New York: Fireside, 1997), 515–517.

3. See also Gina Arnold, *Route 666: On the Road to Nirvana* (New York: St. Martin's, 1993) and Rolling Stone, *Cobain* (Boston: Little, Brown, 1994).

4. Robbins, 549–550.

5. David Fricke, "The Battles of Rage Against the Machine," *Rolling Stone* 826 (November 25, 1999): 42–50.

6. For further analysis, see Robert Wright, "'I'd Sell You Suicide': Pop Music and Moral Panic in the Age of Marilyn Manson," *Popular Music* 19.3 (October 2000).

7. Chris Heath, "Fiona Apple: The Caged Bird Sings," *Rolling Stone* 778 (January 22, 1998): 30–36, 68.

8. Anthony DeCurtis, "2 Live Crew Trial," *The Vibe History of Hip Hop* (New York: Three Rivers Press, 1999), Ed. Alan Light, 268–269.

9. Steven Stancell, *Rap Whoz Who* (New York: Schirmer Books, 1996).

10. Robert Marriott, "Gangsta, Gangsta: The Sad, Violent Parable of Death Row Records," *The Vibe History of Hip Hop*, 319–325.

11. See Stancell, 137–139 and Martin Johnson, "'Cop Killer' and Sister Souljah: Hip Hop Under Fire," *The Vibe History of Hip Hop*, 288–289.

12. Stancell, 122–123.

13. Joe Wood, "Native Tongues: A Family Affair," *The Vibe History of Hip Hop*, 187–199.

14. Stancell, 13.

15. Ibid., 51.

16. Anthony Bozza, "Eminem Blows Up," *Rolling Stone* 811 (April 29, 1999): 42–47, 72.

17. Nancy Collins, "Ricky Martin: The Rolling Stone Interview," *Rolling Stone* 818 (August 5, 1999): 48–52, 82.

18. Ed Morales, introduction, "Hey, Latin Lovers!" *Andy Warhol's Interview* June 1999, 98–105, 118.

19. Fred Goodman, "La Explosion Pop Latino," *Rolling Stone* 812 (May 13, 1999): 21–22.

20. Robert K. Oermann, *A Century of Country: An Illustrated History of Country Music* (New York: TV Books, 1999), 297–298.

21. Ibid., 309–311.

22. Chris Heath, "Spice Girls: Too Hot to Handle," *Rolling Stone* 764 (July 10–24, 1997): 74–82, 138–142.

23. Steven Daly, "Britney Spears: Inside the Heart and Mind (and Bedroom) of America's New Teen Queen," *Rolling Stone* 810 (April 15, 1999): 60–65, 129–131.

24. Chris Mundy, "The Girl Can't Help It," *Rolling Stone* 841 (May 25, 2000): 46–52, 85.

25. David Wild, "Winners Take All," *Rolling Stone* 832 (January 20, 2000): 42–46. 44.

26. Ibid., 45.

27. Jancee Dunn, "The Backstreet Boys Year in Hell," *Rolling Stone* 813 (May 27, 1999): 42–47.

28. Anthony Bozza, "Nsychronicity," *Rolling Stone* 837 (March 30, 2000): 52–58.

CHAPTER 10

1. Joseph Wambaugh, "*Homicide:* The Best Show You're Not Watching," *TV Guide* 44.52 (December 28, 1996): 28–30, 32–33, 38–39.

2. Rent Web site, http://www.siteforrent.com.

3. C. W. E. Bigsby, *Modern American Drama, 1945–2000* (Cambridge: Cambridge University Press, 2000), 163.

4. Ibid., 337.

CHAPTER 11

1. Valene L. Smith and Maryann Brent, eds. *Hosts and Guests Revisited: Tourism Issues of the 21st Century* (New York: Cognizant Communications Corporation, 2001), 8–9.

2. Charles R. Goeldner, J. R. Brent Ritchie, and Robert W. McIntosh, *Tourism: Principles, Practices, Philosophies*, 8th ed. (New York: John Wiley & Sons, 2000), 10–11.

3. Ibid., 138.

4. See, for instance, Smith and Brent, *Hosts and Guests Revisited*, 109.

5. Ibid., 117–120.

6. Ibid., 25.

7. Anne Parr, "The Impact of New Technologies on the Tourist Industry," in *Tourism and Development: Economic, Social, Political and Economic Issues* (Commack, NY: Nova Science Publishers, 1998), Eds. Clement A. Tisdell and Kartik C. Roy, 117–127.

8. Cited in Goeldner, Ritchie, and McIntosh, *Tourism: Principles, Practices, Philosophies*, 119.

9. Smith and Brent, *Hosts and Guests Revisited*, 348.

10. S. Krakover, *The Effects of Terror on the Flow of Tourists to Israel,* Paper presented at the Annual Meeting of the Association of American Geographers, Honolulu, HI, March 23–24, 1999. Cited in Smith and Brent, *Hosts and Guests Revisited*, 367–379.

11. See, for instance, Goeldner, Ritchie, and McIntosh. *Tourism: Principles, Practices, Philosophies.*

12. Alison S. Wellner, *Americans at Play* (Ithaca: New Strategist Publications, 1997), 3.

13. H. Ken Cordell and Gregory R. Super, "Trends in Americans' Outdoor Recreation," in *Trends in Outdoor Recreation, Leisure and Tourism* (New York: CABI Publishing, 2000), Ed. W. C. Gartner and D. W. Lime, 133–144.

14. Smith and Brent, *Hosts and Guests Revisited*, 337.

15. D. B. Weaver, *Ecotourism in the Less Developed World* (Oxon, UK: Cab International, 1998), 13.

16. Smith and Brent, *Hosts and Guests Revisited*, 195.

17. William R. Eadington, "Trends in Casinos and Tourism for the 21st Century," in Gartner and Lime, *Trends in Outdoor Recreation, Leisure and Tourism* 155–163.

18. Smith and Brent, *Hosts and Guests Revisited*, 72.

19. Ibid., 55.

20. Goeldner, Ritchie, and McIntosh. *Tourism: Principles, Practices, Philosophies*, 149–154.

21. Haynes Johnson, *The Best of Times: America in the Clinton Years* (New York: James A. Silberman, 2001), 150–151.

22. James M. Rubenstein, *Making and Selling Cars: Innovation and Change in the U.S. Automotive Industry* (Baltimore: The Johns Hopkins University Press, 2001), 227.

23. Goeldner, Ritchie, and McIntosh. *Tourism: Principles, Practices, Philosophies*, 143–145.

24. Ibid., 146–149.

25. Ibid., 155–158, 220.

26. Wellner, *Americans At Play*, 12.

CHAPTER 12

1. Lisa Phillips, *The American Century: Art & Culture 1950–2000* (New York: Whitney Museum of American Art. 1999), 332.

2. See http://www.aidsquilt.org.

3. Mel Gooding, *Public:Art:Space: A Decade of Public Art Commissions Agency, 1987–1997* (London: Merrell Holberton, 1998), 13.

4. Natalie Nodecker, "Visual Culture: Pop Pride," *American Photo* 11.3 (May/June 2000): 33.

5. Vicki Goldberg and Robert Silberman, *American Photography: A Century of Images* (San Francisco: Chronicle Books, 1999), 223.

6. Russell Hart, "The Future of Photography 1997," *American Photo* 8.6 (Nov./Dec. 1997): 47–48.

7. Goldberg and Silberman, *American Photography*, 225.

8. Russell Hart, "The Artisans: The Next Generation," *American Photo* 8.6 (Nov./Dec. 1997): 49–51.

9. N.E. Thing Enterprises, *Magic Eye: A New Way of Looking at the World,* (Kansas City: Andrews and McMeel, 1993).

10. Carl Machover, "Is It Technology or Art?: The New Tools," *Cyber Arts: Exploring Art & Technology* (San Francisco: Miller Freeman, Inc., 1992), Ed. Linda Jacobson, 39–40.

11. Jeff Berkowitz and Lifesmith Classic Fractals, *Fractal Cosmos: The Art of Mathematical Design* (Oakland: Amer Lotus, 1994).

12. Ron Goulart, *Great American Comic Books* (Lincolnwood, IL.: Publications International, 2001), 328.

13. Ibid., 315.

14. Patrick Daniel O'Neill, "Modern Art," *Hogan's Alley* 5 (1998): 144, 137–139.

15. Scott McCloud, *Understanding Comics: The Invisible Art* (New York: Harper-Perennial, 1993), 126.

16. Goulart, *Great American Comic Books,* 315.

17. For multiple perspectives on *Understanding Comics,* see "Critical Focus: *Understanding Comics," The Comics Journal* 211 (April 1999): 57–103.

18. Cristopher Rapp, "Dung Deal," *National Review* (October 25, 1999).

Further Reading

Adamson, Jim. *The Denny's Story: How a Company in Crisis Resurrected It's Good Name.* New York: John Wiley & Sons, 2000.

Anderson, Sarah, John Cavanagh, Chuck Collins, Chris Hartman and Felice Yeskel. "Executive Excess 2000: Seventh Annual CEO Compensation Survey." http://www.ufenet.org/press/2000/Executive_Excess_2000.pdf (August 30, 2000).

Arnold, Gina. *Route 666: On the Road to Nirvana.* New York: St. Martin's, 1993.

BBC News Online. "Business: The Economy: Woods Holes $90m." http://news.bbc.co.uk/1/hi/business/the_economy/429698.stm (August 25, 1999).

Berkowitz, Jeff and Lifesmith Classic Fractals. *Fractal Cosmos: The Art of Mathematical Design.* Oakland: Amer Lotus, 1994.

Bernstein, Michael A. and David E. Adler, eds. *Understanding American Economic Decline.* New York: Cambridge University Press, 1994.

Bigsby, C. W. E. *Modern American Drama, 1945–2000.* Cambridge: Cambridge University Press, 2000.

Bilstein, Roger. *The Enterprise of Flight: The American Aviation and Aerospace Industry.* Washington: Smithsonian Institution Press, 2001.

Bing, Jonathan. "Sue Grafton: Death and the Maiden." *Publishers Weekly,* April 20, 1998. 40–41.

Blades, John. "David Guterson: Stoic of the Pacific Southwest." *Publishers Weekly,* April 5, 1999. 215–216.

Blakely, Edward and Mary Gail Snyder. *Fortress America: Gated Communities in the United States.* Washington D.C.: Brookings Institute Press, 1997.

Bozza, Anthony. "Eminem Blows Up." *Rolling Stone* 811 (April 29, 1999): 42–47, 72.

Bozza, Anthony. "Nsychronicity." *Rolling Stone* 837 (March 30, 2000): 52–58.

Brooks, David. "The Organization Kid." *The Atlantic Monthly* 287.4 (April 2001): 40–46, 48–54.

Brown, Jane D., Jeanne R. Steele, and Kim Walsh-Childers, eds. *Sexual Teens, Sexual Media.* Mahwah, New Jersey: Lawrence Erlbaum Associates, 2002.

Browne, Ray B. and Pat Browne. *The Guide to United States Popular Culture.* Bowling Green: Bowling Green State University Popular Press, 2001.

Burr, Chandler. "The AIDS Exception: Privacy Vs. Public Health." *The Atlantic Monthly* 279.6 (June 1997): 57–63, 64–67.

Cannell, Michael. "Brain Drain." *Architecture* 88.12 (December 1999): 125–127.

Carver, Reginald and Lenny Bernstein. *Jazz Profiles: The Spirit of the Nineties.* New York: Billboard, 1998.

Charters, Mallay. "The Different Faces of Poetry." *Publishers Weekly,* March 3, 1997. 38–41.

Chase, Alison. "Harvard and the Making of the Unabomber." *The Atlantic Monthly* 285.6 (June 2000): 41–44, 46–50, 51–56, 58–59, 62–65.

Collins, Nancy. "Ricky Martin: The Rolling Stone Interview." *Rolling Stone* 818 (August 5, 1999): 48–52, 82.

Corporate Design Foundation Web site. "Sephora—Liberating Beauty Products." http://www.cdf.org/7_2_index/sephora.html (July 25, 2002).

Covino, Deborah Caslav. "Outside-In: Body, Mind, and Self in the Advertisement of Aesthetic Surgery." *Journal of Popular Culture* 35.3 (Winter 2001): 91–102.

"Craft-Brewing Industry Keeps Growing." http:/www.beertown.org/PR/industry_growth.htm (July 13, 2002).

"Critical Focus: *Understanding Comics.*" *The Comics Journal* 211 (April 1999): 57–103.

Croce, Arlene. *Writing in the Dark, Dancing in* The New Yorker. New York: Farrar, Straus and Giroux, 2000.

Dahlin, Robert. "Expanding the Scene of the Crime." *Publishers Weekly,* April 22, 1996. 38–47.

Dahlin, Robert. "Turning the Page on the 20th Century." *Publishers Weekly,* May 17, 1999. 35–36.

Daly, Steven. "Britney Spears: Inside the Heart and Mind (and Bedroom) of America's New Teen Queen." *Rolling Stone* 810 (April 15, 1999): 60–65, 129–131.

Dean, Andrea Oppenheimer. "Our Critic Goes Behind the Scenes At This Year's AIA Honor Awards." *Architectural Record* 187.5 (May 1999).

Deardorff, David II. *Sports: A Reference Guide and Critical Commentary, 1980–1999.* Westport: Greenwood Press, 2000.

De La Haye, Amy and Cathie Dingwall. *Surfers Soulies Skinheads & Skaters: Subcultural Style from the Forties to the Nineties.* Woodstock: Overlook, 1996.

Dixon, Wheeler Winston, ed. *Film Genre 2000: New Critical Essays.* Albany: State University of New York Press, 2000.

Duany, Andres and Elizabeth Plater-Zyberk. *Suburban Nation: The Rise of Sprawl and the Decline of the American Dream.* New York: North Point Press, 2000.

Dunn, Jancee. "The Backstreet Boys Year in Hell." *Rolling Stone* 813 (May 27, 1999): 42–47.

Dunn, Jancee and Patti O'Brien. "How Hip-hop Style Bum-Rushed the Mall." *Rolling Stone* 808 (March 18, 1999): 54–57, 59.

Dyer, Lucinda. "Love, Thy Magic Spell is Everywhere." *Publishers Weekly,* May 13, 1996. 41–47.

Emmert, Fredric A. "U.S. Media in the 1990s." http://usinfo.state.gove/usa/infousa/media1rd.htm, (November 7, 2002).

Federal Interagency Forum on Child and Family Statistics. *America's Children: Key National Indicators of Well-Being, 2000.* http://www.childstats.gov/.

Fox, Roy F. *MediaSpeak: Three American Voices.* Westport: Praeger, 2001.

Fricke, David. "The Battles of Rage Against the Machine." *Rolling Stone* 826 (November 25, 1999): 42–50.

Frith, Katherine Toland, ed. *Undressing the Ad: Reading Culture in Advertising.* New York: Peter Lang, 1998.

Gartner, W. C. and D. W. Lime, eds. *Trends in Outdoor Recreation, Leisure and Tourism.* Wallinford, U.K.: CABI Publishing, 2000.

Gimlin, Debra L. *Body Work: Beauty and Self-Image in American Culture.* Berkeley: University of California Press, 2002.

Goeldner, Charles R., J. R. Brent Ritchie and Robert W. McIntosh. *Tourism: Principles, Practices, Philosophies.* 8th ed. New York: John Wiley & Sons, 2000.

Goldberg, Vicki and Robert Silberman. *American Photography: A Century of Images.* San Francisco: Chronicle Books, 1999.

Gooding, Mel. *Public:Art:Space: A Decade of Public Art Commissions Agency, 1987–1997.* Introduction. London; Merrell Holberton, 1998.

Goodman, Fred. "La Explosion Pop Latino." *Rolling Stone* 812 (May 13, 1999): 21–22.

Goulart, Ron. *Great American Comic Books.* Lincolnwood, IL.: Publications International, 2001.

Gratz, Roberta Brandes and Norman Mintz. *Cities Back from the Edge: New Life for Downtown.* New York: Preservation Press, 1998.

Hall, Dennis. "Delight in Disorder: A Reading of Diaphany and Liquefaction in Contemporary Women's Clothing." *Journal of Popular Culture* 34.4 (Spring 2001): 65–74.

Halstead, Ted. "A Politics for Generation X." *The Atlantic Monthly* 284.2 (August 1999): 33–34, 36–42.

Hamilton, William. "Suitably Attired." *The Atlantic Monthly* 288.2 (Sept. 2001): 122–125.

Hart, Russell. "The Artisans: The Next Generation." *American Photo* 8.6 (Nov./Dec. 1997): 49–51.

Hart, Russell. "The Future of Photography 1997." *American Photo* 8.6 (Nov./Dec. 1997): 47–48.

Haun, Harry. *The Cinematic Century.* New York; Applause Books, 2000.

Heath, Chris. "Fiona Apple: The Caged Bird Sings." *Rolling Stone* 778 (Jan. 22, 1998): 30–36, 68.

Heath, Chris. "Spice Girls: Too Hot to Handle." *Rolling Stone* 764 (July 10–24, 1997): 74–82, 138–142.

Hischak, Thomas S. *American Theatre: A Chronicle of Comedy and Drama, 1969–2000.* New York: Oxford University Press, 2001.

Hogrefe, Jeffrey. "The Ascent of Glass." *Smithsonian* 32.4 (July 2001): 80–88.

Holtzman, Steven. *Digital Mosaics: The Aesthetics of Cyberspace.* New York: Simon & Schuster, 1997.

Hyde, Harlow A. "Slow Death in the Great Plains." *The Atlantic Monthly* 279.6 (June 1997): 42, 44–45.

Ivy, Robert. "Frank Gehry: Plain Talk with a Master." *Architectural Record* 187.5 (May 1999): 185–192, 356, 359–360.

Ivy, Robert. "Major Museums and Medals: Frank Gehry's Big Year." *Architectural Record* 188.1 (Jan. 1999): 45.

Jacobson, Linda, ed. *CyberArts: Exploring Art & Technology.* San Francisco: Miller Freeman, Inc., 1992.

Jacobson, Michael F. "Liquid Candy: How Soft Drinks are Harming Americans' Health." http://www.cspinet.org/sodapop/liquid_candy.htm.

Johnson, Haynes. *The Best of Times: America in the Clinton Years.* New York: James H. Silberman, 2001.

Johnson, Haynes. *Divided We Fall: Gambling with History in the Nineties.* New York: W.W. Norton, 1994.

Jones, John Philip, ed. *The Advertising Business.* Thousand Oaks: Sage Publications, 1999.

Keating, W. Dennis and Norman Krumholz, eds. *Rebuilding Urban Neighborhoods.* Thousand Oaks: Sage Publications, 1999.

Kilbourne, Jean. *Deadly Persuasion: Why Women and Girls Must Fight the Addictive Power of Advertising.* New York: The Free Press, 1999.

Killheffer, Robert K. J. "Creative Experimentation Reigns." *Publishers Weekly,* June 17, 1996. 34–41.

Killheffer, Robert K. J. "Inter-Galactic Licensing." *Publishers Weekly,* Sept. 25, 1995. 27–31.

Kinsella, Barbara. "Is Oprah Bringing in New Readers?" *Publishers Weekly,* Jan. 20, 1997. 276.

Klensch, Elsa. CNN Online, http://www.cnn.com/STYLE/9812/23/trend.yearender/ (Dec. 23, 1998).

Laiserin, Jerry. "Form Follows Information." *Architectural Record* 187.10 (Oct. 1999): 124–127.

Lamb, Lynette. "Can Women Save Sports?" *Utne Reader* 97 (Jan.– Feb. 2000): 56–57.

Larsen, Elizabeth. "Bossy's Lament." *Utne Reader* 100 (July–Aug. 2000): 18–19.

Lebrecht, Norman. *Who Killed Classical Music: Maestros, Managers, and Corporate Politics.* Secaucus, NJ: Birch Lane Press, 1996.

Lerner, Harriet. "When Bad Books Happen to Good People." *Ms.,* Nov./Dec. 1993. 62–64.

Light, Alan, ed. *The Vibe History of Hip Hop.* New York: Three Rivers Press, 1999.

Lodge, Sally. "Scholastic's Animorphs Series Has Legs." *Publishers Weekly,* Nov. 3, 1997. 36–37.

Marcus, Greil. "Kurt Cobain: Artist of the Decade." *Rolling Stone* 812 (May 13, 1999): 46–48.

Maryles, Daisy. "Connecting the Numbers." *Publishers Weekly,* Jan. 10, 2000. 25–27.

Maryles, Daisy. "The Medium Makes the Sale." *Publishers Weekly,* Jan. 3, 1994. 55.

McCafferty, Dennis. "Breaking New Ground." *USA Weekend* (Aug. 30–Sept. 1, 2002): 6–7.

McCloud, Scott. *Understanding Comics: The Invisible Art.* New York: HarperPerennial, 1993.

Mclellan, Dennis. "Deepak Chopra: The Guru Turns to Fiction." *Publishers Weekly,* July 24, 1995. 43–44.

Merchandisegroup.com Web site. "Aging Baby Boomers Drive Surge in Sales of Personal Care Products." http://www.merchandisegroup.com/password/archive/102102.html (Jan. 21, 2002).

Merrick, Amy. "Tired of Trendiness, Former Shoppers Leave Gap, Defect to Competitors." *The Wall Street Journal* (Dec. 6, 2001).

Milliot, Jim. "Slow Growth Ahead in Consumer Spending on Children's Books." *Publishers Weekly*, Aug. 15, 1994. 24.

Milliot, Jim and Diane Roback. "1996 a Difficult Year for Children's Publishers." *Publishers Weekly*, Nov. 3, 1997. 35–38.

Morales, Ed. "Hey, Latin Lovers!" (Introduction). *Andy Warhol's Interview*, June 1999. 98–105, 118.

Mundy, Chris. "The Girl Can't Help It." *Rolling Stone* 841 (May 25, 2000): 46–52, 85.

Murray, Andy. "Microbreweries Focus on Close-to-Home Connoisseurs." *Eagle-Tribune* online. http://www.eagletribune.com/news/stories/20020303/BV_001.htm (March 3, 2002).

National Center for Policy Analysis. "Crime and Punishment in America: 1998." http://www.ncpa.org/~ncpa/studies/s219/s219a.html.

N.E. Thing Enterprises. *Magic Eye: A New Way of Looking at the World.* Kansas City: Andrews and McMeel, 1993.

Newshour, The Web site. "The Name Game." http://www.pbs.org/newshour/infocus/fashion/namegame.html (July 25, 2002).

Newshour, The Web site. "School Uniforms." http://www.pbs.org/newshour/infocus/fashion/school.html (July 25, 2002).

Nodecker, Natalie. "Visual Culture: Pop Pride." *American Photo* 11.3 (May/June 2000): 33.

Nunn, Joan. *Fashion in Costume 1200–2000.* 2nd ed. Chicago: New Amsterdam, 2000.

Oermann, Robert K. *A Century of Country: An Illustrated History of Country Music.* New York: TV Books, 1999.

O'Neill, Patrick Daniel. "Modern Art." *Hogan's Alley* 5 (1998): 144, 137–139.

Owen, Rob. *Gen X TV: The Brady Bunch to Melrose Place.* Syracuse: Syracuse University Press, 1997.

Parsons, James. "A New World (Made To) Order." *Architecture* 88.5 (May 1999).

Pearman, Hugh. *Contemporary World Architecture.* London: Phaidon Press Limited, 1998.

Phillips, Lisa. *The American Century: Art & Culture 1950–2000.* New York: Whitney Museum of American Art, 1999.

Princenthal, Nancy and Jennifer Dowley. *A Creative Legacy: A History of The National Endowment for The Arts Visual Artists' Fellowship Program.* Introduction by William Ivey. New York: Harry N. Abrams, Inc., 2001.

Public Art Commissions Agency. *Public:Art:Space.* Introduction by Mel Gooding. London: Merrell Holberton, 1998.

Rapp, Cristopher. "Dung Deal." *National Review* (October 25, 1999).

Robbins, Ira A., ed. *The Trouser Press Guide to '90s Rock.* New York: Fireside, 1997.

Rogers, Joel and Ruy Teixeira. "America's Forgotten Majority," *The Atlantic Monthly* 285.6 (June 2000): 66–70, 72–75.

Rollin, Lucy. *Twentieth-Century Teen Culture by the Decades: A Reference Guide.* Westport: Greenwood Press, 1999.

Rolling Stone. *Cobain.* Boston: Little, Brown, 1994.

"The Rolling Stone Poll: Young America Talks Back." *Rolling Stone* 799 (November 12, 1998): 79–80.

Rubenstein, James M. *Making and Selling Cars: Innovation and Change in the U.S. Automotive Industry.* Baltimore: The Johns Hopkins University Press, 2001.

Rubinstein, Ruth P. *Society's Child: Identity, Clothing, and Style.* Boulder: Westview Press, 2000.

Russell, James S. "Profound Forces are Reshaping American Cities: Is There a Place for Architecture?" *Architectural Record* 188.3 (March 2000): 76–82, 206–208.

Rutter, Nancy and Owen Edwards. "Ready to Ware." *Forbes ASAP,* April 5, 1999. 30–32.

Schneider, Barbara and David Stevenson. *The Ambitious Generation: American Teenagers, Motivated but Directionless.* New Haven: Yale University Press, 1999.

Schlosser, Eric. *Fast Food Nation: The Dark Side of the All-American Meal.* New York: Houghton Mifflin, 2001.

Scholsser, Eric. "The Prison-Industrial Complex." *The Atlantic Monthly* 282.6 (December 1998): 51–52, 54–58, 62–66, 68–70, 72–77.

Schrag, Peter. "The Near-Myth of Our Failing Schools." *The Atlantic Monthly* 280.4 (October 1997): 72–74, 76, 78, 80.

Shand-Tucci, Douglass. *Built in Boston: City and Suburb, 1800–2000.* Amherst: University of Massachusetts Press, 1999.

Smith, C.E. Kidder. *Source Book of American Architecture.* New York: Princeton Architectural Press, 1996.

Smith, George and Nicola Walker Smith. *New Voices: American Composers Talk About Their Music.* Portland: Amadeus Press, 1995.

Smith, Valene L. and Maryann Brent, eds. *Hosts and Guests Revisited: Tourism Issues of the 21st Century.* New York: Cognizant Communications Corporation, 2001.

Sommerer, Christa and Laurent Mignonneau, eds. *Art @ Science.* New York: SpringerWien, 1998.

Spaulding, John. "Poetry and the Media: The Decline of Popular Poetry." *Journal of Popular Culture* 33.2 (Fall 1999): 147–153.

Springhall, John. *Youth, Popular Culture and Moral Panics: Penny Gaffs to Gangsta-Rap, 1830–1996.* New York: St Martin's, 1998.

Steel, Jon. *Truth, Lies, and Advertising.* New York: John Wiley & Sons, 1998.

Stossel, Scott. "Sport: As American as Women's Soccer?" *Atlantic Monthly.* 287.6 (June 2001): 89–93.

Taylor, Paul. "Stumped Speech." *Mother Jones* (May/June 2000).

"This is Your Government on Drugs." editorial, *Rolling Stone* 794 (Sept. 3, 1998): 43–44.

Tisdell, Clement A. and Kartik C. Roy, eds. *Tourism and Development: Economic, Social, Political and Economic Issues.* Commack, NY: Nova Science Publishers, 1998.

True, Cynthia. "Master of the Game." *Rolling Stone* 800 (Nov. 26, 1998): 94, 99–101.

Twitchell, James B. *Twenty Ads That Shook the World: The Century's Most Groundbreaking Advertising and How it Changed Us All.* New York: Crown Publishers, 2000.

Udovitch, Mim. "Breasts, Reassessed." *Esquire* 131.2 (Feb. 1999): 86–89.

United States Census Web site. http://www.census.gov.

Wambaugh, Joseph. "*Homicide:* The Best Show You're Not Watching." *TV Guide* 44.52 (December 28, 1996): 28–30, 32–33, 38–39.

Warde, Alan and Lydia Martens. *Eating Out: Social Differentiation, Consumption and Pleasure.* New York: Cambridge University Press, 2000.

Weaver, D. B. *Ecotourism in the Less Developed World.* Oxon, UK: Cab International, 1998.

"Weaving a Web of Horror, the Author Lures Millions into His Spooky Parlor." *People Weekly* v. 44 (Dec. 25, 1995): 102–103.

Wellner, Allison S. *Americans at Play: Demographics of Outdoor Recreation and Travel.* Ithaca: New Strategist Publications, 1997.

Wild, David. "Winners Take All." *Rolling Stone* 832 (January 20, 2000): 42–46. 44.

Williams, Donald C. *Urban Sprawl: A Reference Handbook.* Santa Barbara: ABC-CLIO, 2000.

Wilson, William Julius. *When Work Disappears: The World of the New Urban Poor.* New York: Knopf, 1996.

Wines, James. *Green Architecture.* Koln: Taschen, 2000.

Woodward, Kenneth. "Angles." *Newsweek,* December 27, 1993. 57.

Wright, Robert. "'I'd Sell You Suicide': Pop Music and Moral Panic in the Age of Marilyn Manson." *Popular Music* 19.3 (October 2000).

Zeff, Robbin and Brad Aronson. *Advertising on the Internet.* 2nd ed. New York: John Wiley & Sons, 1999.

Zolo, Peter. *Wise Up to Teens: Insights into Marketing and Advertising to Teenagers.* 2nd ed. Ithaca: New Strategist Publications, 1999.

Zuckerman, Mortimer B. "The Illiteracy Epidemic." *U.S. News & World Report.* June 12, 1989. 72.

Index

About the Author

MARC OXOBY received his BA from San Jose State University and now lives in Reno, Nevada, where he is a doctoral candidate in the University of Nevada, Reno English Department. He has worked as a disc jockey and as the editor of the small-press literary journal *CRiME CLUB.* He currently teaches English and Humanities classes at UNR. A regular contributor to the scholarly journal *Film and History,* he has also written for several other periodicals, as well as for *The St. James Encyclopedia of Popular Culture* and *The International Dictionary of Films and Filmmakers.*

DATE DUE